# The dream that kicks

Film has taught us to see the world afresh, but it could not picture its own birth. In *The Dream that Kicks*, Michael Chanan puts forward a theory of invention as a type of *bricolage* to show how cinematography was a product of the growing forces of nineteenth-century capitalist production and traces the development of British cinema from its popular origins to its emergence as a cultural commodity.

*The Dream that Kicks* combines astute textual analysis of individual films with detailed archival work of the industry. It situates cinema within its wider context to produce a thought-provoking exploration of its cultural and ideological implications. This new edition of *The Dream that Kicks* had been thoroughly revised and updated to take into account other recent work on early cinema.

**Michael Chanan** is a film maker, writer and teacher. A music critic in the early 1970s, when he directed documentaries on music for the BBC, he went on to make several films in Latin America during the 1980s. He is the author of *The Cuban Image* (on Cuban cinema) and of *Musica Practica* and *Repeated Takes* (on the social practice of music and the recording industry) and he is a member of the editorial board of *Vertigo*, an independent film and television magazine.

# The dream that kicks

## The prehistory and early years of cinema in Britain

Second edition

Michael Chanan

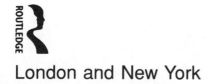

London and New York

First published in 1980 by Routledge & Kegan Paul Ltd

This edition first published 1996
by Routledge
11 New Fetter Lane, London EC4P 4EE

Simultaneously published in the USA and Canada
by Routledge
29 West 35th Street, New York, NY 10001

Phototypeset in Times by Intype, London
Printed and bound in Great Britain by
TJ Press (Padstow) Ltd, Padstow, Cornwall

*British Library Cataloguing in Publication Data*
Chanan, Michael.
    The dream that kicks : the prehistory and early years of cinema in
Britain / Michael Chanan. – 2nd edn.
       p.    cm.
    Includes bibliographical references and index.
    1. Motion pictures – Great Britain – History.
    2. Cinematography – History.   I. Title.
    PN1993.5.G7C44   1996
    791.43′0941 – dc20   95–14953

*Library of Congress Cataloging in Publication Data*
A catalogue record for this book has been requested

ISBN 0–415–11750–X

*In memory of my father,*
*and of Solomon Abramovitch Trone,*
*and to Olympia Qhari Qhari*

# Contents

# Author's note (first edition)

This book grew out of a suggestion by Miguel Cabezas. I first met him a year or so after the coup d'état in Chile in 1973. Before the coup he had worked in the Chilean State Publishing Company, Quimantú, set up by Popular Unity. After the coup he became involved in a new publishing endeavour in Rosario, Argentina, for which he commissioned a book from me on British cinema. I am only sorry he was unable to publish the end result of his initiative – although this book is rather different from the one he proposed: but he was forced to leave Argentina too by another military coup.

This book is also very different from the one I discussed with Dan Omer and Shanee Marx in Jerusalem in a memorable conversation which helped me sort out my ideas at an early stage. My brother Gabriel has seen it through more stages of growth than anyone else apart from myself and I very much hope it echoes at least something of his critical watchfulness. It would be an impossible task to name individually everyone who helped with general or particular bits of advice and criticism. I thank them all. My special thanks, however, to Anthony Friese-Greene for access to his family files on his grand-father, William Friese-Greene, and for permission to reproduce the notes on pp. 92–3, and the letter on p. 90; to Olivia Harris and John Mepham, who read substantial sections of the manuscript and made valuable comments; to Michael Engelhard for translating an article on Haggar from Welsh; to Noel Burch for discussion about early films; and to my brother Noel for the use of his collection of early books on cinematography. Finally my thanks to Marian Shapiro for help in compiling the (original) index; to the staff of the BFI Library and Jeremy Boulton of the National Film Archive; and to David Godwin for his particular enthusiasm for the book.

*Michael Chanan*

# Preface to the second edition

The centenary of the birth of cinema in 1895 provides an apt excuse for the second edition of this book. When it was first published in 1980, early cinema was just beginning to make a come-back in academic circles. In the preceding dozen or fifteen years, the study of film had turned to other disciplines (linguistics and semiotics, psychoanalysis and structural anthropology) to reconstitute itself and its object in accordance with a new critical agenda. Film scholars reached back, in the process, to the beginnings of the theory of film in the 1920s, especially in the Soviet Union, and it was largely through those eyes that the shadowy world of early cinema was seen. Since the 1920s, writers on film had speculated about the early self-discovery by film of its artistic capacities, and pointed to its dual nature: the seizure of physical reality on the one hand, the seduction of fantasy on the other; but for the most part they saw the process as unproblematic. The 1970s changed all that, and several new studies of early cinema which have appeared since this book first came out show interesting results. One reason for a new edition, then, rather than just a re-issue, is in order to revise the account I gave then in the light of this new work.

It is not as if I have changed my mind about anything substantial, but there were examples and connections which I overlooked or misplaced, and passages where I could have expressed the argument more succinctly. I have therefore done a thorough textual revision from beginning to end. Least affected are Chapters 3–7, covering the dialectic of invention. The second chapter, however, I have almost entirely rewritten. The new versions of the last two chapters are not so drastic; the material is the same but has been re-ordered, and some new passages added. At the same time I have taken the opportunity to do the opposite of what most new revised editions usually do: instead of adding anything, I have greatly compressed sections of the original. In particular, Parts Three and Four of the first edition (comprising Chapters 9–14) were a rather sprawling attempt to explore the complexity of aesthetic influences which affected the beginning of cinema. To make it more focused and more readable, I have considerably pruned the text and combined six chapters into two, transposing paragraphs and removing passages which were tangential to the main line of the argument. This edition, therefore, is in four parts with thirteen chapters, instead of six parts with seventeen.

One of the things that surprised me about the reception of the first edition was that it was much more sparsely reviewed in Britain than in the United States. In North America, lengthy and generally positive reviews appeared in film journals over a couple of years. At home there were short friendly notices in the trade press and one or two leftist publications, one very hostile review in *The Economist* (which I greatly enjoyed) and not much else. The book was ignored by both *Sight and Sound* and *Screen* – in other words, by both the right and the left wing of the principal institution of film culture in Britain – the BFI. For the one, I suppose, I was too radical; for the other I was out of line: I was unsympathetic to certain aspects of the new film studies. I agreed entirely with the need to reconstitute the history but considered suspicious the abstraction of the issues from historical material-ism. A very sympathetic review in *Radical Philosophy*, however, demonstrated that my theoretical framework was not, after all, just my own invention.

In 1995, the climate is rather different (though remarkably, all four of the publications just mentioned still survive). In the centennial celebrations of the cinema, amid the welter of screen-ings and television programmes and their fallout in the press and on the radio, a book like this is but a single small voice. (Worse still, a book about the invention of cinema without any pictures.) The media, which thrive on anniversaries, will celebrate the cen-tenary as a 'true fact' of history, spewing out a panoply of images to allure us. What I argue in this book – which covers the whole period of gestation, going back before photography, and the early years, when film production was still undercapitalized and arti-sanal – is that what led up to this invention and remains hidden behind these images had a crucial influence on what it grew into.

For anyone interested in these origins and beginnings, these pages are intended to provide a space away from the screen, for reflection on the source of its promises and attractions.

Miguel Cabezas, who asked me to write the book which turned into this one, was never able to return to his native country; he died some years ago in Sweden. I dedicate the second edition to his memory.

*Michael Chanan, London, March 1995*

## ACKNOWLEDGEMENTS

The author and publishers would like to thank the following for permission to reproduce copyright material:

Constable and Dover Books for extracts from E. F. Bleiler's *The Best Tales of Hoffman*; Anthony Friese-Greene for unpublished notes and family letters relating to William Friese-Greene; A. M. Heath and Mrs Sonia Brownwell Orwell for an extract from *'New Words'*, *Collected Essays, Journalism and Letters of George Orwell*, published by Secker & Warburg; David Higham Associates for the poem 'Our Eunuch Dreams' by Dylan Thomas, published in *Collected Poems* by J. M. Dent and New Directions Inc.; Manchester University Press for an extract from R. Roberts, *The Classic Slum*.

# OUR EUNUCH DREAMS

## I

Our eunuch dreams, all seedless in the light,
Of light and love, the tempers of the heart,
Whack their boys' limbs,
And, winding-footed in their shawl and sheet,
Groom the dark brides, the widows of the night
Fold in their arms.

The shades of girls, all flavoured from their shrouds,
When sunlight goes are sundered from the worm,
The bones of men, the broken in their beds,
By midnight pulleys that unhouse the tomb.

## II

In this our age the gunman and his moll,
Two one-dimensioned ghosts, love on a reel,
Strange to our solid eyes,
And speak their midnight nothings as they swell;
When cameras shut they hurry to their hole
Down in the yard of day.

They dance between their arclamps and our skull,
Impose their shots, throwing the nights away;
We watch the show of shadows kiss or kill,
Flavoured of celluloid give love the lie.

## III

Which is the world? Of our two sleepings, which
Shall fall awake when cures and their itch
Raise up this red-eyed earth?
Pack off the shapes of daylight and their starch,
The sunny gentlemen, the Welshing rich,
Or drive the night-geared forth.

The photograph is married to the eye,
Grafts on its bride one-sided skins of truth;
The dream has sucked the sleeper from his faith
That shrouded men might marrow as they fly.

## IV

This is the world: the lying likeness of
Our strips of stuff that tatter as we move
Loving and being loth;
The dream that kicks the buried from their sack
And lets their trash be honoured as the quick.
This is the world. Have faith.

For we shall be a shouter like the cock,
Blowing the old dead back; our shots shall smack
The image from the plates;
And we shall be fit fellows for a life,
And who remain shall flower as they love,
Praise to our faring hearts.

*Dylan Thomas*

# Part 1

# The arrival of moving pictures

The Cinematograph, which is the invention of MM. A. and L. Lumière, is a contrivance belonging to the same family as Edison's Kinetoscope and the old 'Wheel of Life', but in a rather higher stage of development. The spectator no longer gazes through a narrow aperture at the changing pictures, but has it presented to him full size on a large screen. The principle, however, is much the same, consisting simply of passing rapidly before the eye a series of pictures representing the successive stages of the action of the changing scene that has to be reproduced.

*The Times*, 1896

It was outside a derelict greengrocer's shop. The hawk-eyed gentleman on a fruit-crate was bewildering a sceptical crowd. In that shuttered shop there was a miracle to be seen for a penny, but only twenty-four could enter at a time, there wasn't room for more. His peroration was magnificent. . . . 'You've seen pictures of people in books, all frozen stiff. . . you've never seen pictures with people coming alive, moving about like you and me. Well, go inside and see for yourself, living pictures for a penny, and then tell me if I'm a liar!'

One of my pennies went suddenly; I joined twenty-three other sceptics inside. Stale cabbage leaves and a smell of dry mud gave atmosphere to a scene for Hogarth. A furtive youth did things to a tin oven on iron legs, and a white sheet hung from the ceiling. We grouped round that oven and wondered. Suddenly things happened, someone turned down a gas jet, the tin apparatus burst into a fearful clatter, and an oblong picture slapped onto the sheet and began a violent dance. After a while I discovered it was a picture of a house, but a house on fire. Flames

and smoke belched from the windows, and miracle of miracles, a
fire-engine dashed in, someone mounted a fire-escape, little
human figures darted about below, and then ... Bang! ... the
show was over. Exactly one minute. ... I had been to the cinema!

George Pearson, *Flashback*

'What do you think we've come for?' she asked; and then, without
waiting for a reply, she added, 'We've come to take you with us
to see the cinematograph.'

'Oh, jolly!' cried Bobbie, clapping his hands. He hadn't the
remotest idea what a cinematograph was, but anything which
would afford him an opportunity of going out in the evening was
hailed by him with delight. ...

In a very short time Langham Place was reached, and they had
taken their seats in the Small Hall, where, before the platform,
an enormous white sheet was stretched.

Of course you all know, so I need not tell you, that the cinematograph pictures are very like those of the magic lantern, with
the exception that in the former case the figures in the pictures
all move in the most natural manner possible – exactly as though
they were alive.

Well, Bobbie had been highly delighted in seeing several of
these wonderful pictures, representing a fire-engine tearing off to
a fire, a troopship filled with soldiers going out to the war, the
King witnessing the trooping of the colours at Whitehall, and a
lot of other interesting and exciting scenes, when a certain picture
was shown which attracted Bobbie's attention more than any of
the others.

It represented a country railway station with a tiny black tunnel
in the distance, from which, while Bobbie watched, first one and
then another little puff of white smoke appeared, and at last, out
came a tiny little train rushing along at a rare rate, till finally it
tore into the station, stopping just in time, so Bobbie thought, to
prevent the terrible accident which must have occurred had it
gone a little further forward and crashed in among the audience.

What a jolly little train it was, to be sure, as it stood there
puffing and snorting, and letting off steam, just like a real train,
while the passengers got in and out, and the porters bustled about
on the platform in the most delightfully natural way.

Bobbie never knew how it was, but suddenly – without stopping
to think whether it were right or wrong – he made up his mind

that he would go and see for himself if the doors of the carriages opened and shut.

No sooner thought of than done, and Bobbie found himself amongst the crowd on the platform.

Yes! Hurrah! The doors did open, and Bobbie had just stepped into the carriage, when pop! flash! and a curious feeling as though he had suddenly 'gone out' and as suddenly been lighted again, and Bobbie found himself tearing off goodness knew whither in the cinematograph train.

G. E. Farrow, *The Cinematograph Train and Other Stories*, 1904

Hungry Willie, who has not tasted food for some days, espies a splendid leg of mutton hanging outside a butcher's shop, and while the master's back is turned he snatches it off the hook and bolts down the street. The fun now commences, and the chase which ensues is one of the funniest yet produced. New obstacles are introduced and the subject is one long laugh from beginning to end. A screaming comedy!

Synopsis of *Lost! A Leg of Mutton*, 1906

The directors of the earliest movies often did queer things. One of the most curious was their habit of showing you people riding about in a taxi, then piling out and walking away without paying the driver. They'd ride all over town, have fun, or go to a place of business, and that was the end of that. No payment necessary. It was very much like most of the books on the Middle Ages that go on for pages and pages about knights and ladies all decked out in shining armour and gay dresses, at tournaments and games. They always live in splendid castles and have plenty to eat and drink. You get very little hint that someone had to provide all these things . . .

Leo Huberman

An image is not a picture, but a picture can correspond to it.

Wittgenstein

# Chapter 1

# The site of film

One beam in a dark place hath exceeding much refreshment in it.

Oliver Cromwell

In spite of the extensive documentation which exists concerning the early days of film there is a sense in which the origins of film are obscure. Film has taught us to see the world anew, but it seems that the one thing it could not properly picture was its own birth. What we see in the earliest films is the beginning of a new way of seeing. What we don't seem to see is how that way of seeing was first seen.

Sometimes there are anecdotes we can grab at, like the story of Hepworth and the parson. Cecil Hepworth was one of the English film pioneers. He was the son of a magic lantern lecturer and had an inventive turn of mind: his first contacts with the cinematograph came when another pioneer, R. W. Paul, bought from him some hand-feed arc lamps of his own design after Hepworth approached him at Olympia, where Paul gave his first paying film shows in March 1896. This was one month after the first public presentation in Britain of the cinematograph invented by the Lumière brothers in France. Hepworth soon began his own film career, inauspiciously, touring the country lecturing like his father, but with film instead of slides. On one occasion, in a church hall, in order to parry the displeasure of a suspicious parson over the prospect of a film of an exotic dance by a well-known music hall artiste, Hepworth had a brainwave and announced it as a film of Salome dancing before Herod! 'Everyone was delighted', he wrote later, 'especially the parson. He said in his nice little speech afterwards that it was a particularly happy idea to introduce a little touch of bible history into an otherwise wholly secular entertainment. And he added that he had no idea that the cheenimartograph had been invented so long' (Hepworth, 1967, p. 39; a slightly different version of the story is told in Hepworth, 1951). The parson's sarcasm notwithstanding, there were indeed a great many people who were simply credulous before the phenomenon of film.

But what kind of credulousness was it and how did it arise? Could they not see a two-dimensional screen and a machine casting light and shadow upon it? To wonder how this effect could be achieved would not have been a surprising response, but to be taken in, as we know some of the early audiences were, as if this were some kind of magic – how was that possible? And then, when the first shock of the apparition was past, to accept the image as a full and complete picture of reality no matter what it left out – how could that have happened? Do these questions seem odd? Perhaps that's only because the credulousness which greeted cinema at the beginning has survived to our own time.

We must go back into the prehistory of film if we want to understand the influences which were already affecting cinema in its earliest days. This prehistory has two main aspects. They can be looked at separately only if we also remember that they interacted in various ways at the same time. On the one hand, there's the lengthy process of the invention of the apparatus itself which in turn must be examined from at least two more interrelated aspects – technical and economic; and then there's the development of cultural forms and popular entertainment during the nineteenth century and its legacy, which shaped the first films and created a dominant series of attitudes and expectations which audiences brought with them when they came to see them. The main link is obviously photography, but other forms are equally important, and again there's more than one aspect to consider: traditions, attitudes and expectations differed in the different social classes, and it is therefore necessary to try and sort these out.

The basic principles of cinematography are not difficult to describe. A scene is exposed to a camera which takes photographs in rapid series at the rate of at least sixteen per second (though modern sound film speed is faster: 24 or 25 frames per second). In order to accomplish this, the film is mounted on a roll with perforations down the edge: between each exposure, a sprocket engages a perforation and pulls the film down to the next position, or frame; whereupon the shutter opens and closes and the process is repeated. The film is viewed by using the same kind of mechanism to project light through it on to a screen. (The Kinetoscope which Edison introduced in 1894 lacked projection: it was a peepshow device.) The machine which achieves this consists of a number of components engineered to a high degree of precision – lens, shutter, sprocket, etc., and the film itself – which only trial and error over a period of several years brought to fruition in the first functioning prototypes of 1895 and 1896.

In studying the technical origins of cinema it isn't as if the only thing that matters is to settle the exact chronology, to sift the evidence and agree who invented what when (even though some arguments still take place on this score), and it will not be the approach of this book to deal with things in that sort of way. Basically, these things can tell us nothing by themselves that we don't already know, namely, that film was invented somehow. To explain *how* cinematography came to be invented, how the inventors arrived at their inventions in the sense of what the process was and what were their motivations – this is another matter altogether. It cannot be achieved by passing blandly from one 'fact' to another. It hasn't been achieved by those so-called histories which, as Geoffrey Nowell-Smith has put it, 'accumulate facts or merge facts and impressions into linear narratives with scant regard for any process of definition, or delimitation of the area, or rigour of deduction' (Nowell-Smith, p. 8).

Nowell-Smith belongs to a generation of critical film theorists who argue that it's impossible to write a history of film unless you make it a primary task in so doing to confront the problem of how the institutions of cinema – the industry, the star system, the idioms, styles, genres, etc. – how these were constituted, instead of taking them for granted as 'natural' forms of evolution. I share this concern. How is it, I want to know, that cinema became a system in which moving images (later combined with recorded sounds) are assembled in various ways, according to various conventions, so that on the surface, as it were, the screen appears to be a kind of 'window' on to reality – whereas what is really screened is a world apart, both illusory and imaginary, which produces its own meanings, the genres which form our modern myths, legends and fantasies?

To realize this disjunction, the disjunction between process and appearance, leads to a conception of cinema not just as an artistic form but also an ideological one, where the screen obscures as much as it reveals and in the process represents not reality but an ideological version of it. What does ideology mean here? It is not just a set of 'mistaken ideas' about the social world, of which we accuse our political opponents, which correspond to their specific political interests and may or may not be present in a film. An ideology is rather a form of representing reality, expressed in art, philosophy, religion, political and legal systems, etc., which is largely the unconscious product of the organization of the social world and the position of the individual subject within it. This does not mean that ideologies are reducible to the effects of the economic base, a mechanical idea propagated by those whom Sartre called lazy Marxists, which was never advanced by Marx himself. Nor does it mean that ideology is never conscious, never intentionally constructed (at least in part) so as to represent economic or political self-interest; plainly it often is. But the formation of ideology is an extremely complex phenomenon and I don't want to write a theoretical dissertation on the subject as a precondition for approaching the history of cinema. The truth is that an ideology and its effects cannot be studied apart from historical instances. One of the reasons for this, as we shall discover, is that many ideological elements are fundamentally remnants of previous ways of thinking which have been superseded in particular branches of knowledge but which retain their influence within general consciousness.

Nevertheless, these reservations made, I agree with those theorists who maintain that ideology is not just an added ingredient in a film but enters into the conception of a moving picture, and conditions the very nature of that conception. Conditions but not determines. For lazy Marxists, it was enough to describe the ideology of the capitalist film industry in some such formula as 'the true interest of the bourgeoisie is that cinema should make up for what people do not have in real life', which not only suggests a mechanical and deterministic explanation of the relationship between economic forces and ideological effects but seems to eliminate concern for cinema as an art form, not just an ideological one. Now it is perfectly true that the film industry after a hundred years is mostly concerned with providing the audience with pure escapism. But when you start asking more definite questions such as how the economic structure of the industry actually produces these results – when you begin the historical examination of these problems – such assertions quickly appear simplistic, and themselves ideological in form, rather than being serious critical attempts to grasp the nature of social and historical processes. The question, if it is true, is how it came about. And what is it about cinema that lends itself to such use? This book will, I hope, shed some light on these questions through an examination of the origins of cinema, cultural, technical and economic. The question that inevitably follows – Is it redeemable? belongs elsewhere.

Concrete historical evidence tends to explode a whole series of myths and misconceptions about these origins which come from jumping to unhistorical conclusions. André Bazin, for example, foremost critic from an earlier generation, claimed that the idea of cinema existed fully grown in the inventors' minds when they started. Certainly there came a point when some of the inventors had a pretty good idea of what it was they were trying to invent, and they said so. But many of those who contributed to the dialectic of invention were quite uninterested in the idea of moving picture projection. Men like Janssen, Muybridge and Marey, whose work is described below, weren't trying to invent cinematography: they were involved in a search for quite different discoveries, in the fields of astronomy or the investigation of animal locomotion; they used rapid series photography as an instrument or tool of scientific research. Bazin knows about these men and to sustain his thesis therefore has to discount their contribution as somehow incidental; but this is merely to look away from what it is inconvenient to see. In fact, the developments they made in the techniques of rapid series photography became vital steps towards the achievement of cinematography. A fundamental question therefore arises here concerning connections that may exist in the methods and instruments involved in the processes of discovery and invention in different fields. A question about the twin processes of discovery and invention and the relationship between them. What do you need to discover in order to be able to invent something? What do you need to invent in order to be able to discover something?

Inventions don't just happen, they don't just drop from the skies or appear out of a vacuum in the mind of the inventor. In the first place, any invention depends on prior discoveries of some kind – discoveries which in some way dictate the initial purpose the invention is intended to serve. In the second place, the step from discovering something to an invention which embodies it and thence to its application for purposes previously unimagined also has to be explained. The invention normally has to be motivated in some way. Very few inventions are ever the result of mere disinterested curiosity, and they're usually impractical if they are. The primary motivation is usually either economic necessity, or, as in the case of cinema, economic opportunity. In either case economic conditions play a determinate (but not determining) role, corresponding to the state of development of the technological conditions for the new invention.

In this respect cinematography is no different from other inventions of the nineteenth century. Devices which contributed to the invention grew out of a variety of contexts and found uses in other contexts before anyone arrived at the idea of moving pictures as we now know them. The same thing happened in all those branches of production which led to new devices, new machines, new instruments and new industries. During the 1850s, for example, piano manufacturers were trying to develop larger and more sonorous instruments suitable for the new large concert halls and for accompanying larger orchestras. One of the weaknesses of the original design of the piano which had become a major problem by the 1840s was that the strings kept breaking as more was demanded of them. Finally a new method of producing copper wire was invented in Britain in 1854. But this new kind of wire immediately proved to suit not only piano strings but also a whole range of industrial purposes, from agricultural machinery to suspension bridges. The invention of cinematography was similarly linked to technological progress, often as the by-product of such different developments as the search for new types of explosives, the industrialization of agriculture, and the invention of a new material for printers' rollers.

Then comes the process of discovery which takes place once the invention has been achieved. What this largely consists in is the discovery of ways of using the invention which the inventors had not actually been trying to provide for, because these are uses which the invention itself has made possible, and which could not therefore have been envisaged beforehand. This is certainly true of the invention of cinematography. Cinema, the institution and the industry which we now have, was not in the minds of the inventors and could not have been. Film, that is, cinematography, was invented; but the cinema grew.

*

The starting point for the history of cinema must therefore be (as Nowell-Smith also argues) an acknowledgement that cinema (or film), before it acquired any identity of its own, was immersed in a series of histories which conditioned the process of invention. These histories are those of the relevant aspects of science and technology, economics, aesthetics, and so on; and the prehistory (and, later, history) of cinema is interwoven with them. What the relevant aspects of these histories are cannot be assumed beforehand; they can only be discovered by historical research. In other words, none of these histories is sufficient in itself; they each invoke the study of those further histories to which they are in turn related.

Historical research can also be carried out too narrowly by failing to consider what it was people saw, or thought they saw, when they first saw a film; in other words, what the subjective experience of seeing films for the first time was like. This is a deficiency in many historical studies of the origins of cinema, which sort through historical records without ever really grasping film as a new form of cultural production. And so for the most part we haven't got beyond the stage of seeing the first films as curious historical records – records of historical interest simply because they're the first films. We still see many of the scenes which film was exposed to at the beginning as a kind of historical dumb-show, descended from the peep-shows and panoramas, magic lanterns and dioramas, of the nineteenth century, where people saw the reconstruction of battles and volcanoes, famous historical scenes and natural wonders, in short, every spectacle under the sun.

The peep-shows of the nineteenth century were miniature forms, popular in fairgrounds and on the streets, but often quite elaborate in their lighting and perspective effects; their origins are lost. At the other end of the scale, the panorama, originally created in the late eighteenth century, and the diorama which followed, were evolved to cater for the more refined tastes and susceptibilities of the bourgeoisie, and then expanded to attract a more popular audience. The diorama was devised by Daguerre some years before he invented photography. In fact his interest in the idea of photography grew out of it: he was looking for a new way of producing the naturalistic scenic drops which the diorama employed. He had begun as a scene-painter at the opera, so he knew what kind of spectacle would tantalize the bourgeois audience: the diorama was a system of producing illusions by means of changing lights, so that various parts of the scene, or certain elements within it, appeared and disappeared. Within a few years dioramas had opened in leading cities throughout Europe, together with many imitations. In some places there were almost as many of them as there were cinemas a century later.

The magic lantern, which is particularly important in the origins of film because it involved projection, first appeared in the seventeenth century – Pepys bought one in London in 1666 – as a development of the camera obscura, which artists used as an aid. The lantern employed a lens and lamp to project the image on a slide on to a screen. In the nineteenth century it became a public form of entertainment when new sources of illumination (limelight, gas light and later electricity) extended the throw and allowed projection before larger audiences, stimulating improvement of the lantern itself, the slides they showed, and the whole mode of presentation. Multiple lanterns and mechanical slides were developed capable of sophisticated effects including simple types of movement; the slide show became an entertaining (though always moral and edifying) lecture with musical accompaniment. In many ways it provided a crucial model for the development of the mass media over the following century, the first mass entertainment medium to inject a uniform view of the world into the heart of existing institutions such as the family and the school, thus moulding them from within, while at the same time reaching beyond the confines of any particular social class. Other entertainments, like music and theatre, adapted themselves to the social predilections of different audiences; in the case of the magic lantern it was fundamentally the same style of presentation which offered itself to all classes. The magic lantern was thus a key element in the process, which subsequently embraced all the media, of creating the myth of the average member of society, 'the man (!) in the middle', the model citizen of the modern democratic state.

As a pair of modern commentators have put it, 'The magic lantern was widely used as a domestic toy, but was also an engine of public instruction' (Martin and Francis in Dyos and Wolff, eds, p. 239). Indeed, its educational importance was recognized at the time by, for example, the Victorian popularizer of science John Henry Pepper, who spoke of it thus in his book *The Boy's Playbook of Science*:

> No other optical instrument has ever caused so much wonderment and delight, from its origin to the present time, as this simple contrivance. For a long time its true value was overlooked, and only ridiculous or comic slides painted, but its educational importance is now being thoroughly appreciated, not only on account of the size of the diagrams that may be represented on the disc, but also from the fact that the attention of an audience is better secured in a room when the only object visible is the diagram under explanation.

The popularization of science was one of the practices which the magic lantern, though not initiating it, certainly made its own, through the projection of 'general interest' slides on which the lecturer gave a somewhat anecdotal running commentary. Audiences for these presentations varied in size from little more than family groups to the capacity of a large hall; in 1891, 1,500 people attended a lecture at the Crystal Palace by D. W. Noakes, official lanternist at the Royal Albert Hall. In this way the magic lantern lecturer took his place as a mediator between the general audience and the nineteenth-century tradition of the scientific gentleman amateur, which played such a large role in the progress of science during the Victorian era. Later on, when film replaced the magic lantern, it took this tradition over, and for several years often retained the presence of a lecturer to provide a commentary, a practice which has since passed to television. At the same time, the magic lantern lecturer and the scientific amateur tradition occupy a special position in the prehistory of film on technical grounds, since many of the suggestions and discoveries which led to the invention of cinematography came from the scientific amateurs and were taken up by the lanternists in their desire to improve on the dumb-show they projected to their avid audiences.

Stimulated by a widespread demand, the popularization of science became a practice with particular ideological effects. For example, it helped to give science a safe and tame appearance at a time when it was increasingly to be feared by ordinary people

with only an informal education, because of the threatening role
it played in the technological development of the increasingly
alienating industrial system. But when film came along it was, for
the vast majority of people who saw it, not so much a new kind
of dumb-show as a wonder of science in its own right. It was so
mysteriously alive and vividly intense that it almost seemed to
speak with its own voice, even if it was difficult to make out what
it was saying. Considered as a wonder of science, film must certainly have seemed the crowning achievement in a line of scientific 'toys' based on optical illusions which resulted from the
investigations of the scientists and also fed the the process of its
invention. Many of these devices had been taken up by theatrical
showmen. Many of the early film showmen were professional
magicians, and early film culture owes a great deal to the ambiv-
alent position which film held somewhere between science and
magic – that is, a sense of the objective reproduction of the world
on the one hand, and the magical creation on the screen of
separate worlds on the other. In many ways film has never lost
this ambivalence.

However, new-fangled magic isn't always acceptable. People
are often as likely to disbelieve it as they are to be taken in by
it. William Friese-Greene used to tell a story about a woman at
one of his earliest moving picture demonstrations who went and
poked her fingers at the image on the screen of a girl's face,
convinced that the whole thing was an impossible illusion, and
that there were holes in the screen for the eyes of a real girl
standing behind it. The issue is not whether this story is factually
true – or all the other stories like it. The interest of these stories
is that they comprise a kind of myth of origins which reveal
crucial subjective aspects of the reception of early film. And in
fact there are some early films which turn such incidents into
jokes, making fun of the likes of country bumpkins on seeing
their first films.

*

Film had a radical effect on people's sense of history. Our sense
of history has changed – obviously in all sorts of ways and for
all sorts of reasons – but partly as a result of film. First, it made
many aspects of the world which to most people were distant and
unseen, immediate. Immediate but at the same time mediated.
Although film conjured up the apparent presence of something

which was absent, you saw it with your own eyes, and you knew you could go back and see it again. Because a camera happened to record them, the moments film was exposed to thus became historical moments of a new order. In a sense, therefore, film made history out of the present; it turned the present into a kind of immediate history. Film was thus an entirely new mode of production of human perception; it created a new mode of vision, provided a new way of looking.

The modern world almost seems to have begun with the birth of film, at any rate in retrospect. Because we're used to seeing film images of the First World War, the First World War seems to be part of the modern period. Anything more than twenty years earlier belongs to an era which we easily feel to be lost. Even if we have photographs, they are static, the portraits clearly posed, in short, more of an artefact than a historical record.

Of course, film was not unique in changing the social perception of the world. A host of new inventions during the course of the nineteenth century contributed to the same effect. The decade following the invention of photography – the 1840s – also saw the spread of the electric telegraph. The year 1876 saw Bell's original patent for the telephone and 1877 was the year in which Edison constructed the first primitive phonograph. Add to these the invention of the electric light bulb, also at the end of the 1870s, and the consequent expansion of the electrical industry, leading to wireless telegraphy at the end of the century, and what you have is a series of related but initially separate industries covering the fields of electrical goods, electronics and telecommunications, which by the mid-1920s have begun to converge in the hands of all-powerful transnational corporations, a convergence in which all the mass media are now embedded and which, since the Second World War, has come to constitute the fastest growing area of surplus profits within the whole domain of capitalism.

Some of these companies date back to the decades before the First World War. They include General Electric, Westinghouse, Siemens, Philips and a number of others, and already before the Russian Revolution, Lenin, an astute observer of these things, identified the electrical industry as the most typical in the 'new stage of world concentration of capital and production, incomparably higher than the preceding stages' (Lenin, p. 79). The early history of the film industry weaves in and out of, and is finally totally intertwined with, the history of these companies. Take Edison, for example, known as 'The Wizard of Menlo Park', famous as *the* inventor of the nineteenth century. Menlo Park was in fact a highly efficient research laboratory employing dozens of highly skilled tehnicians in which work was conducted on several projects simultaneously – for example, at the end of the 1870s, on the telephone and the phonograph as well as the electric light. General Electric grew out of the Edison Electric Light Company, founded in 1878. The Electric Light Company was formed a year before he applied for his successful patent, on the strength of his new-found fame as inventor of the phonograph, in order to provide the funds for the necessary research. In other cases he funded research through the income on work which had already proved profitable through the sale or licensing of patents. This was how he financed his pioneering work in the field of cinematography during the early 1890s, when he produced the moving picture camera which he called the Kinetograph, and the Kinetoscope for viewing the results, a 'what the butler saw' machine and forerunner of cinema proper. And in the same way that General Electric proceeded to engage in restrictive arrangements with other producers over the various patents involved, so too Edison's cinematography patents lay at the centre of the Patents' War during the early years of the film industry in the United States.

There is a critical difference, however, between the techno logies of film on the one hand, and, on the other, telegraphy and the telephone, which in part is the difference between the reproduction of images and the instantaneous communication of coded messages or speech itself. The telegraph, the telephone and the wireless telegraph (which led to radio) answered to quite different economic and social needs and opportunities from the parallel cases of the phonograph and cinematography. The growth of capitalism in the early nineteenth century had created pressing demands for improved commercial intelligence. The big banking houses like Rothschild's ran their own communications using couriers and carrier pigeons, and legend quickly transformed the Ostend boat which Nathan Rothschild's agent caught on the way to London just after Waterloo, so that Rothschild's were the first to hear the news of Wellington's victory and were able to speculate on it, into a specially chartered schooner. But it wasn't only news of political and military events affecting the market that the capitalists needed. *The Times* established its own network of regular information on market prices in different centres of trade, and Havas in France made the reputation on which his news agency was later based by supplying the Bourse with the European exchange rates. On the day that the Prussian state telegraph line opened between Berlin and Aachen, 1 October 1849, two new contenders set up in business, Bernard Wolff at the Berlin end, and at the other end, Paul Julius Reuter. As the European telegraph network was extended, Reuter preceded it. In 1851 he established himself in London in order to exploit the brand new submarine cable link between Dover and Calais. Reuter worked hard to gain the custom of the newspapers – and with the expansion of the British press in the 1850s following the repeal of stamp duties, he succeeded – but they were not his principal clients. On the contrary, his business, as it expanded to cover the globe, mainly served private commercial users, and right up to the First World War the supply of news to newspapers alone failed to produce a profit. (Today Reuter's is once again a major supplier of financial and trading information to business, nowadays transmitted instantaneously across the globe by satellite.)

The telephone similarly served to accelerate business, beginning as an object of individual consumption among the well-off which was both an aid to commercial transactions and also a luxury item in its own right. According to a circular published by the Bell Telephone Company when it set up in business in London in 1879:

> The development of the telephone in England although it has not made such rapid strides as in America, has, since its introduction, been advancing slowly and surely. A large number of instruments are now in constant use, and it has been found that the more accustomed one becomes to the telephone, the more its advantages are appreciated. But in the former country, by means of the central system, one communicates with one's tradesmen, calls cabs, transacts business of all kinds, without going out of the room.
>
> (Robertson, p. 16)

A year earlier, Bell himself had written in a prospectus addressed to 'The Capitalists of the Electric Telephone Company' – that is, to his prospective investors, that the telephone should immediately be brought prominently before the public, as a means of communication between bankers, merchants, manufacturers, wholesale and retail dealers, dock companies, water companies, police officers, fire stations, newspaper offices, hospitals and public buildings, and for use in railway offices, in mines and diving operations. Agreements should also be speedily concluded for the use of the telephone in the Army and Navy and by the Postal Telegraph Department.

(ibid., p. 12)

These inventions created new markets for the new types of communication they provided. These markets, and the inventions which served them, were intimately related, and stimulated each other's growth, like the telegraph and the massification of the press; and they created a certain ethos which conditioned the reception of moving pictures. The development of telegraphic news agencies played a major role in the shaping of the press at the very moment of its commercial expansion, when the introduction of new steam-driven presses made for hugely increased print-runs. The total circulation of daily papers in the United Kingdom in 1854 was less than 100,000, of which *The Times* claimed 51,000. Sixteen years later, during the Franco-Prussian War, the *Daily News* alone had reached a figure of 150,000, and Mowbray Morris of *The Times* instructed his correspondents abroad that 'the telegraph has superseded the newsletter, and has rendered necessary a different style and treatment of public subjects'.

According to one historian of Reuters, 'The sympathies of the majority of this new reading public were far more in tune with the "spot" news and short political messages, in which Reuter was to specialise, than with the longer and more reflective "correspondents' letters" of the more conservative *Times* and *Morning Post*' (Storey, p. 18). This, however, puts the cart before the horse. These 'sympathies' were actively produced by the press, through the way they played on people's political and cultural susceptibilities. Reuter himself very cleverly insisted not only that his telegrams should bear his name but also that they should be carried with no alterations at all in the wording, in order to avoid the political manipulation of his service by newspapers of different persuasions which could only damage his reputation. Reuter thus served Capital and Empire as a whole, rather than any particular party or interest group. And at the moment when the growing hegemony of scientistic values was promoting new notions of objectivity, the first step was thus taken in the construction of the modern ideology of 'objectivity' in the media, an idea that, in the case of film, succours the naïve belief that the camera doesn't lie.

*

Establishment history has it that it was the Education Act of 1870 which taught the masses in Britain how to read and thereby laid the basis for the new mass press. It is false, however, to imagine that before the introduction of universal elementary education the working classes were essentially illiterate, as the extent of the radical press in the first half of the nineteenth century makes clear. In the excited political atmosphere which developed in Britain following the French Revolution, when skilled artisans formed the social, cultural and political vanguard of the working classes, the printed word was deeply feared, and this vanguard formed an important part of its audience. Thomas Paine's *Rights of Man* is sometimes estimated to have sold one and a half million copies in a cheap edition; its first publication at the more expensive price of three shillings sold 50,000 within weeks, already an enormous figure for a book at that time. Here also was the readership for the radical press. When newspaper stamp duty was raised to fourpence in 1815 in an attempt to suppress the radical papers, William Cobbett, dropping news and concentrating on opinion, sold his weekly *Political Register* for twopence and achieved a sale of 44,000 copies – which meant nearly half a million actual readers. The repeal of the stamp duties in the 1850s was intended to reduce the price of the capitalist newspapers to enable them to compete more effectively with the radical papers. Obviously the improved news coverage which the telegraph news agencies made possible gave the capitalist press further advantages. What occurred in the process was a weakening of the culture of the early-nineteenth-century proletariat which had produced the political movement that the radical papers had served.

By this time the entry of cultural production into a capitalist market was already well under way, but mainly within the middle classes, since they alone could afford to pay profitable amounts of cash for their culture. I am thinking of such activities as the rise of the novel, portrait painting as a business, the growth of music publishing to exploit the amateur music makers in the middle-class salons, the practice of public concerts to a paying audience, and so forth, which all appeared long before capitalist development took hold of popular entertainment forms like music hall or created the mass press. When these things happened, the middle classes had already experienced the effects of commercialized culture at first hand, as consumers.

Around the middle of the century, British capitalism entered a new phase of buoyancy and expansion. Parliamentary reform was followed by the repeal of the Corn Laws and the victory of the free trade doctrine, and free trade enabled British capital to extract the maximum advantage from its increasingly powerful international trading and financial position. The consensual radicalism of the Chartist movement now waned, while the reign of Empire waxed. The result was a rise in the real value of working-class incomes and the beginning of a gradual reduction in the length of the working day – conditions essential for developing the mass exploitation of leisure. Changes now began to take place in working-class culture. A key area for us is music hall. By the mid-century, music hall was establishing itself as the major form of urban working-class diversion, drawing on various traditions in popular theatrical and musical entertainment going back a very long way. Now began the commercialization of the halls. The radicals had always spurned the halls and their antecedents, the traditional forms which E. P. Thompson spoke of, in *The Making of the English Working Class*, as belonging to the more 'rowdy' elements in working-class culture. As the radical tradition now became more institutionalized and self-contained, it also became more cut off from those untutored sections of the working class for whom the culture represented in the music hall was so central. Here then was a cultural situation where commercial interests were able to insinuate themselves all the more easily.

The music halls were one of the major sites where early films were exhibited. The commercialization of the halls over the preceding half-century constituted, as I shall show, an important model for what happened in cinema. Our analysis will trace the scope of this influence on both the aesthetics and the political economy of early cinema; in so doing, our attention will be drawn to a number of idiosyncrasies which distinguish film from the performing arts and give it a different economic system. These idiosyncrasies are only expectable. In material terms, as commodities available on the market, every art form manifests its own peculiarities, which stem from the material characteristics of the object in question: the oil painting is different from the fresco; the book is different from the manuscript. These differences give rise to distinctive traits in both the means and relations of production, and the modes of distribution and consumption. The oil painting as an object could be bought and sold, extending the market for the artist's skills; the book expanded enormously a market for literature which copyists had been unable to satisfy. Both gave the creator the opportunity for independence from direct patronage, and thus promoted the artist's individualism, until, in the nineteenth century, he often became the hero of his own work (the paradigm of the nineteenth-century artist being always male).

The new media born of the technology of the Industrial Revolution created new types of cultural commodity and new forms of access to the public. The photograph, the film, the gramophone record and the radio and television programme are products which reach their audiences in several different ways. In conventional terrestrial broadcasting, a single source may reach an effectively infinite domestic audience which pays nothing for the reception of the programme. What the audience in this system of free reception pays for is the apparatus, the radio or television set. The programmes themselves, from the audience's point of view, are not strictly speaking commodities. They are commodities only from the point of view of the companies which buy and sell them to each other. Different political regimes found different answers to the problem of financing a system of broadcasting in which the products are free at the point of delivery. America adopted the commercial methods of sponsorship and advertising. Europe, with some exceptions, opted for funding by government, either directly or by means of a licence fee.

In the case of the gramophone record, both the apparatus needed to reproduce it and the record itself are proper commodities: both are sold to the public directly, for domestic consumption. In its early days, however, the phonograph reached the public in ways more readily associated with cinema. Showmen, with their own apparatus, charged admission for the public to come and listen. (This even happened with television. My brother tells me that he first saw television as a child in the 1930s in the East End of London in the back of shop where you paid a penny to get in.) The public presentation of the phonograph disappeared when cylinders gave way to discs and the record market emerged at the turn of the century. The film, however, thrived on the audience, which rendered it unnecessary ever to consider the option of selling directly to the public for domestic consumption. The institution of cinema is constituted by the fact – and its consequences – that neither the apparatus nor the film itself passed directly into the hands of the consumer as a commodity. What the film audience paid for was the right of admission, and the model of exploitation is derived from music hall and theatre because the mode in which the individual exhibitor generates income is that of the box office.

If music hall was the dominant form of popular entertainment at the moment of the birth of film, the dominant mass medium of the day was the press. The massification of publishing in the nineteenth century came about through improvements in the means of both production and distribution: the development of rapid printing techniques using the steam press, and the advantages for distribution, both of speed and geographical dispersion, provided by the railways, of which book publishers also took advantage. As Raymond Williams has explained: 'it was in the bookstalls at the new stations, notably those of W. H. Smith, that the public could be reached in a new way. The cheap Parlour Library, and then the Railway Library, poured through this new outlet; the yellow-backs, with glossy covers, illustrated in colour, and carrying advertising on their backs' (R. Williams, 1965, p. 190). In the 1850s a new situation was clearly emerging: 'Defoe's description of writing as a "very considerable Branch of the English Commerce", and of its organisation in the typical forms of capitalist industry, had been an accurate foresight of a situation which only fully revealed itself when the market became really large' (ibid., p. 189). The result was, in Matthew Arnold's words at the time, 'a cheap literature, hideous and ignoble of aspect, like the tawdry novels which flare in the bookshelves of our railway stations, and which seem designed, as so much else that is produced for the use of our middle-class seems designed, for people with a low standard of life' (quoted ibid., p. 190). Arnold is specific: this is a middle-class phenomenon. It thus turns out that many of the characteristics later projected on to working-class culture were first encountered before the working class became the primary audience, but under middle-class tutelage.

The press was not homogeneous. The radical Sunday newspapers which began to appear in the 1820s tapped the same readership as the 'unstamped press' but without the politics. Instead they continued the traditions of popular literature in the shape of ballads, chapbooks, almanacs, accounts of murders and executions, and the like. Out of this stable came George Newnes's *Tit-Bits* (or, to give it its full title, *Tit-Bits from all the Most Interesting Books, Periodicals and Newspapers of the World*), which first appeared in 1881. According to Northcliffe, who introduced the halfpenny *Daily Mail* fifteen years later, 'The man who has produced this *Tit-Bits* has got hold of a bigger thing than he imagines. He is only at the beginning of a development which is going to change the whole face of journalism' (quoted ibid., p. 196).

The idea of the newspaper as a miscellany was succoured by the growth of the news agencies and the supply to the developing bourgeois press of a flow of translations of significant news and choice items from other newspapers in other countries. The Sunday press had adapted the same principle to the range of material in popular literature. Then came Newnes, not a journalist by profession but rather more aptly a representative of a fancy goods firm, to produce what one historian of the press called a predigested literary breakfast food for all the family. Basing his entrepreneurial skills on the recent advances in the technology of rapid printing, he was able within a few months to achieve a weekly sale of 800,000 – three times the circulation of the *Daily Telegraph*. The figure itself, though enormous, was not unprecedented. Much earlier in the century James Catnach, one of the most successful broadsheet publishers, reached a sale of 1,166,000 copies of the 'Last Dying Speech and Confession' of William Corder, the murderer of Maria Marten. What Newnes did was to show that you could sustain this kind of circulation from week to week.

A new generation of advertisers rushed to fill the channel which thus opened up directly to the mass market. A new style of news agency quickly appeared to supply the copy, which discarded Reuter's carefully nurtured principle of objectivity. The new newspapers were no longer competing for a market with the established bourgeois press; they were not concerned with supplying intelligence for sectors of the ruling classes; they didn't need to bother about objectivity, accuracy and precision. The result was the birth of 'human interest' and 'yellow' journalism: there was an increase in sensationalism and rumour, particularly from abroad and especially from the United States. Typical of the stories which now began to appear, among the old staple of crimes both famous and infamous, were tales of cyclones and the ravages of wild animals in obscure North American townships, and items such as the German Emperor's premature announcement of the remarkable powers of one Dr Koch's tuberculin as a cure for certain forms of consumption. This was the climate in which the inventors of cinematography were at work, egged on by the promise of commercial gain to produce ever new scientific wonders. None of them was better at exploiting the new publicity than Edison, who manufactured for himself a reputation the world over as 'the Wizard of Menlo Park'.

In short, the milieu which determined the reception of moving pictures was a world of miscellanies. Constrained by the technical limits of the device, each film lasted only a minute or so and early film culture hardly amounted to more than a miscellany of visual tit-bits. As if cinema at its birth were no more than a form of disconnected visual display. Anecdotal, and apparently ill-adapted to serving immediate purposes of intelligence, film was readily susceptible to the ethos of the new mass press, in which the reader is reduced to a kind of generalized stupidity. As Siegfried Kracauer was to put it. 'In the illustrated magazines the public sees the world whose perception of it is hindered by the illustrated journals themselves' (quoted in Frisby, p. 154). Meanwhile the 'quality' press, the serious small-circulation newspapers of the educated reader, more or less ignored it. After covering the first Lumière show at the Regent Street Polytechnic in 1896, *The Times* carried no further reports of the cinematograph for eight years. By that time, however, moving pictures had spread to virtually every corner of the land, becoming a familiar sight in popular milieux like music halls and the fairground; and within the commercial anarchy which characterized this process, the medium of film was beginning to acquire the aesthetic and ideological properties which were to make it so potent. John Grierson tells us that the cinematograph at first escaped the constrictions of his Calvinist elders because they accepted it as essentially different from the theatre. Sin still, somehow, attached to play acting, but, in this fresh new art of observation and reality, they saw no evil. I was confirmed in cinema at six because it had nothing to do with the theatre, and I have remained so confirmed. But the cinema has not. It was not quite so innocent as our Calvinist elders supposed. Hardly were the workmen out of the factory and the apple digested than it was taking a trip to the moon, and, only a year or two later, a trip in full colour to the devil. The scarlet women were in, and the high falsehood of trickwork and artifice were in, and the first fine careless raptures were out.

(Grierson, p. 132)

For the petit bourgeois film pioneer of the type that dominated the early cinema, the pull of music hall created a dilemma. These men, with imaginations formed and limited by Victorian lower-middle-class mores, were driven, by their very business sense, into association with a seedy world. Music Hall operated according to principles of aesthetic diversity, seen as late as 1910 in a programme for the Palace Theatre in London:

1 Marche Russe.
2 Miss Lily Hayes, Comedienne.
3 Vickey Delmar, Novelty Dancer.
4 Christie Duo, Eccentrics.
5 Selbo, Club Juggler.
6 The Palace Girls.
7 La Contadina, Italian Violinist.
8 Albert Whelan, The Australian Entertainer.
9 The Great Goldin, with a series of new illusions.
10 Orchestral Selection.
11 Miss Margaret Cooper and her piano.
12 Special engagement and first appearance in England of Anna Pavlova and Michael Mordkin, Russia's acknowledged greatest dancers and the famous leaders of the Imperial Russian Ballet, supported by a specially selected company of premieres danseuses.
13 Kinemacolor – Paris, the Gay City and Choosing the Wallpaper, and Urbanora Bioscope – Arrival of Lord Kitchener at Southampton, Mr Graham White's Great Aeroplane Flight, and Punchestown Races.

(Illustration in Pearsall, 1975, p. 54)

Commercial interests may have tried to fumigate music hall and
dissociate it from its popular origins, but it was far too deeply
tainted. As the century grew older, more feverish and more aim-
less, the night-time city drew into its net not only all those
elements which were already stigmatized by bourgeois respectability, including those who needed to escape into the demi-
monde of sexual corruption and thereby lived a double life
because nothing was worse than exposure. It also drew into itself
the impious intelligentsia, refined and sensitive persons, attracted
by a sordid romanticization of sin. Painters such as Walter Sickert
found here the same inspiration which Toulouse-Lautrec had
found at the Moulin Rouge, and Degas backstage among the
ballet dancers. Sickert painted Katie Lawrence on stage in Agos-
tino and Stefano Gatti's velvet-cushioned restaurant in the
Strand, and the scenes at the Bedford Palace of Varieties. As far
as the respectable bourgeois was concerned, if that's where artists
sought their inspiration this only proved that art was rooted in a
disgusting craving for abjection and it was best to have nothing
to do with it. But film was not an art and commercial motives
were bound to win out. Many of the early film makers had the
sound commercial sense of the tradesman, and went to the music
halls because that's where they found the audience or, rather, the
entrepreneurs willing to invest in the magic they offered.

Economically, the rapid spread of film involved the discovery
of its peculiarities as a commodity. Film is different from the
performing arts, from books, newspapers and magazines, from
paintings and printed graphics, gramophone records, and not least
photographs too. From the introduction of the Kodak camera in
the 1880s, the mass consumption of photography has been based
on the sale of both camera and photographic film backed by the
provision of commercial developing and printing facilities. In this
domain, which is mainly domestic, photographs are hardly
thought of as commodities at all. On the contrary, their delight
lies in their personal, apparently non-commoditized identity. In
comparison, the gramophone record, sold directly to the public
as a ready-made object, behaves like the book. Film is different
from both. People paying to see a film do not buy a copy of it.
(That only happens when video comes along.) Instead it is viewed
collectively, by audiences, and its exchange value is realized
through gate-money, in which it is the right to admission and not
the object itself which is sold. This makes it a cousin of theatre

but with a crucial difference: a film can be exhibited in many places at the same time. It does not require the presence of performers. The only productive human labour required to show a film is that of the projectionist. Moreover, the film is not economically consumed, used up, in a single act of consumption which removes it from the market as with regular commodities. Each copy of the film remains available for continued exploitation until it is eventually consumed physically only by being too scratched or torn or in some other way disfigured to be viewable any more. Hence the unprecedented speed of its dissemination.

What we pay for when we go to the cinema is not a material object we expect to carry away with us, but a promise, the promise of being startled, excited, teased, made to laugh or to cry or simply to be caught in a look of amazement, the promise of some kind of aesthetic pleasure. There is nothing unique about film in this respect. But if the first viewers could not have known the first time that this is what film would offer, the rapid growth of the audience only shows how easy it became.

# Chapter 2

# The sight of film

What appears on the screen, which our sensibility works on, is not reality, but a sign. The great error which has been committed regularly, is to embark on the study of film as if the spectacle of cinema placed us in the presence of a double of reality. It should never be forgotten that film is constituted by images, that is to say, objects which are fragmentary, limited and fleeting like all objects. What materialises on the screen is neither reality, nor the image conceived in the brain of a film maker, nor the image which forms itself in our brain, but a sign in the proper sense of the term.

Pierre Francastel

Film, like photography, is clearly different from earlier kinds of visual representation such as painting, and not just in the manner of its consumption and the audience to which it is directed. It has at least one material quality which makes its images members of a different order of representation: the mechanism of the camera means that it records whatever it's exposed to automatically. In the language of semiology, the representational painting is iconic. The relationship it bears to the scene it pictures is one of similarity between chosen features, coded according to the conventions of the style employed. Umberto Eco mentions a thirteenth-century artist who claimed to be copying a real lion, and yet reproduced it according to the most obvious heraldic conventions of the time. The photographic image, however, has the guarantee of likeness, so to speak, built in, because it is not just an icon but also an index. Index is the term employed by C. S. Peirce for a sign which, while it is not produced intentionally by a human emitter, nonetheless has a human receiver, like meteorological and medical symptoms. The photograph is an index to the extent that the signifier is produced by a mechanical and chemical process. It can only be faked by some kind of trickery (which in the age of digital image processing becomes ever easier). Trick films, which make impossible things happen, were a favourite genre of early cinema, as if there were a compulsion to see how far you could go with it.

The indexical attributes of the photographic image can be submerged, however, by the subjective control of the photographer. The stylistic choices the photographer makes can so inflect the subject of the image as to imbue the representation with all sorts of artistic hues. It can even transform the ugly into the beautiful. If it continues nevertheless to command our acquiescence, then, as Dai Vaughan puts it, this is because its visual idiom reassures us not only that this is the way it looks, but 'more fundamentally, that an object of which this is a representation must have existed in the first place' (Vaughan, 1995).

In short, the photograph is an iconic index (or indexical icon), objective and subjective at the same time. To employ the terms introduced by Etienne Souriau in the 1950s, the indexical aspect corresponds to the profilmic event: the objective appearance of the scene in front of the camera; while the subjective corresponds to the filmographic, which comprises all those elements that result from the manipulation of the camera and the process of editing.

Imagine, then, by way of example, a film which purports to show, according to the commentary – a thoroughly filmographic device – a supposedly primitive society. Look carefully at the implements used by the subjects in the film. Do they till the ground with iron hoes they couldn't possibly have made for themselves and probably got from a trader? Perhaps their oil lamps are made from old food cans. The way the film is shot, the way it's edited and presented, perhaps with music and commentary, may make these things almost imperceptible, but if they're there, the camera cannot avoid recording them. Perhaps the film makers never noticed them. But if the film makers had been painters, the fact that they never noticed them would mean that they would never appear in the painting.

This is not all. The photograph, by fixing the momentary sight of the object, gives vision a new dimension. On the one hand, it is able to render the moment magical – to grant the representation the power, for example, to evoke buried memories, or sometimes the imagining of remembrance. On the other hand, it makes it available to repeated scrutiny and directs attention to the inconspicuous. As Walter Benjamin puts it, in his 'Small History of Photography',

> it is another nature that speaks to the camera than to the eye: other in the sense that a space informed by human consciousness gives way to a space informed by the unconscious. Whereas it is commonplace that, for example, we have some idea what is involved in the act of walking, if only in general terms, we have no idea at all what happens during the fraction of a second when a person *steps out*. Photography... reveals the secret. It is through photography that we first discover the existence of this optical unconscious, just as we discover the instinctual unconscious through psychoanalysis.
>
> (Benjamin, 1979, p. 243)

This quality is enlarged by cinematography. As Benjamin explains in the companion essay, 'The Work of Art in the Age of Mechanical Reproduction':

> film has enriched our perception with methods which can be illustrated by those of Freudian theory. Fifty years ago, a slip of the tongue passed more or less unnoticed. Only exceptionally may such a slip have revealed dimensions of depth in a conversation which had seemed to be taking its course on the surface. Since the *Psychopathology of Everyday Life* things have changed. This book isolated and made analysable things which had heretofore floated along unnoticed in the broad stream of perception. For the entire spectrum of optical, and now also acoustical, perception the film has brought about a similar deepening of apperception. It is only an obverse of this fact that behaviour items shown in a movie can be analysed much more precisely and from more points of view than those presented in paintings or on the stage.
>
> (Benjamin, 1969, pp. 235–6)

This capability of the screen, the capacity to draw attention to the pregnant moment and the significant detail, lies at the root of its narrative powers. But it formed no part of the inventors' intentions for their invention, and could hardly have done so. It was beyond their imagination. As Arago said, speaking in the French Chamber of Deputies in 1839 on behalf of photography,

'When inventors of a new instrument apply it to the observation
of nature, what they expect of it always turns out to be a trifle
compared with the succession of subsequent discoveries of which
the instrument was the origin.' The capabilities of the camera had
to be learnt – just as its economic peculiarities had to be understood – in order to bring them to fruition. The early history of
cinema is the history of this learning.

\*

In contrast to Edison, whose early Kinetoscope subjects were all
taken from vaudeville, Louis Lumière photographed the world
around him. His first subjects were short actuality films of factory
workers streaming out through his own factory gates, members
of a photographic convention disembarking from a river trip,
princes and heads of state on official visits. The world seen
through the eyes of a successful bourgeois. One of the first Lumière films shows a train drawing into a station, approaching the
camera from a distance. To the first audiences, the train seemed
almost to steam right off the screen into their midst – there are
reports of the way people recoiled when the train got right close
up to the camera. That is to say that they didn't yet see the
screen *as a screen*.

The range of subjects filmed by Lumière and his team of
cinematographers is much greater than that of newsreel; many
are common everyday sights and some are not actuality at all,
but little staged scenes. Indeed, the very first film poster showed
an image from a comic sketch called *L'Arroseur arrosé* or *Watering the Gardener*, which Lumière included in his first screening
to the Photographic Club in Lyons in June 1895, and which, like
so many early films, seems to have been remade several times
(sometimes under different titles). This film tells a simple tale: a
young rogue steps on a gardener's hose, the water stops, the
gardener peers at the hose, the boy takes his foot off, the water
spurts in the gardener's face, who turns and chases the boy and
finally spanks him; all this in a single shot of barely a minute by
an immobile camera, which arguably fulfils the minimum conditions of narrative established in the work of Propp, namely,
beginning, continuation and conclusion. Yet it is not always easy
to sustain a clear distinction between the real and the fabricated.
Should we describe as fiction or actuality such mundane scenes

as those set up by Hepworth on the Thames at Walton around the turn of the century in which people fell out of boats? Orthodox film history contrasts Lumière's 'realism' with the 'fantasy' of Méliès, as if they represented alternative and fundamentally distinct modes of human consciousness. This distinction is based partly on historical testimonies. Lumière told Méliès that he regarded film as nothing more than a scientific toy. (Perhaps so, but the remark must also be understood in its context: Méliès wanted to buy one of the Lumière machines and Lumière was trying to put off a potential competitor.) And when Méliès did set up in the film business, buying his apparatus from the Englishman R. W. Paul, his first prospectus of 1897 announced that he specialized 'mainly in fantastic or artistic scenes, reproductions of theatrical scenes, etc. . . . thus creating a special genre which differs entirely from the customary views supplied by the cinematograph – street scenes or scenes of everyday life'. It is not much more than a year since the debut of the cinematograph and Méliès speaks of 'customary' scenes and 'a special genre'.

Siegfried Kracauer, in his *Theory of Film*, comments that 'Méliès's tremendous success would seem to indicate that he catered to demands left unsatisfied by Lumière's photographic realism', and considers that the two of them represent thesis and antithesis in a Hegelian sense, in other words, as if they were dialectical oppositions whose synthesis lies at the root of film as art (Kracauer, pp. 30–3). There is indeed a sharp contrast between Lumière and Méliès, but Kracauer's Hegelianism is almost too static and rigid a view of the relationship between them. It is not as if Lumière's films left unsatisfied part of the audience's hunger, but that they created new appetites. Lumière's films are now adjudged to be realistic, but we know how fantastic they seemed to their first viewers, with the train about to steam into the midst of the audience. Gorki once said about *Teasing the Gardener* that the image carried such a shock of truthfulness that 'you think the spray is going to hit you too, and instinctively shrink back'. He also wrote that the screen was a kingdom of shadows, no sounds, no colours, everything grey – earth, trees, people, water, air: 'This is not life, but the shadow of life, and this is not movement but the soundless shadow of movement' (Taylor and Christie, p. 25).

Kracauer offers as the antithesis of Lumière's *Arrival of a Train* the Méliès film *An Impossible Voyage*, in which we see 'a toy train as unreal as the scenery through which it passes'. Yet if the first audiences saw Lumière's train as if it could detach itself from the screen, then in a way Méliès's film – in which a cut-out of a train flies through the skies and vaults across the ravines of painted cut-out scenery – was simply the film of a train which had so detached itself and now traversed the world severed from its rails by the artfulness of the film itself. It is like a filmic metaphor for the effect on the audience of the Lumière film. (Perhaps then, we do see, after all, how films were first seen.) The next move was a synthesis of the magical animation of Méliès with the manipulation of the objective image in the trick film, where photographic realism behaved in impossible ways. In this manner – though this is very schematic – film began to surpass the simple reproduction of the world – the one we live in – and became the projection of another, more or less similar, but with its own laws.

The process was not just dialectical, but as the Russian literary theorist Bakhtin would call it, dialogical. The rapid circulation of early films, in the form both of multiple prints and remakes, quickly established a repertoire of different types of moving views, an extended community of film makers communicating in a new kind of artistic speech, a realm of visual utterances characterized, as in all cultural media, by a variety of genres. The natural condition of speech, says Bakhtin, is dialogue, and every utterance is inherently responsive, a link in a complex chain of other utterances, of the same kind and of other kinds. Early film is thus a world where social, cultural, aesthetic and ideological influences are all jumbled up with the discovery of the idiosyncratic properties of cinema itself. The genres of early cinema are mostly adapted unthinkingly from other sources, mainly popular. This is one reason why there is so much continuity between the ideological tensions that soon surrounded film and those of traditional popular entertainment, which authority had always viewed with suspicion, as an expression of the rudeness, lack of culture, and anarchism of the teeming and uneducated masses.

*

If the forms and genres of early cinema were adapted from other forms of entertainment and then redeveloped in cinematic terms, we must ask about not only technical precursors of cinematography but also the popular milieux where film made its appearance and from which it borrowed many of its subjects: music hall, the variety theatre and vaudeville, the circus, the fairground, itinerant theatre, the amusement arcade. We must ask what kinds of expectation audiences in these places would have brought to film, not only in terms of content but also visual form and iconography. For example – and as I shall later show in some detail – to locate the early cinematograph within the tradition of music hall is to draw attention to the inheritance of the stereotypes of pantomime and *commedia dell'arte*. Similarly, to emphasize its relation to stage magic and visual illusionism is to see the issue of realism in another light. Realism à la Lumière and fantasy à la Méliès are thus only two among various orders of imagery which populated early cinema.

Yet even when these various influences are acknowledged, another idea remains: the notion that early cinema was somehow 'primitive'. As Virginia Woolf put it in the 1920s, expressing a common prejudice of the literary elite, it was 'as if a savage tribe ... had found scattering the seashore fiddles, flutes, saxophones, trumpets, grand pianos by Erard and Bechstein, and had begun with incredible energy, but without knowing a note of music, to hammer and thump upon them all at the same time' (Woolf, 1950). This sort of notion has come under suspicion since anthropologists demonstrated the charge of primitivism to be little more than ideological prejudice against conquered colonial peoples. (Woolf was a feminist, but still an upper-class Englishwoman born at the height of the British Empire.) The early film makers were far from primitive: the pioneers were mostly middle or lower-middle-class businessmen with a good technical education and a conventional sense of the aesthetic. The only sense in which their films might be called primitive is that the equipment they used to make them consisted in working prototypes with no elaboration and extremely limited scope. It would be better to speak of early film as artisanal. Nevertheless, some very sophisticated film theorists continue to use the term primitive.

To most people nowadays, early film looks naïve. The first historians of cinema thought of it as a childlike time when film makers were learning the language of film (they did not say where the language of film came from, but give the impression it was somehow divined). Modern theorists see it as the period before the creation of the classic codes of visual narrative, or what Noel Burch calls the Institutional Mode of Representation

(IMR), which is to say those rules of film language that were institutionalized by the studio production system, especially in Hollywood, which evolved in the decade of the First World War. In contrast, says Burch, the first ten or fifteen years inhabit a Primitive Mode of Representation (PMR), with a distinct quality of its own. But if the contrast between early cinema and classical narrative is a real one, there are several problems in defining it. The first difficulty with Burch's construal, as he himself acknowledges, is that it leaves open the issue of how the one turned into the other: a question which I shall address in a later section of the book. The second problem is that usually such definitions are either idealized or too schematic, even when, as with Burch, they are hedged around with qualifications.

The characteristic visual form of the Primitive Mode of Represention in Burch is the tableau, with a fixed frame around a scene played frontally to the camera, in which composition and movement is centrifugal, and filmed in a single long take. The shot has duration but no internal rhythm. Players are anonymous. The tableau form has two sources. On the one hand it corresponds to the single continuous shot of the first cameras mounted on their tripods. On the other, it imitates the form of both the visual illustration and the presentation of an act on a proscenium stage. The viewer, like the camera, is external to the scene; the composition of the image is so arranged as to be fully contained within the frame. As a description of the *mise-en-scène* of early one-shot sketches, comic and melodramatic, this is accurate enough, at least if you accept that when the action spills out of the frame, as it often does, this is usually because of the camera operator's lack of experience and finesse in handling the camera and instructing the performers how to move.

What happens, however, when the scene is not an acted one, but actuality? According to Burch it is then unburdened by narrative content, and accordingly has no closure. In other words, the film doesn't conclude, it just stops, in the same way that it didn't begin, it merely started. There are many early films which display just this kind of fragmentary form, but not, as it happens, the first of the Lumière films, which frequently observe a definite action or activity clearly chosen because it can be shown complete in more or less the available length of the film in the camera. This is not yet narrative, but it does represent the conscious segmentation of time which is one of the definitive proclivities of film, and one of the conditions for narrative.

It is particularly misleading to call these early films primitive when you consider the question of visual composition. The actuality genre initiated by Lumière modelled its sense of visual composition on the genres of the photographic view and the picture postcard, which as Thomas Elsaesser puts it, 'quite self-consciously worked with composition and perspective' (Elsaesser, p. 22). Hence the placement of the camera in films like the train arriving at the station to produce a sense of perspective; and the use of light to give a sense of space. The whole approach is that of the practised amateur, neither primitive nor crude but civilized and well-behaved – like the photographers arriving for a congress in another early Lumière film, who doff their hats at the camera.

The effect of these compositions when they sprang into movement is critical. The train steaming towards the audience loomed larger and larger and made the first spectators wince. Running the film of a wall being demolished backwards was eerie and funny at the same time. These movements drew the eye in different directions. As Richard deCordova puts it, 'The Lumière films fall solidly within the rules of perspective representation, but the elements are in constant flux' (Elsaesser, p. 78). The workers leaving the factory move across the screen in random motion. Cyclists, masked by the crowd, appear at a stroke in the middle of the scene (such an act of appearance was impossible in painting or photography). In short, the flux of movement produces a tendency to discomposition of the perspective system that had been dominant in painting since the sixteenth century and which photography so easily imitated.

This hardly mattered with actuality, which, as Burch correctly puts it, 'was a matter of "catching" an action, known in its overall lines beforehand, predictable within a few minutes, but random in all its details' (Burch, 1990, p. 15). In the enacted scene, however, random movement becomes a form of noise, interrupting the flow or distracting attention away from the intended actions of the film. Thus, as soon as the action in front of the camera was 'made up', as soon as the profilmic scene became a profilmic event specially set up for the camera to film, the frame begins to bear down on the scene, trying to organize it into an intelligible point of view. This was usually done by centring the composition within the frame, thus re-enforcing the form of the tableau, but even simple actions easily burst the tableau asunder. In Lumière's *Watering the Gardener*, for example, the rules of 'good' composition are violated at almost every turn. As it begins, the gardener is on the left, facing out of the frame. When he chases the boy, both of them disappear from view for a moment. When he captures him he pulls him into the centre of frame in order to spank him, but then returns to his original position while the boy turns to exit frame right, unbalancing the composition again.

Gestalt psychologists such as Rudolf Arnheim have argued that the principles of artistic composition favour balance and harmony, and stigmatize discord and disorder. Perhaps early film can be seen as a testing ground for this proposition, in which we witness the first film makers beginning to learn the values of 'good' composition. At the same time, however, part of the pleasure of early cinema lies in the simple sight of movement and activity, and great delight was taken in traits like the chaos of the typical comic film, in which characters chase each other backwards and forwards across the screen in a frenzy which would lend its energy to slapstick. To call examples like this primitive carries with it (as Tom Gunning has pointed out) the connotation that it shows only 'an elementary or even childish mastery of form in contrast to a later complexity' (Elsaesser, p. 96). And this elides with a more sinister sense, in which it manifests a state of underdevelopment, a lack of some kind in relation to what followed: for example, a lack of editing, camera movement and variation of framing. However, it is not as if accounts of early cinema from this perspective are mistaken in identifying the typical features of the early film idiom. The problem is that of viewing things with hindsight, for, as Cavell puts it in another context, hindsight is of its essence blind to the past.

*

The early film has the appearance of a moving photograph projected by a new kind of magic lantern. The photographic quality was the essence of the marvel. The film was a real likeness of living reality, not an animated painted slide. The evidence of real life, so to speak. Painting is not evidential or veridical in this way: it cannot be taken as genuine evidence of what was in the scene. Painting gives us the subjective vision of individual painters; there is no way of knowing how far this diverges from objective reality, which is captured, however, by the camera. On the other hand, reproducing the world automatically is not quite the same thing as reproducing it faithfully or objectively. There is human choice involved in the operation of the camera and the result is therefore full of the subjective, socially conditioned and class-bound point of view of the film maker.

In this respect, film and painting are not so far apart. In both there is another level of organization of the image, which is not immediately visible, not on direct display in the visual representations in the work. It lies rather in a particular way of ordering these representations, the structural relationship between the elements they contain within them. The order of representation is the combined product of the properties of the medium and the historical situation in which the piece is produced. Each medium and each historical age produces its own sense of order, imbued with its own sense of time and space, or what Bakhtin calls the chronotope. The term, which means 'time-space', is borrowed from Einstein's Theory of Relativity, he says, 'almost as a metaphor (almost, but not entirely). What counts for us is the fact that it expresses the inseparability of space and time (time as the fourth dimension of space).' Applied to artistic forms it therefore indicates the way in which 'time, as it were, thickens, takes on flesh, becomes artistically visible' while 'space becomes charged and responsive to the movements of time, plot and history'; and how each genre possesses its own typical chronotope, the organizing structure of the narrative where 'the knots of the narrative are tied and untied' (Bakhtin, pp. 84, 250). The mere description of the concept sounds like the very definition of the art of film, which is the organization of spatial images through time, and of segments of time through spatial images, in short, of time and space in terms of each other.

Where in this grid of relations is the individual subject who creates the work located? Michel Foucault opens his book *The Order of Things*, with a pertinent account of Velasquez's painting *Las Meninas*. Foucault finds that Velasquez captured here something about the structure of the classical form of representation which cannot normally be explicitly conveyed within that form of representation itself. The painting shows us the painter painting a portrait of the king and queen of Spain, who are seen only as a reflection in a mirror facing us in the painting. The mirror hangs behind the painter and those around him who are all facing the king and queen – and us. On the left we see the back of the canvas which the painter is painting. Everyone in the painting in front of us is thus looking directly out of the canvas, the painter, the reflected king and queen, the subjects of the painting within the painting (which we cannot see because it is facing away from us), whom we see in the mirror facing us. In this way, the spectator – that's us – is connected to the king and queen in the centre of the scene, although, like them, absent, merely a reflection which ought to be a reflection of ourselves (and would be if this were a photograph) but isn't, but which transposes us into the position of the royal couple. The painted reflection serves to draw into the interior of the painting something which is necessarily (Foucault says 'intimately') foreign to it: the gaze of the viewer for whom the painting is displayed. Velasquez thus appears to do the impossible: to include the viewing eye in what it views. He even manages to include himself within the painting, leaving us to wonder how he painted this strange self-portrait. Foucault calls the painting a kind of depiction of the classical form of representation, and of the structure of its supposed objectivity.

If the photograph imitates the painting, film, as the animation of the photograph, redoubles the effect. The camera records the scene automatically, but the scene may be set up and the camera has to be pointed and turned on; and the sequence of images unfolding before our eyes appropriately arranged. The person who points the camera and arranges the sequence is necessarily absent – unless they choose to include themselves, as Velasquez did in *Las Meninas*, by means of some special kind of artifice. But unless reminded in this way of the absence which determines what is seen, viewers are apt to forget themselves as well. In early cinema, the camera assumes the view of the spectator in front of a scene; in acquiring the resources of art, the plasticity of the altering frame and of montage, the spectator assumes the vision and ubiquity of the camera. As Stanley Cavell has put it, we feel not just that the screen is something which holds a projection but also that it screens us from the world which is viewed. What is on the screen is present to us, but we are not present to it. The relationship between viewer and screen is therefore a curious one, not unlike the relationship of dreamer to dream: not so much an absence as a kind of invisibility.

The screen makes us invisible to the people who people it; it seems to turn us into voyeurs, as if to satisfy a wish to be able to see without being seen. The seductive power which film exerts over us comes from this condition, for seeing the world unseen absolves us of all responsibility for what goes on in it. We are no longer engaged in the world as actors who have the possibility, however limited, of affecting the course of events. This is not just philosophical speculation. There are early films which make fun of the naïve who fail to recognize the nature of the screen, like a Biograph scene of 1902 called *Uncle Josh at the Moving Picture Show*, where according to the catalogue a 'country bumpkin . . . becomes so overwhelmed by watching his first motion picture from a stage box that he tears down the screen in his enthusiasm to help the heroine of one of the films'.

If cinema calls on the same suspension of self which is mobilized in one form or other by every art form, the screen intensifies the experience by emulating the condition of the dream. As Christian Metz noted, the film encourages narcissistic withdrawal and the indulgence of fantasy, including temporary suspension of concern for the exterior world. In the words of George Orwell:

> Everyone must have noticed the extraordinary powers that are latent in the film – the powers of distortion, of fantasy, in general of escaping the restrictions of the physical world. I suppose it is only from commercial necessity that the film has been used chiefly for silly imitations of stage plays, instead of concentrating as it ought on things that are beyond the stage. Properly used, the film is the one possible medium for conveying mental processes. A dream, for instance . . . is totally indescribable in words, but it can quite well be represented on the screen. Years ago I saw a film of Douglas Fairbanks', part of which was a representation of a dream. Most of it, of course, was silly joking about the dream where you have no clothes on in public, but for a few minutes it really was like a dream, in a manner that would have been impossible in words, or even in a picture, or, I imagine, in music. I have seen the same kind of thing by flashes in other films. For instance in *Dr Caligari* – a film, however, which was for the most part merely silly, the fantastic element being exploited for its own sake and not to convey any definite meaning. If one thinks of it, there is very little in the mind that could not *somehow* be represented by the strange distorting powers of the film. A millionaire with a private cinematograph, all the necessary props and

a troupe of intelligent actors could, if he wished, make practically all of his inner life known. He could explain the real reasons of his actions instead of telling rationalised lies, point out the things that seemed to him beautiful, pathetic, funny, etc. – things that an ordinary man has to keep locked up because there are no words to express them. In general, he could make other people understand him.

(Orwell, p. 25)

It is no accident, then, that the lavish cinemas erected when the business became industrialized were called 'dream palaces', where films were shown produced by movie moguls who behaved like millionaires with a private cinematograph, dreaming what they thought were the dreams of the common folk. By reproducing the condition of dream and fantasy in commercialized form, film seems not only to absolve us of responsibility for the world, but also to absolve us of responsibility for our dreams and fantasies, or at least to drive them further inside us instead of awakening them. This is a critical key to the powerful ideological effects of cinema.

In the words of Cavell, 'It is our fantasies, now all but completely thwarted and out of hand, which are unseen and must be kept unseen. As if we could no longer hope that anyone might share them – at just the moment that they are pouring into the streets, less private than ever' (Cavell, p. 102).

But as Orwell adds:

Of course, it is not desirable that any one man, short of a genius, should make a show of his inner life. What is wanted is to discover the now nameless feelings that men have *in common*. All the powerful motives which will not go into words and which are a cause of constant lying and misunderstanding, could be tracked down, given visible form, agreed upon, and named. I am sure that the film with its almost limitless powers of representation, could accomplish this in the hands of the right investigators, though putting thoughts into visible shape would not always be easy – in fact, at first it might be as difficult as any other art.

(Orwell, p. 25)

# Part 2

# The dialectic of invention

# Chapter 3

# The conditions of invention

The re-reading of my excerpts bearing on the history of technology has led me to the opinion that, apart from the discovery of gunpowder, the compass and printing – those necessary prerequisites of bourgeois development – the two material bases on which the preparations for machine-operated industry proceeded within manufacture during the period from the sixteenth to the middle of the eighteenth century (the period in which manufacture was developing from handicraft into large-scale industry proper) were the clock and the mill (at first the corn-mill, specifically the water-mill). Both were inherited from the ancients. (The water-mill was introduced into Rome from Asia Minor at the time of Julius Caesar.) The clock was the first automatic device applied to practical purposes, the whole theory of the production of regular motion was developed through it. Its nature is such that it is based on a combination of semi-artistic handicraft and direct theory. Cardanus, for instance, wrote about (and gave practical formulas for) the construction of clocks. German authors of the sixteenth century called clockmaking 'learned (non-guild) handicraft' and it would be possible to show from the development of the clock how entirely different the relation between science and practice was on the basis of handicraft from what it is, for instance, in modern large-scale industry. There is also no doubt that in the eighteenth century the idea of applying automatic devices (moved by springs) to production was first suggested by the clock. It can be proved historically that Vaucanson's experiments on these lines had a tremendous influence on the imagination of the English inventors.

Marx to Engels, 28 January 1863

Inventions very rarely appear out of the blue. Take the case of the electric light. Most people know it was invented by Edison, and a few will give you the date: 1879. One or two – the type who go in for television quiz games – might even tell you that it was 'also' invented by an English chemist, J. W. Swan, but unfortunately Edison beat him to the British Patent Office. In fact the incandescent lamp has a long prehistory, obscured by the fragmented way these subjects are conventionally taught. The principles on which the electric light is based were established by Humphry Davy in 1802, following discoveries two years earlier by Alessandro Volta. Drawing current from a voltaic cell, Davy produced an arc light at the interrupted point in a circuit with a pair of wooden charcoal electrodes. He also passed a current through a platinum wire and through a carbon rod and in each case showed that they glowed until consumed by oxidization. Swan made experimental lamps in 1860, but they were impractical because he was unable to prevent oxidization. In 1877, however, the German chemist Herman Sprengel produced a vacuum pump, and the British scientist William Crookes discovered how to apply it to making a vacuum in a glass bulb. Together with Charles Stearn, another specialist in vacuum pumps, Swan returned to the problem and by 1880 they succeeded in bringing the electric lamp to the point where commercial production could begin. Edison only turned to the problem for the first time in 1878, and the rapid progress which he made was principally due to the sophisticated organization of his research laboratory (he already had twenty men working for him at the time, a figure which grew considerably during the 1880s) and his successful record in producing commercially viable 'inventions' which enabled him to draw on considerable financial backing. He formed the Edison Electric Light Company, with a capital of $300,000, on the strength of the invention of the photograph, a year before he applied for the successful patent, precisely in order to provide funds for the necessary research.

The invention of cinematography followed a broadly similar pattern, reaching fruition through an accelerating series of discoveries which fed into each other, some of which (like the vacuum pump in relation to the electric lamp) were made quite independently. Again the invention employed a number of elements, such as the arc lamp, which were already pretty widely known and used, even though they were rather recent. And again, Edison played a key role in the process, demonstrating the importance of properly funded research and development. Thus it was Edison's assistant, W. K. L. Dickson, who constructed the first successful prototype, the kinetograph, in which moving pictures were taken on celluloid roll film which was moved intermittently through the camera by means of perforations; these films were not projected, however, but viewed by one pair of eyes at a time through the eye-piece of a viewing machine, the kinetoscope, which made its debut in the entertainment arcades in 1894, seven years after Dickson started working on the project. But one sight of the kinetoscope was enough to prompt several well-equipped competitors into activity, including the Lumières in France, Paul in England, Skladanowsky and Messter in Germany and Armat in the United States, who one by one each came up with workable projectors within a year or two.

Arc lamps were used in large-scale magic lantern and panorama projection, and the invention of film was partly the result of attempts to develop and 'improve' these popular forms. Many of the early film showmen came out of this magic lantern tradition, which they soon began to replace, while many of the principles which the inventors called on entered the popular scientific culture of the nineteenth century through a number of devices and toys which made use of optical phenomena discovered by scientists earlier in the century. You therefore get different types of film pioneer, depending on what their background was and how they were drawn into their fascination with moving images.

Broadly speaking, the pioneers were either industrial or artisanal producers involved in photography or some related branch of production, or else they came from popular commercial entertainment. Some were practising photographers; some were already involved in another new device of entertainment, the phonograph. Some were popular showmen, especially magicians. Their class of origin, when they were not popular entertainers, was predominantly petit bourgeois. The type is exemplified by those from the magic lantern tradition, such as Cecil Hepworth, who combined the skills of a presenter with technical know-how and were therefore equipped to handle the new apparatus. Hepworth, as already mentioned, invented a new type of arc lamp which he offered to R. W. Paul when he saw Paul's moving pictures at Olympia in March 1896. Later on he invented a printing device, one of the first to carry the film on rollers and sprockets, made with parts taken from a projector. Plenty of other lanternists were similarly involved in the early days. When David Devant, the first person to purchase one of Paul's theatrographs – the first projector produced commercially in Britain – toured Scotland with a conjuring and musical troupe in which moving pictures figured as one of the main attractions, his operator was a certain C. W. Locke, an experienced lanternist well known in the lantern world for his numerous innovations in optical projection. It was important to have such a man on hand, able to repair the apparatus from his own expertise when something went wrong (quite a frequent problem in the early days).

Devant's role points us towards the 'magic' half of the magic lantern tradition. When he first became interested in Paul's apparatus, he was junior partner to J. N. Maskelyne at the Egyptian Hall in Piccadilly, 'England's Home of Mystery'. Maskelyne had not been very enthusiastic over the idea of moving pictures (indeed, many people were sceptical about it), which is why Devant ended up buying the apparatus by himself. But then later he changed his mind, and when he did so he tried to design a projector of his own. It was not particularly successful, but the point is that he was a clever enough mechanic to attempt it, since he had himself designed many of the illusions used in the performances at the Egyptian Hall, which were constructed in his own backstage workshop. And he had the resources to attempt a projector because magic had long since been mechanized. There is thus a link between the development of mechanical gadgetry and the traditional appeal of illusion as entertainment, to which magic had been reduced with the rationalization of religion that came with the growth of bourgeois society. The modern imagination has not exactly lost the old sense of mystery and awe – which goes back to pagan sources – at the power of the human intellect to master alien forces. But with the development of science and technology this fascination grew more secular, giving constant employment among itinerant and popular entertainers to those who presented the latest gadgets, and demonstrated the latest scientific wonders: from the electrical machine which Goethe saw at a fair as a child well before the French Revolution, to the demonstrations of X-ray photography which Friese-Greene gave on the music hall stage almost a century and a half later, after success with the projection of moving pictures eluded him.

The magic lantern was especially popular in Britain, France and Germany, but conditions for the more sophisticated development of the medium, in terms of both content and technology, were especially favourable in Britain. Elaborate multiple projectors were devised, capable of superimposing pictures and dissolving them into each other – even, by such means, simulating simple effects of movement, such as the ripple of waves or the drift of clouds, or physical actions like the movement of a limb. The latter effects were usually achieved by means of a mechanical device on the slide itself. Lanternists were forever trying to improve these effects, and because of this many of them were technically adept at manipulating both mechanical and optical equipment. In other words, they were adept at the practice of aspects of the same amateur scientific curiosity which they projected in many of their slide shows.

This helps to explain why film spread so quickly once the basic principles were established and the first demonstrations had taken place. Indeed, without these human resources the process would have been much slower, for in spite of their entrepreneurial intentions the first commercial manufacturers of the necessary projection apparatus were quite unprepared for the speed with which the new medium caught on. But there were plenty of people around who were equipped to try and construct the apparatus themselves – and not only lanternists. Thus Monty Williams, another who entered the field at the start in 1896, explained that he was inspired by the Trewey show of the Lumière cinematograph at the Polytechnic, where he was a student. He teamed up with a friend of his who was a mechanic. They copied down the design of the Lumière machine which was on display at the Poly. They visited the Patent Office and found out about the Maltese cross (one of the means of achieving the intermittent movement of the film past the lens). They inspected Edison's kinetoscope and finally they built their own projector. And then, when they started to make their own films, since raw film coming from the manufacturer in the early days had no perforations, they built a perforation machine by copying a postage-stamp perforator. How can we characterize this kind of activity?

The French have a word for it: *bricolage*. This refers not, as in the chain of superstores on the outskirts of Paris called 'M. Bricolage', to do-it-yourself, but to the much more subtle art of knocking something together from whatever happens to be at hand. Lévi-Strauss has used the term *bricolage* to describe a distinct type of cultural practice which is distinguished from engineering proper. It involves the true *bricoleur* in what he calls a 'dialogue' with his 'treasury' of bits and pieces, which allows for a process of substitution in construction. For example, 'a particular cube of oak could be a wedge to make up for the inadequate length of a plank of pine, or it could be a pedestal which would allow the grain and polish of old wood to show to advantage' (Lévi-Strauss, 1972, pp. 18–19, and ch. 1 *passim*). The procedure is necessarily limited, either by features of the pieces to be used which are already determined by the uses which they were originally designed for, or by the modifications which they have already undergone. Nevertheless an amazing range of products can be constructed in this way.

Since the *bricoleur* pays individual attention to each product, and it is virtually impossible that any two prototypes can be turned out which are identical, *bricolage* is evidently a method of production which is exactly the opposite of the mass production methods of modern industrial society. Someone like Maskelyne, who probably only needed one of each of his devices anyway, must have been a master at it. But not just the Maskelynes of the nineteenth-century world. *Bricolage* must have been a necessary procedure in one form or another at various stages in the process of technological development during a large part of the nineteenth century.

*Bricolage* becomes most necessary when attempting to develop inventions in areas that are not yet industrialized, especially when capital starts to be available for investment in these areas and sets off a rush of activity to try and grab hold of the new opportunity. This is exactly what started happening in the latter part of the nineteenth century. As Ernest Mandel has explained, 'The growing concentration of capital and the rising costs of new investments in spheres that had already been industrialised . . . inevitably meant a rapid increase in the volume of capital pressing for new fields of investment' (Mandel, p. 81).

When the process of industrialization was still only beginning, not only was there no established body of knowledge to go by in constructing new machines for new purposes, but there were no established means for producing these machines either. Machines had to be built individually and by hand. In a sense every machine was a prototype and therefore had to be built by means of *bricolage*. To some extent new machines could be built by bringing together the skills of different traditional crafts; this is a kind of *bricolage* on the level of the organization of the project – one of the practical characteristics which marks out the classical entrepreneur. At the same time, workers had to develop new skills and abilities, so the new engineering industry had to create its own technicians and workers 'who trained themselves as they produced the new machines', as J. D. Bernal puts it. There is a certain *bricolage* here too, since they proceeded to solve theoretical problems in practice before they were solved in theory, so that 'the new engineering industry did not so much depend on science as create it' (Bernal, pp. 26–7).

The next stage was building machines to produce machines. In his inaugural address as president of the British Association in 1861, William Fairbairn recorded that when he first went to Birmingham in 1814 all machinery was made by hand. By the time of his address, however, 'everything is done by machine tools with a degree of accuracy which the unaided hand could never accomplish' (quoted in Derry and Williams, p. 344). Yet according to Bernal, the development of techniques for accurate metal machining depended even less than the development of the steam engine on scientific knowledge. It was still a product of practical skills.

However, 'The new ability to machine metals accurately', Bernal continues, 'in turn made possible the series production of identical parts that could later be assembled' (Bernal, p. 28). Large-scale machine production of interchangeable parts began in the United States (where there was a particular shortage of skilled labour) where it was first applied to the manufacture of armaments. These included the revolver, invented in the 1830s by Samuel Colt, which belongs to the prehistory of film because its mechanism inspired Janssen's photographic revolver in the 1870s, one of the important experimental devices on the way towards cinematography. Later, the 'American system', as it was known, was extended to the production of such machines as harvesters, typewriters and sewing machines, while the commercial production of machine tools (that is, the machine manufacture of machines to make machines) led to increasing standardization in the production of many different goods. Yet even this did not eliminate *bricolage* from the process of invention, even in the machine world. The typical inventor of multiple-part machines, says Bernal, 'was usually a workman or amateur who contrived to find the most convenient arrangement of wheels, rollers, cogs and levers to imitate the movement of the craftsman at higher speed and using steam power' (Bernal, p. 28). There is still much of the *bricoleur* described by Lévi-Strauss in this. The art still lies in the trial-and-error assembly of available parts to perform a certain function or series of functions, so that the machinery is hardly designed but more or less designs itself (and looks that way).

All told, then, it is inconceivable that cinematography could have been invented earlier, not only because it would not have attracted anyone's attention as an opportunity for investment, but also because the technological means did not exist. Indeed, the film apparatus depended not only on a degree of precision engineering which had simply not been attained fifty years earlier, but also on advances in other areas, such as chemistry. And not only those aspects linked to photography. The science of chemistry in the nineteenth century was closely related to developments in several different industries – textiles, which saw technical innovations in the processes of bleaching and dyeing; armaments, with the discovery of new explosives; and agriculture, through the production of fertilizers.

The creators of this science were strongly practical men. Lavoisier in France died on the guillotine not so much for a lack of sympathy with the Revolution but, as Hobsbawm puts it, for being a big business man. In England, Dalton and Priestley (who had his house sacked and his books and laboratory destroyed by a 'Church and King' mob in 1791 for excessively sympathizing with the Revolution) both had links with a variety of practical men of their time through societies such as the Manchester Literary and Philosophical Society and the Lunar Society of Birmingham respectively. The research agenda which these chemists followed was largely set by the practical problems of industrialization. Thus around the middle of the century, the accumulation of new knowledge produced the invention of new synthetic materials called plastics, of which the first was celluloid, which, as we shall see, was crucial to the accomplishment of cinematography.

In short, there is no single line of development which leads unerringly from the earliest scientific experiments in optical phenomena to the invention of film. On the contrary, the process was divided between two wings: the scientists and the entrepreneurs. Of the latter, generally the most successful were technically educated businessmen, who could only approach the scientific knowledge involved in the pragmatic spirit of the *bricoleur*. Scientific discoveries had accumulated over several decades, but so had gaps in scientific theory. Different bits of scientific knowledge, especially in practical fields, lay in disparate relationship to each other; nor was scientific research yet organized – as multinational corporations, following the model created by Edison, organize it today – to achieve the practical results of invention. In short, the invention of cinematography involved a form of intellectual *bricolage*, which knocked together bits of theory and practical know-how to being the photograph to life. With what effects and implications will emerge more clearly if we now go back to those early experiments and the beginnings of the scientific theories of perception which have been held to account for the way film works.

# Chapter 4

# Theories of perception

The human body is the best picture of the human soul.

Baudelaire

Many histories of the origins of cinema have pointed out that its technical gestation includes a good deal of scientific work, such as the investigations of Roget and Faraday into the nature of visual perception, and that these investigations are linked to scientific 'toys' based on stroboscopic phenomena devised by Plateau, Stampfer and others. But it isn't enough to give the chronology, name the inventors and the inventions, try to settle claims for priority and assume that the connections will be clear. They aren't. And it says nothing in particular to add, as some writers have done, that observations on optical phenomena go right back to the tenth-century Arab astronomer Al Hazen, and even further to Ptolemy. Yet some writers simply repeat these isolated pieces of information without trying to understand them. This is one of the ways in which science becomes mystified.

Because you cannot arrive at an understanding of the process of invention in this way, film historians easily fall into confusion, in the course of trying to explain the cinema's technical origins, over the theory of perception which allegedly explains the phenomenon of film. What they do is reproduce the inadequate state of the theory of perception which prevailed at the end of the nineteenth century when cinema was born. They fail to take note of the huge developments in the theoretical understanding of the processes of perception which have occurred since then. As a result they have missed something about the dialectic of invention which, on the other hand, the suggestion of *bricolage* is more than capable of explaining: namely, that theories can be wrong, but the inventions 'based' on them can still work.

Film is commonly said to be explained by a phenomenon called 'persistence of vision', sometimes paraphrased as 'retention of image'. This is the notion that in certain conditions the retina retains an image of the impressions it receives for a short period after the object viewed is removed or changed. Although the origins of the theory go back at least to Newton, it was firmly established only by the Belgian scientist Joseph Plateau in 1829. The phenomenon was then associated with what we now know as the retinal afterimage, the image which you see after looking at a bright light and then turning away and looking at, say, a blank wall. Indeed, in the course of his researches, Plateau stared at the midday sun for twenty-five seconds, and went temporarily blind. Newton had once done the same thing, and, like Newton, Plateau took some time to recover, passing the time in a darkened room. (In the end he seriously damaged his eyes and went permanently blind in 1842.)

Plateau followed closely the experiments and observations of his contemporaries, especially the group of English scientists which included Roget, Faraday, Herschel and Wheatstone. In part, however, he developed the work of an earlier scientist, the Frenchman d'Arcy, who had presented a paper on retinal persistence to the French Academy of Sciences in 1765. In this paper, d'Arcy had tried to measure the familiar effect produced when a point of light, swung rapidly in a circle, looks like a continuous circle of light. Plateau wrote: 'Whenever we look at objects which are moving rapidly, the persistence of impressions modifies appearances' (Sadoul, vol. 1, p. 9).

The explanation of film on the basis of this theory goes something like this. A sequence of images is projected; between each image the screen is blanked out to allow the film strip to be moved on to the next one. This intermittent movement of the film strip takes place so fast – at least sixteen frames per second – that owing to persistence of vision, or retention of image, we never notice the gap between the images (unless the mechanism is uneven or imperfect for one reason or another, in which case a flicker can be seen. This was common enough in the early days, hence the term 'flicks', one of the original slang names for cinema). The notion of persistence of vision is invoked here in order to explain what appears to be a failing in our perception:

our failure to notice the gaps between successive images. The image is said to persist during these gaps. As we shall see, this attempts to explain the wrong thing. And it doesn't explain why we get the impression of movement, which requires an assumption that the sequence of images is integrated in some way.

This account reflects major difficulties in the invention of the apparatus, although it would be wrong to imagine that these difficulties were always understood theoretically before their solutions were attempted. One problem was what the film strip should be made of and how to control its movement, how to devise a method of effecting the intermittent movement of the strip at considerable speed and be able to maintain correct registration of the image. This had to be constant in both the camera and the projector, because any inconstancy in either would make the image on the screen wobble. The relevant parts of the apparatus therefore had to be finished with a high degree of accuracy, and this is what makes it inconceivable that film could have been invented in an earlier period when such accurate machining was not ordinarily possible. Many of the design problems here have been studied in considerable detail, but much less attention has been paid to the problem of the material the film strip was made of. Early experiments were carried out using paper treated with castor oil to make it transparent, but the paper kept tearing. The problem was only solved with the production of celluloid in sheets that were sufficiently thin to be both transparent and flexible. Later on I shall look at the history of the quite independent invention of celluloid, and the enormous implications which its conditions of manufacture had for the development of the film industry.

*

One of the first of the nineteenth-century scientific 'toys' commonly cited by film historians is the thaumatrope, which consists of nothing more than a smallish disc, held by pieces of string and spun between the fingers. It has two drawings, one on either side, which merge into one when the disc is spun. One drawing, for example, might consist of a winter tree with its branches bare, the other of its summer foliage. When the disc is spun, the image you see is of a tree in leaf. (Obviously the drawings on opposite sides must be placed in the correct position relative to each other.) Frequently the drawings were designed to produce comic effects and were accompanied by comic or witty epigrams. One which the film historian Deslandes quotes consisted of a rose-bush on one side and a flower pot on the other, with the inscription 'This is the tree of liberty, planted by revolution' (Deslandes, vol. 1, p. 28).

Frederick Talbot, author of one of the first classic accounts of cinema, published in 1912, credits the invention of the thauma-trope to the astronomer John Herschel, but it was a Dr Paris who popularized it. Paris, a well-known London physician, the author of several treatises on medicine, a friend and later biographer of Humphry Davy, manufactured the toy, and wrote about it in a book published in 1827, whose title is sufficient indication of its relation to the popularization of science which I've already spoken about: *Philosophy in Sport Made Science in Earnest*. Paris considered the device might serve educational purposes. He thought it could be used, for example, to illustrate the metamorphoses of Ovid.

The source which led Talbot to credit the invention to Herschel may have been an account by Charles Babbage (the mathematician who first conceived the computer) of a dinner party which Babbage attended with Herschel (*Passages from the Life of a Philosopher*, 1864). The two of them were old collaborators, starting in 1813 with experiments on electricity. According to Babbage, Herschel demonstrated the principle of the thaumatrope at the dinner table using a coin. Babbage says he told a Dr Fitton about it, and Fitton produced a disc with drawings on it. Fitton was a doctor, geologist and astronomer who led the campaign for Herschel's election to the Royal Society. A few months after the dinner party, says Babbage, he heard someone at a Royal Society dinner talking about a 'marvellous invention' called the thaumatrope, credited to Dr Paris and on sale for the price of seven shillings and sixpence at the Royal Institution, where Faraday worked.

Deslandes has questioned some of the details of Babbage's account. Be that as it may, two things are clear. First, Paris was the man who cashed in on the thing; and second, we're dealing here with a close-knit group of gentlemen scientists who amused each other in their social chit-chat with anecdotes and puzzles which issued from their scientific work. It is impossible to find a single original author for games of this sort; they are a kind of folklore, whose 'invention' cannot be traced to any single individual. Someone – presumably Dr Paris – coined the name, but what this name applies to is the commercial development of what was obviously a socially well-established piece of knowledge among the scientists.

Another optical illusion which attracted the attention of the scientists around the same time was the effect of stroboscopic movement. In 1824, a few years before the thaumatrope appeared, the mathematician Roget (also known as the original author of the *Thesaurus*) presented a paper to the Royal Society, *Explanation of an optical deception in the appearance of the spokes of a wheel seen through vertical apertures.* It seems that Roget had noticed when looking idly through a Venetian blind at traffic in the street outside that the spokes of a wheel on a passing cart appeared to stand still. The explanation of the phenomenon is this. The slats of the blind interrupt our continuous vision of the wheel going round. They act, in fact, like a kind of shutter. The effect works when both the distance between the slats, and the speed at which the wheel revolves, are such that each time we catch sight of the wheel it has revolved by an angle precisely equivalent to the angle between a whole number of spokes, so that the wheel does not appear to have revolved on its axis at all. (Another version of the effect, familiar to everyone who watches Westerns, is produced when the angle of revolution is not equal to a whole number of spokes: in that case, in each successive film frame, the spokes of the wheel have moved a distance short of a complete segment and the total effect is of reverse movement; that is, the wheel appears to be going backwards although the wagon is moving forwards. A similar effect can often be noticed in shots of aeroplane propellers as they begin to revolve, which suddenly seem to stand still and then reverse their motion until they become a blur.)

These curious observations were very often made by scientists outside the main field of their work. A few years later, for example, Faraday was struck by virtually the same effect at just the time when he was reaching his first great discoveries in electro-magnetism. Leading scientists at the time supplemented their official, but small, institutional salaries by working as consultants for industrialists. 'Being at the magnificent lead mills of Messrs. Maltby', Faraday wrote, 'two cog-wheels were shown me moving with such velocity that if the eye were retained immovable no distinct appearance of the cogs in either could be observed; but, standing in such a position that one wheel appeared behind the other, there was immediately the distinct though shadowy resemblance of cogs moving slowly in one direction' (quoted in Crowther, 1940, pp. 124–5). Faraday then constructed a device which illustrated the principle, just as Roget too had constructed a laboratory apparatus for the purpose of closer study. Faraday's device, known as the Faraday wheel, consists of two matching wheels mounted on the same axis with spokes around the perimeter. When the spokes of the further wheel are viewed through the spokes of the nearer one during rotation, the viewer's sight of them is interrupted in the same way as the slats of the Venetian blind in the effect which Roget noticed interrupt our view of the wheel. And as Faraday also observed in his 1831 paper, *On a peculiar class of optical deceptions*, where he gave an account of the matter, the same effect is also produced with a single wheel whose revolution is viewed in a mirror through its own spokes.

The Faraday wheel is an example of a peculiar class of scientific experiment. In the orthodox view, scientific experiments are derived from hypotheses, and are intended to measure precise values which it is the function of the hypothesis to designate beforehand. The hypothesis, in turn, is derived from an overall theoretical framework, or paradigm, as T. S. Kuhn has called it. Sometimes, however, puzzling observations are made virtually by chance, which command a scientist's attention even without the existence of a proper theoretical framework into which they can be fitted. In that case, experiments may be designed not so much to gather information of a kind which has been predesignated, but in order to re-create or simulate the conditions of the chance observation so as to be able to study it in isolation. The Faraday wheel is just such an experiment, and indeed so are many of the experiments on visual perception in the early part of the nineteenth century which belong to the prehistory of cinema. As Kuhn has explained in his study *The Structure of Scientific Revolutions*, this is often inevitable in the early stages of discovery in a new scientific field, before it becomes a unified territory of study.

In the absence of a paradigm or some candidate for paradigm, all of the facts that could possibly pertain to the development of a given science are likely to seem equally relevant. As a result, early fact gathering is a far more nearly random activity than a theory makes possible, and more recondite aspects are usually overlooked. The resulting pool of facts contains those accessible to casual observation and experiment together with some of the more esoteric data retrievable from established crafts, like medicine, calendar making and metallurgy. Because the crafts produce data that have not been discovered casually, technology has often played a vital role in the emergence of new sciences (Kuhn, p. 15). This accounts precisely for the condition in which the early discoveries in optical illusion were made at the beginning of the nineteenth century, including the casual observations made by both Roget and Faraday. All they needed to make these observations was their formation as scientists, which made them readily observant, and opportunities like that provided by Maltby's lead mills. The branch of science which later developed to contain these observations is concerned with the nature of observation: the psychology of perception.

Plateau took the principle of the Faraday wheel further. (Again Deslandes has investigated who influenced whom, and he remarks that Plateau reproached Faraday for failing to cite his own experiments of a few years earlier. However, according to one of Faraday's biographers, J. G. Crowther, Faraday had not known of Plateau's work when he produced his own paper.) What struck Plateau was first that it was possible to reduce the appearance of any object with a periodic (i.e. repetitive) movement to immobility by viewing it through the spokes of a single Faraday wheel. But he also noticed how if you altered the speed of the wheel so that it was no longer precisely equivalent to the rate of repetition in the object under examination, the movement of the object reappeared, but extremely slowly. This was what Faraday actually observed in Maltby's lead mills: the 'shadowy resemblance of cogs moving slowly in one direction'. In 1832, Savart, remembered today for his work in acoustical physics, used this method to examine the patterns of the vibration in the string of a musical instrument. (This, of course, is always the way science proceeds: discoveries in one field are applied to researches in another. We shall meet with this again.) Plateau drew from these facts the conclusion that the phases of a movement could be reconstructed by inverting the process.

What Plateau did was to reverse the various effects in a series of experiments aimed at synthesizing images rather than breaking down the appearance of objects in motion. This led him to the invention of one of the most important devices in the prehistory of cinema, which came to be known as the phenakistoscope (from the Greek, *phenax*, 'deceptive', and *scopein*, 'view'). You take a disc, he said, and divide it up into equal segments by cutting slots in it like spokes. You then draw an identical image in the same relative position in each segment. On viewing the revolving disc through the slots, in a mirror, with the side carrying the images facing the mirror, the images appear to stand still like the spokes of a Faraday wheel. But if instead of using an identical image you drew a series of figures each representing a different position in a sequence of movement, such as a dancer doing a pirouette, you would then see a perfect representation of the movement which the series of drawings represented. This was how he explained it:

> It is a natural consequence of the well-known phenomenon of the persistence of the sensations of vision. Each time an opening passes in front of the eye, it allows one to see the image of the disc and the figures it carries for a very short moment. The same effect is produced by each of the slits. A series of images results which appear successively before the eye. It only remains that these figures . . . differing slightly in form and position, serve easily to become integrated, which results in the illusion in question.
>
> (Quoted in Sadoul, vol. 1, p. 18)

The paper in which he described these findings was published early in 1833. But already a few months earlier he had sent the apparatus to Faraday in London. It was soon copied and sold as a toy, like the thaumatrope. The copies were imperfect, and Plateau protested, eventually marketing his own more accurate model. A similar device was produced at about the same time, but quite independently, by an Austrian geometrician, Simon Ritter von Stampfer. He called his apparatus by the name stroboscope (from the Greek, *strobos*, 'whirl'; *scopein*, 'view'). This is the word which has remained current for a revolving disc carrying lines arranged like spokes, intended to produce a static image at a certain speed, later used to test the speed of a turntable. (The coincidence of discovery by people working independently is another thing we shall come across again.)

Various 'improvements' to the invention were soon devised. In 1834, the English mathematician Horner produced a version which he named the zootrope. Instead of a disc, it consists of a band of images mounted inside a drum and viewed from the outside through slots in the drum as the drum rotates. (This eliminates the need for a mirror, though later versions brought it back, placing a series of mirrors at the centre of the drum so that the viewer looked at a reflection rather than the side of the drum opposite the slit. This increased the number of people who could view the toy at the same time.) The zootrope was the apparatus which received the popular name 'Wheel of Life'.

*

In the thaumatrope, two different rapidly repeating images merge into one. In the Faraday wheel, the effect is produced by the rapidly repeating interruption of a single continuously repeating stimulus. In the wheel of life, these two effects, which Talbot called the reverse of each other, have been synthesized. A series of discontinuous images merge into continuity, because the images are presented at a speed too fast to differentiate. This is not the same as persistence of vision – but, in the absence at the time of any real theory of perception, for reasons that were hardly apparent.

The idea of persistence of vision was the only explanation of the phenomenon of film available in its early years. The most sophisticated version is found in the 1912 book by Frederick Talbot. Talbot was for long a major source for writers on cinema, and possibly, therefore, the failings of subsequent accounts may be due at least in part to people trying to summarize his explanation – and making a mash of it. According to Talbot,

> The brain is somewhat similar to the sensitized emulsion of the photographic plate upon which the image is impressed in a latent manner, and so takes time to assert itself under the developing process. In the work of reconstruction the brain is relatively sluggish; hence after it has reformed the picture it will retain that impression after the reality has disappeared from before the eye.
>
> (Talbot, p. 4)

It is this which he called persistence of vision, though in line with late-nineteenth-century psychology he believed this to operate not in the retina itself but in the cortex. The problem with this account is that in proposing the mechanism of the camera as a model for the working of the brain, it presupposes what it purports to explain.

One element in Talbot's explanation, however, has been upheld in modern theories of perception: the fact that observation is a cortical process. The receptor – the eye – has to signal its sensations to the parts of the brain which interpret them. We now know that this process of interpretation consists of various stages, and is interactive in character. As A. R. Luria (p. 229) explains:

> The psychology of the nineteenth century regarded perception as a passive imprint made by external stimuli on the retina, and later in the visual cortex. . . . Modern psychology attempts to analyse perception from quite different standpoints. It regards perception as an active process of searching for corresponding information, distinguishing the essential features of an object, comparing the features with each other, creating appropriate hypotheses, and then comparing these hypotheses with the original data. . . . It begins with the analysis of the structure perceived, as received by the brain, into a large number of components or cues which are subsequently coded or synthesized and fitted into the corresponding mobile systems. This process of selection and synthesis of the corresponding features is active in character and takes place under the direct influence of the tasks which confront the subject. . . . During the perception of familiar objects, firmly established in past experience, this process is naturally contracted and takes place by a series of short cuts, whereas during the perception of new and unfamiliar or complex visual objects, the process of perception remains full and uncontracted.

The stages of analysis of visual data begin in the eye itself, in the rods and cones of the retina. A discovery of more recent times, this has a variety of consequences which Talbot or anyone earlier could not have been aware of. The rods and cones respond to different kinds of stimulus. Because they are sensitive to different wavelengths, the cones provide us with colour vision while the rods, attuned to twilight vision, are monochrome. The rods are especially geared to the detection of contrast, and thus of movement, for changes of contrast mean that something is moving. As the neuroscientist Susan Greenfield puts it, 'contrast means edges, edges mean form, form means shapes, shapes mean significance' (Greenfield, 1994). Thus, a moving object stimulates rows of rods as it passes across the visual field, firing them one after another, on and off, as the light strikes each row of rods successively. The rods thus trace, through their successive stimulation, the passage of a shape in a movement. The brain distinguishes displacement in the retina caused by objects moving from displacement caused by the continual movement of the eye itself, by feeding back information about these eye movements which can then be cancelled out. In short, the signals which the eye sends to the interior of the brain themselves contain information about movement. This is clearly different from the film strip.

The problem originates with the notion of 'persistence of vision' itself: an unfortunate misnomer especially when para phrased as 'retention of image'. There is, in fact, no retention at all, but the inability of the eye to distinguish rapidly repeating stimuli beyond a certain threshold (which varies according to the circumstances). As R. L. Gregory (p. 109) explains:

> Persistence of vision is simply the inability of the retina to follow and signal rapid fluctuations in brightness. If a light is switched on and off, at first slowly and then more frequently, one will see the light flashing until at about thirty flashes per second, it looks like a steady light. If the light is bright, the Critical Fusion Frequency (as it is called) is considerably higher, and may reach about fifty flashes per second.

What we see on the cinema screen is a succession of patterns of fluctuating brightness flashing on and off at a rate something above sixteen a second.

Talbot's explanation of how this turns into the perception of movement is based on the notion that the brain recognizes movement by constructing and comparing successive pictures relayed from the eye as if they were like the individual frames of a film. But this already assumes an answer by supposing that the way we synthesize movement from the successive frames of the projected film strip is the same as the way we generally perceive movement. Film, as it were, fools the brain, according to Talbot's explanation, by presenting successive pictures at a rate which roughly corresponds to what he calls, by analogy with photography, the latency period in the brain itself. Each new image is superimposed on the previous one just as the previous image fades (a bit like the construction of a television picture, as we might suppose nowadays). This superimposition produces the illusion of movement. In the case of a man walking, for instance, the brain perceives in the second picture the changed position of the left foot of the man in relation to the stationary objects, and this part of the first picture dissolving into the second picture causes the brain to believe that it actually witnessed the depression of the man's foot and the slight forward movement of his whole body.

(Talbot, p. 7)

There is something in this account which is curiously reminiscent of eighteenth-century automata, those clockwork models of human figures which reproduce the complex movements of acrobats, magicians and musicians. Beautifully modelled on the outside (the heads, in particular, were modelled by specialists), they have insides consisting of an extraordinary system of cogs, levers and pulleys. Originally little more than an extension of the blacksmith's craft, they developed, especially in France, into a branch of the intricate workmanship of clockmakers and jewellers. They were toys for the rich, costing in France up to a thousand francs each at a time when the average income was as low as twenty francs a year. In the present context, the most teasing thing about them is the idea they seem to represent of the interior workings of the human being: the idea of the human being as a fantastically intricate but completely mechanical object.

However, if the eye actually transmits information about movement to the interior of the brain, then it cannot be like a movie camera after all. Neurophysiologists now believe that the optically perceived world is indeed 'reconstructed' in a projection area within the cortex, but the process they describe is far from mechanical.

According to modern experimental psychology there are two separate phenomena. Gregory says that the effect of film depends on the interaction of the two of them: 'persistence of vision' properly understood in terms of threshold (or critical fusion frequency), and the phenomenon of apparent movement. This is the general term now used for the effect which was isolated in the early part of this century by the psychologist Max Wertheimer and labelled by him the 'phi phenomenon'.

The simplest method employed in the laboratory to demonstrate apparent movement uses an apparatus similar to the one which demonstrates the critical fusion frequency. Here, instead of one light flashing on and off, there are two, placed near each other and flashing alternately. When the flashes alternate at a speed which goes beyond the threshold, the viewer no longer sees two lights flashing alternately, but a single light oscillating between two points. (This, of course, recalls the circling light effect.) (See Gregory, p. 110.)

Another piece of laboratory equipment is used to produce a different version of the effect. It consists of a paper band passed in front of an aperture (like a film strip passing in front of a lens, but here without a shutter). Identical shapes are located at regular intervals along the band, which is lit from behind; the distance between them is such that only one of the shapes can appear in the aperture at the same time. The dominant effect produced when the band is moved is of apparent reverse movement. According to one laboratory witness, the shape appearing in the aperture begins to look like a bouncing rubber ball; according to another, like a sledgehammer in action. This is due to the fact that the shape appears at the bottom of the aperture only a tiny interval after disappearing from the top – again the interval is beyond the threshold – so that the thing appears to oscillate between the two points (see J. F. Brown, in Vernon, p. 257). Obviously this is very close to film. You can insert a shutter to eliminate the reversal effect. If you then replace the identical images with a sequence, you get an apparent movement created by the continual slight displacement of the images in the frame, which merge into continuity when their speed of presentation passes the threshold (just like the wheel of life).

If these principles do not yet explain the phenomenon of film, they tell us something about the perceptual processes involved. On the basis of their investigation of apparent movement, Wertheimer and others produced the first hypotheses about what was going on inside the cortex, though these are not now generally accepted. As Luria pointed out, the terms of explanation which scientists have been developing have changed. Hence 'persistence of vision', as the nineteenth century understood it, is an archaic notion.

'Persistence of vision' refers to what Gregory calls the 'visual fact' that there is a threshold. The phi phenomenon is an effect that occurs under certain conditions beyond it. This would explain why it was so easy to confuse the two. But there is also another question involved – that of rapid repetition. This is the phenomenon known in information theory (one of the new disciplines produced by the changing terms of explanation) as statistical periodicity. Crudely, this means the repetition of a stimulus at a rate which is too fast to be perceived.

Information theory (developed in the mid-twentieth century by Claude Shannon, Norbert Wiener and others) consists largely in the application of mathematics to processes of communication. It can be applied to the psychology of perception because, according to information theory, communication means the passage and exchange of information, which is the basic aspect of all neurophysiological processes; that is, the passage of signals through the central nervous system.

Periodicity, defined by mathematics, is the regular repetition of a phenomenon at the end of a certain interval of time, called the period. However, information theory makes a distinction between the occurrence of periodicity at a rate where it can be perceived phenomenologically (i.e. as a recognizable quality of the object) and its occurrence at a faster rate where this is no longer possible. The beat in music is an example of the former. Beyond the threshold periodic repetition dissolves into continuity. It ceases to be perceived as such and becomes statistical periodicity. This is the domain of musical pitch, where the term 'frequency' refers to the statistical periodicity of the sound waves which make up the note. Abraham Moles says, 'periodicity only appears on our temporal scale. It disappears when the rhythms become more rapid than 16 to 20 per second (as in the movies or in "musical" sounds). ... We know that the essence of the moving picture for us is continuity, not the periodicity which concerns only the engineer or technician' (pp. 67–8).

Periodicity, at the phenomenological level, creates the forms of expectation which find expression in our sense of rhythm. Here, says Moles, 'The phenomenological approach ... opposes the scientific a priori, for it suggests to us the concept of the length of the present – the perceptual threshold of duration.' What Moles means by the 'perceptual threshold of duration' is the minimum length of time a stimulus must last in order for us to be aware that it is lasting any time at all. We cannot be aware of duration in any stimulus which lasts less than this period of time. That doesn't mean we cannot perceive stimuli which last for shorter durations. We can, even when unaware of it, as in subliminal perception. It means that presented with two or more signals at a rate beyond the threshold we cannot perceive them as distinct.

So the threshold we're speaking of here is not a threshold of perception but of the perception of duration.

It is because the process of observation is not instantaneous that this threshold exists. Observation involves a series of 'mental' operations in the handling of signals. Obviously the system cannot process incoming information faster than it can transmit it internally. This speed is determined in the last instance, therefore, by the rate at which synapses and other parts of the nervous system operate. The fastest speed at which the system can handle information determines what has been called the minimum perceptual delay, and this determines what Moles calls the perceptual threshold of duration.

Film depends on the interaction between the perceptual threshold of duration and the statistical periodicity of projection. Experiment has shown that a second signal following the first at an interval smaller than the threshold has the effect of masking the first one, as if the system compensates for the likelihood of change during the period of minimum perceptual delay by allowing incoming signals within this period to correct earlier ones. This is known as 'backward masking' (see Haber, and Haber and Hershenson). It is precisely because of this faculty of the brain for instant correction of incoming signals that Luria speaks of 'mobile systems', characterized by feedback between different levels. (Indeed, it is now known that there is a particular part of the visual cortex devoted to the task of synthesizing movement. Susan Greenfield has mentioned the case of a woman with damage to the visual cortex such that she could see form and colour but not movement: moving objects would not change size smoothly but in jumps – the tea pouring from a pot would look frozen; a vehicle approaching would be small one moment and the next, alarmingly large (Greenfield, 1994). One wonders what this unfortunate woman makes of watching a film or television screen.)

In sum, information about change and movement is incorporated at a primary level, while the process of observation on more complex levels continues uninterrupted. This is why, beyond the perceptual threshold of duration, periodicity in the incoming signal is read automatically and unconsciously as part of the structure in which the message is encoded. What of the gaps, the jumps between one frame and the next? For information theory they are not interruptions in the message but part of the encoding. The reason why we don't notice the gaps is very simple: they carry no information. A gap cannot mask the image which precedes it. And as long as each successive image arrives at an interval within the period of minimal perceptual delay, the gaps simply disappear A gap can only impinge on our attention if it lasts long enough for us to perceive duration in it separately from the images which surround it. This explains the flicker caused by the slow and uneven projection speeds of the early days; they were slow because films were originally shot at sixteen or eighteen frames per second instead of the modern 24 they were uneven because most early projectors were hand-cranked, and some of the gaps became a little too long.

# Chapter 5

# Photographic development

Photography does not possess the advantages of perfection any more than other human inventions. Had it been left where we found it when the discovery was announced, it would have remained a beautiful, but almost useless thing, a philosophic toy, which lent a little assistance to the cultivation of taste, but afforded none to the economy of manufactures: whereas now it promises to be of important use to many of the arts of industry. The multiplication of pictures from an original photograph is the great end of the art.

Robert Hunt, *A Popular Treatise on the Art of Photography*, 1841

A popular parlour game in the early nineteenth century, derived from a simple chemical experiment, involved attaching objects like flowers and leaves to pieces of paper treated with silver salts. When the paper was exposed to sunlight, the objects left an outline on the paper, although the image quickly disappeared because there was no means of fixing it. Joseph Niepce discovered how to do this, using sunlight on silver chloride to inscribe a design on metal automatically. According to Sadoul, Niepce, who was not a very a good artist, came to this idea through the difficulty he experienced in obtaining lithographic stones, which induced him to try replacing the stone with metal (Sadoul, vol. 1, p. 26). But to obtain results required extremely long exposures. The photograph he submitted to the Royal Society in 1827 needed eight hours, and two years later economic necessity forced Niepce into partnership with Louis Daguerre, who was carrying out similar experiments with the object of improving an already profitable business in designing dioramas. It was Daguerre alone who achieved the breakthrough, after Niepce's death, though the technique he achieved was of little use to him for the purpose for which he originally intended it.

The invention of photography by Niepce and Daguerre (who gave his name to the daguerreotype) in France, and, in England, quite independently, by Fox Talbot (who called his process the calotype), became public in 1839. The long-term future of photography lay with the development of the calotype process, since the calotype produced negative images, from which copies could be made, while the daguerreotype produced only a single positive image. Partly because of its initially superior image quality, however, the daguerreotype was the dominant process for quite some time – although this also had to do with the action of the French government in purchasing the rights of the invention in order to make it public, and the difficulties this created for the competitive exploitation of Fox Talbot's British patent.

A number of commentators have suggested that it was only a matter of time before the idea arose of using photographs instead of drawings in the various animated optical devices which appeared from the 1840s on. Perhaps so, but the adaptation was fraught with problems. To begin with, exposures were too slow. Daguerre himself claimed, as early as 1844, that one could photograph galloping horses and birds in flight – at a time when the minimum exposure periods were uncomfortably long for human sitters. The typical portrait pose of the 1840s, with the elbow resting on a convenient support and the hand brought up to the face as if the sitter were in a pensive mood, was necessary in order to help keep the head steady. A little later, in some of the earliest attempts to produce photographs for animation, subjects were required to pose in a series of successive positions which were supposed to make up a simple movement, like the series of drawings they were modelled on. Even with the gradual reduction in exposure time, many of these poses were pretty awkward and impracticable. Moreover, in constructing these series, photographers knew no better than painters what the correct intermediate positions were. It isn't surprising, then, that when faster exposures were first achieved, one of the first uses they were put to was the analysis of human and animal locomotion. This, as we shall see, played a singularly important role in the progress towards cinematography.

Meanwhile the commercial development of photography

gathered pace. While the first street photographers were appearing in the working-class districts of the cities, the *carte de visite*, or photographic visiting card, made its appearance, a new kind of keepsake with or without more elaborate mountings. According to the vivid account in Mayhew's survey of London:

> Within the last few years photographic portraits have gradually been diminishing in price, until at the present time they have become a regular article of street commerce. Those living at the west-end of London have but little idea of the number of persons who gain a livelihood by street photography.
>
> There may be one or two 'galleries' in the New-road, or in Tottenham-court-road, but these supply mostly shilling portraits. In the eastern and southern districts of London, however, such as in Bermondsey, the New-cut, and the White-chapel-road, one cannot walk fifty yards without passing some photographic establishment, where for sixpence persons can have their portrait taken, and framed and glazed as well.
>
> It was in Bermondsey that I met with the first instance of what may be called pure street photography. Here a Mr. F—1 was taking sixpenny portraits in a booth built up out of old canvas, and erected on a piece of spare ground in a furniture-broker's yard.
>
> Mr. F—1 had been a travelling showman, but finding that photography was attracting more attention than giants and dwarfs, he relinquished the wonders of Nature for those of Science.

As G. H. Martin and David Francis explain, the trade in photographs

> rapidly extended its range from personal portraits to views, and then to celebrities, to curios, and to any other theme acceptable to popular taste ... the historical importance of these small glazed prints overrides their artistic and technical significance, even though many of them were of the highest quality. To the historian they speak of the mass-market that they commanded; their consequence lies in their numbers and diffusion.
>
> (Martin and Francis in Dyos and Wolff, eds, p. 234)

By the beginning of the 1860s, when faster exposures became possible and photographs became more or less instantaneous, people began to express wonder at the new pictures of street scenes which showed 'omnibus horses with uplifted legs without a blur, and foot passengers in every stage of action perfectly defined' (Scharf, p. 102). The age of the snapshot – the term was first used by Herschel in 1860 – had arrived. The photochemistry for achieving these instantaneous images was obviously a prerequisite for taking photographs in rapid series. But if such series photographs were intended for the wheel of life, there were other problems to be solved as well.

The immediate difficulty was that photographs were taken on plates and the images in the wheel of life were contained on a circular band, usually paper (so that it could be replaced – an important factor in the commercial exploitation of the device: like the gramophone, where records are sold separately from the record-player). Some of the methods proposed for taking rapid series photographs suggested dropping plates rapidly in front of one another. This left the problem of transferring the images to a continuous mounting. Around 1860, one Henry Du Mont filed a series of patents in Belgium, France and England for an apparatus specifically intended to produce photographs for a wheel of life. He thought of mounting miniature photographic plates on a drum and revolving the drum intermittently from one plate to the next – an idea which was later tried (unsuccessfully, one should add) by Edison's assistant Dickson. Ducos de Hauron, in a patent filed in 1864, spoke simply of mounting the plates on a 'band of black material', although as yet there was nothing suitable. The most advanced design was that of Wordsworth Donisthorpe, who was granted an English patent twelve years later for a device intended to take photographs on glass plates arranged as a pack, each plate dropping out of the way after exposure. Pictures were taken at the rate of eight a second and the patent specified that the pictures were to be finished on paper, spaced equidistantly. The strip would then be mounted in a zootrope or phenakistoscope; or, according to a contemporary account, it could be 'wound on a cylinder, to be unwound from it at a uniform speed to another cylinder, and so carried on past the eye of the observer, any ordinary means being used for insuring that the pictures shall be exposed only momentarily to the observed' (quoted by Theisen in Fielding, ed., p. 118).

There lies the rub, of course. If this is to be taken as a partial prototype of the cinematograph, then the means employed 'for

insuring that the pictures shall be exposed only momentarily'
turned out not to be ordinary at all, but to require a quite
novel solution, in the form of perforations which allowed a claw
mechanism to move the film strip one frame at a time. And if
this was hardly yet apparent in the 1870s, nor could the writer
of this account have known that eight images per second would
not be fast enough to achieve a smooth movement, or that a new
material would be needed to carry the images. These things,
which are all connected, were only discovered by trial and error.
Even then, there remained no suitable material until the photo
graphic industry discovered on its own account the benefits of
replacing plates with roll film, which was first produced on paper;
and then improved on paper by adopting a new synthetic material
invented in 1869 called celluloid.

Some inventors, meanwhile, were inspired by a method already
devised for the magic lantern in order to animate painted slides,
which consisted in mounting a series of pictures in a circle round
a revolving disc. This technique still suffered, like that of the
wheel of life, from the limitation of any method which carried
images in a repeating circle: it was obviously restricted to movements which also repeated themselves exactly, like skipping with
a rope. But if this is an example of the limits of *bricolage* which
Lévi-Strauss pointed out – in adapting elements at hand, you're
constrained in the results you can achieve by the functions which
those elements were originally designed for – nevertheless, the
revolving disc would make a vital contribution to the gestation
of cinematography.

*

The development of new photographic techniques, particularly
new types of emulsion, progressively reduced exposures, which
in turn prompted changes in the design of the camera, especially
improvements in shutter design. In the early 1870s, using the new
gelatin-bromide process developed in England, a faster range of
exposures became possible, which greatly exceeded the human
eye's perceptual threshold of duration. These photographs went
beyond the snapshot and produced a number of shocks and
surprises, among which was what they revealed about the positions of human and animal limbs in the course of movement. It
appeared, for example, that the painters' traditional 'flying gallop'
position, which showed all four of the horse's legs off the ground

at the same time, splayed out forwards at the front and backwards at the back, was quite simply wrong. The man who demonstrated this was Eadweard Muybridge. As Aaron Scharf has commented, 'The meaning of the term "truth to nature" lost its force: what was true could not always be seen, and what could be seen was not always true' – a dichotomy which moving pictures would only exacerbate (Scharf, p. 111).

Muybridge began his experiments in 1872. About five years later he obtained personal financial backing from Leland Stanford, the governor of California, and, using wet collodion plates and shutter speeds around 1/1000th of a second, was able to obtain definitive results, He arranged a series of cameras alongside each other in a row, and the horse itself took the photographs as it passed by, triggering off trip-wires connected to each camera. (Later he devised a way of triggering the cameras electrically.) However, the photographs were taken against a blank background. This was because the object was to show the movements of the horse's anatomy but not its motion, that is, its movement in relation to the environment. Clearly the method could not have been used to show this, because each camera was in a different position and therefore the background, if it had been included, would not have remained static when the photographs were viewed in succession. Nor did they accurately preserve the passage of time, for the timing of the exposures was governed by the spacing of the cameras, not by equal temporal intervals, and as Marey pointed out, the speed of a running horse isn't uniform.

The experiment was successful, however. It showed that there is a moment – but not the one which people had previously thought – when a galloping horse has all its legs off the ground. Indeed, many people at first refused to believe what the photographs showed. Nevertheless, they were soon being used commercially as bands for the zootrope, and Muybridge himself devised an apparatus, the zoopraxiscope or zoogyroscope, for their projection.

The French painter Meissonier regarded Muybridge's work as particularly important for painters concerned with correct anatomical drawing. He arranged for Muybridge to demonstrate his equipment in Paris in 1881. One of the people Muybridge met when he went to Paris was the physiologist E. J. Marey, who had already been in correspondence with him following the publication of his results. Marey was also in contact with the astronomer Janssen, who had devised a photographic revolver in 1874 in order to take pictures of the transit of Venus across the sun on 8 December of that year. These partial eclipses of the sun by Venus occur in pairs eight years apart at intervals alternately of 105½ and 121½ years. The transit of 8 December 1874 was the first of such a couple. The second of the previous pair had occurred in 1769. The transit of 1874 was therefore keenly awaited by astronomers who had become interested in measuring the distance of the sun from the earth. It was believed that by examining the transit and the shadow of the planet which was cast on the earth, accurate measurements would be possible. Expeditions set out for advantageous locations at a cost which was estimated at nearly a quarter of a million pounds. A total of eighty observation posts were set up round the world; Janssen journeyed to Japan. Of all those planning to use photography, it was Janssen who hit on the problem of timing. He realized that with ordinary photographic methods it was likely that the observer would fail to obtain a photograph of the precise moment of contact between the two heavenly bodies. The problem was that taking an ordinary photograph depended on a subjective judgement as to when to release the camera shutter. Janssen's photographic revolver was designed to overcome this, by taking a series of exposures at intervals of seventy seconds. The mechanism was modelled on that of the pistol revolver introduced by Colt in 1837, although on a much larger scale: Janssen's machine was much too big to be held in the hand. In Janssen's equipment, a series of photographs was taken at regular intervals, by means of clockwork, round the outside of a revolving plate. By setting off the machine shortly before the moment of contact, he reasoned that one of the photographs in the series would be bound to show the moment of contact with pretty fair exactitude, or at any rate the necessary calculations could be made with ease.

It turned out that photography didn't help, but showed up new problems connected with the imprecision of the photographic image, for several reasons including the luminosity of the planet. Janssen's invention proved to have another significance, however. He himself realized that it could be used for purposes other than astronomy, but it was Marey, the physiologist, who saw that it could be adapted for the analysis of animal movement, Muybridge-style, to improve on Muybridge's method with problematic subjects such as the flight of a bird. Marey developed the equipment accordingly, producing a photographic gun which, unlike Janssen's instrument, could be held in the hands. (The term 'shooting' film, a metaphor deriving from this action of aiming the camera and 'triggering' it, is directly embodied in these photographic guns.)

Marey developed the photographic gun (*fusil photographique*) in 1882, but he didn't stop there. In the same year, the French state and the city of Paris appointed him director of a research station with a budget of 60,000 francs, and with this he was able to proceed to fresh experiments. The physicist Mach had underlined the importance of the stroboscopic methods of Plateau and Stampfer in the analysis of moving objects, and Marey used this knowledge in his work. He developed a system known as chronophotography, in which the successive stages of movement were recorded on a single photographic plate. But he also realized that in trying to mount a series of separate images on a revolving plate you were limited to only a small part of the series. This problem was only relieved when the first roll film was produced in 1884, and indeed Marey later wrote that he 'profited from this commercial idea'. Of course, the use of roll film immediately presented another problem – the problem of devising an intermittent movement for the film strip. By October 1888 Marey had made sufficient advance to be able to present to the French Academy of Sciences a band of sensitized paper carrying a series of images realized at a rate of twenty per second – greater, he said, than he needed. One thing here which might be underlined, the intermittent movement of the strip was not so much a theoretical necessity, understood in terms of the theory of persistence of vision, as a practical one. Photographs, however instantaneous, have to be taken with the film still, otherwise they blur.

Marey had not yet produced proper moving pictures in the sense we now know as cinema. For one thing, he attached no particular importance to the projection of the film, because he was interested in the analysis of movement rather than its photographic synthesis. His concern with animal movement was a development of his interest, as a physician, in the circulation of the blood; his particular line of research, according to Sadoul, was developing graphic analogues of various kinds of physiological movement. The first graphs, he observes, appeared in France as an illustration in the translation of an English work of economics, the 1789 edition of Playfair's *Linear Arithmetical Tables of*

*Commerce, Finances and the English National Debt.* 'The date, the origin and the subject of this work are triply important: the graph was really one of the indices of a new order' (Sadoul, vol. 1, p. 61). Marey addressed the question of analogical graphs traced automatically through some device linking the tracing with the actual movement under examination. He was not bothered by the fact that his images weren't properly centred, that is, their registration was uneven (one of the imperfections Plateau had complained about in the imitations of his phenakistoscope).

It was Edison and his assistant Dickson who solved this problem, but Marey's work was their main stimulus. Edison saw Marey's apparatus when he visited the Paris Exhibition of 1889 (where he went to exhibit his new electric lamp). He had by this time already filed three motion picture caveats (US terminology for a provisional patent), but there were so many unsolved problems that this work had almost ground to a halt. Marey's apparatus set off new trains of thought in Edison's mind which, on returning to the United States, he communicated to Dickson, who was in charge of the project, and his fourth caveat is the first to introduce the idea of a film strip and of perforations. These were to be used not merely as part of the intermittent drive, but also to guarantee correct registration of the image.

The machine which resulted from this work, the kinetoscope, or 'what-the-butler-saw' machine, still did not involve projection. After seven years' work, Edison held back from further delaying the launch of the device because he conceived its exploitation on the model of the phonograph in the amusement arcades: a diversion to be consumed individually in a booth. Perhaps his sights were limited because his original idea had been to provide the phonograph with a visual accompaniment, and the early phonograph was an equally limited apparatus, with no means of amplification. But if skilled technicians such as Lumière, Paul and others were able to devise their improvements so quickly, then perhaps it is not only in hindsight that this seems like a missed opportunity. Indeed, the projection of moving images had already been accomplished. As early as 1845, one Baron von Uchatius, an Austrian artillery officer, began experimenting with the projection of images produced in a wheel of life, thinking of the usefulness this would have for purposes of military demonstration. Von Uchatius published his results in 1853 and many other methods were developed in subsequent years. The Victorian *Boy's Play-*

*book of Science* describes two such pieces of apparatus, called the kalotrope and the photodrome, produced by a Mr Thomas Rose of Glasgow. The most successful method was devised by the Frenchman Emile Reynaud. One of the imperfections of the wheel of life which Reynaud sought to improve was that the images lost some of their luminosity in movement. The praxinoscope he devised overcame this by using reflected light to illuminate the image. Then he added an attachment which restricted the viewer's field of vision to just one of the images, framing it in a kind of miniature proscenium arch. He called this the praxinoscope-theatre. The next step was to find a method of projecting a single reflected image. Achieving this, he replaced the circular band with a continuous strip, which immediately enabled him to devise a new style of entertainment which owed a great deal to already established shadow plays. Thus he arrived at his *Théâtre Optique*, in which, at the Musée Grevin in Paris from 1892 to 1900, he presented a series of 'luminous pantomimes', portraying animated scenes ranging from *commedia dell'arte* to modern risqué subjects like 'Around a Bathing Cabinet'. If these can be correctly called the first animated films, then it is merely one historical irony among many that they predate the debut of cinema proper.

# Chapter 6

# Patent business

Of the twenty-eight of whom precise details are given among the successful 'men of invention and industry' immortalized by Samuel Smiles, fourteen came from small property-owners or yeomen farmers, master-weavers, shoemakers, schoolmasters and the like, six came from quite prosperous middle-class circumstances, and only eight seem to have had any trace of working class origin. Of the eight out of the twenty-eight who became capitalists of any importance, only one . . . was of working class origin. . . . The other seven were men who belonged to the lower middle or middle class.

Maurice Dobb

Janssen, Muybridge and Marey do not belong either to the popular show traditions or to the traditions of the scientific amateur. On the contrary, they were professional scientists of one kind or another, interested in developing photographic methods for research purposes. But this also distinguishes them from the earlier scientists whose discoveries belong to the ancestry of cinema. In the case of the generation of Faraday and Plateau, optical phenomena were themselves the subjects under investigation, and the devices they invented which relate to the prehistory of cinematography were first thrown up as experimental demonstrations of their observations, and then given a popular form by the process of commercial exploitation. For Janssen, Muybridge and Marey, on the other hand, the subjects they were investigating were not optical phenomena, although their method was photographic scrutiny, and it is another historical irony that they are nowadays remembered much more in connection with cinematography than with anything else. (This is not entirely true in Janssen's case. He has several first-time observations to his credit and, according to one biographical dictionary, achieved 'immortality' in 1868 when he observed a strange spectral line during a total eclipse of the sun: he sent the data to the English astronomer Lockyer, who attributed it to a new element which he called helium.)

The relationship between these two generations of scientists is the relationship between different stages in the historical development of modern science – stages in a protracted revolution in scientific thought and method, beginning in the fields of astronomy and physics in the seventeenth century, which altered the relations between different types of knowledge. During the course of this revolution, the fields of science expanded through the discovery of new tools of enquiry, both theoretical and practical, which generated new problems as well as providing new ways of looking at old ones. Few specialist instruments were available to aid visual research in the earlier period, although these included lenses, which had been known to the Arabs (Al Hazen, author of *The Elements of Optics*, lived from 965 to 1038); they arrived in Europe during the late thirteenth century. Throughout the early period, therefore, scientists employed tools and instruments which were produced outside the field of science altogether, for purposes other than experimental investigation. The practice of science was then much closer to the direct knowledge of materials characteristic of the craftsman and the *bricoleur*, from which it becomes increasingly separated during the course of its development, as it produces not only its own theoretical knowledge, but also its own specialized instruments.

In the cases of Janssen, Muybridge and Marey, the problems they were engaged in had reached a stage where they needed new tools in order for further advances to be made. These tools were provided by a marriage between the direction of their work and the recent development of photography. But since photography had not made the means available in just the form they needed, they still had to adapt it to their own purposes; and in this way they ended up contributing to the gestation of the apparatus of cinematography. If this participation was forced on them by the growing sophistication of the equipment they needed for their research, for the same reason the costs of research were going up, as they must do when more and more specialized equipment has to be designed and built. Muybridge needed

Stanford's financial backing, just as the astronomers needed the quarter of a million pounds they spent observing the transit of Venus, and Marey needed the 60,000 francs he got from the French state. In short, scientific advance was beginning markedly to need a new level of organization and technological support.

But the backing Muybridge received from Stanford was of quite a different order from that which Marey received from the French state. Stanford was a self-made West Coast capitalist who joined with other self-made men to form a group known as the Pacific Associates, to exploit the new business possibilities of the developing West. Their major enterprise was the Central Pacific Railroad, which relied on Stanford's position as governor of the new state of California to ensure the support of the state government and of the towns and counties along the route. 'Confronted with all the awkward delay and uncertainties inherent in democratic institutions', Matthew Josephson has written, 'the Associates, who were compelled to act with promptitude and union in such a great public work, quickly developed a technique of political action such as the situation demanded and, indeed, justified in their eyes. Breaches were opened in the defenses of the law; clubs were improvised to swing over the heads of a constituency unaware of its interest and slow or doubtful in its policy' (Josephson, 1962, pp. 82–4). It was with the same kind of brashness that Stanford one day backed Muybridge, in order to settle a bet with a colleague about whether a horse ever had all its legs off the ground at once while galloping.

In contrast, the French state which gave Marey his funds was among the first to undertake the formal organization of scientific and technical education and investigation. The Revolution had set up new scientific institutions, like the Ecole Polytechnique, or revived old ones, like the Académie. The spirit of state patronage of scientific works had operated in the Assembly's decision to purchase the rights on the daguerreotype for the country. Reforms of this kind did not take place in Britain, however. While the Polytechnique was imitated across Europe and even in the United States (in Massachusetts, for example), in Britain the state took no such steps to organize scientific education. The Regent Street Polytechnic, where Trewey presented Lumière's cinematograph in 1896, was already in existence at the time photography was invented, but it was a private charitable institution by origin. So too was the Royal Institution, founded in 1799 by a Count Rumford, whom Hobsbawm (p. 338) describes as a 'peripatetic illuminist adventurer', which provided Humphry Davy and Michael Faraday with something of a research laboratory.

The absence in Britain of state organization in the sciences can be explained largely by the fact that the development of a state prerogative was no more acceptable in this field than it was in economic production or its regulation. Meanwhile, although the uneven rate with which the separation of scientific disciplines from handicraft knowledge takes place is partly determined by the internal tensions which arise within the logic of science itself, it is also determined externally by the state of development of the practical knowledge involved in each branch of production as industrialization proceeds. The first great inventions of the early part of the Industrial Revolution were the empirical products of practical and often uneducated men, based on their craft and industrial knowledge. Hobsbawm describes George Stephenson, 'the hero of the British railway revolution', as 'a scientific illiterate, but a man who could smell what would make a machine go: a super-craftsman rather than a technologist' (ibid., pp. 337–8). The pace of change during the earlier part of the nineteenth century being dictated mostly by general movements of the economy, inventions came about, or at any rate were seriously developed, mostly in response to economic necessity. Like many of the problems in those branches of science which were most closely related to economic production, they represented attempts to find a supplement or substitute for some process where existing methods could not keep pace with the demands of an expanding market. On the whole, inventors did not act, or the social conditions did not encourage them to act, unless the need was already clear, indeed pressing. Samuel Lilley remarks that 'The idea of invention as good in itself ... could only arise in a world that had passed through an industrial revolution and discovered ... that new techniques, in sufficiently affluent societies, create their own demands' (Lilley in Cipolla, ed.).

But as Maurice Dobb has explained, the mere solution of a problem in principle is not enough for a successful invention: 'We also have to remember that the qualities and experience needed for successful synthesis and application are often those of an industrial organiser rather than of a laboratory worker ... until economic development has reached a certain stage neither the

type of experience and quality of mind, nor the means, material
or financial, to make a project an economic possibility are likely
to be present, while the problem will probably never be formu-
lated in the concrete form which evokes a particular industrial
solution' (Dobb, p. 269). In short, in the early part of the Industrial Revolution, when invention was not only a highly empirical
affair but was successfully accomplished without any particular
intellectual finesse, progress was served by the patronage of a
small number of cultured aristocrats and enlightened entrepreneurs. By the second half of the nineteenth century the situ
ation had changed. The practical activity of invention was
increasingly motivated by the idea of creating new opportunities
for commercial gain. The key to commercial exploitation of an
invention is protection of the techniques involved. This is not a
question of the kudos attaching to scientific originality, but of
owning the rights. One of the reasons we know as much as we
do about the inventions leading up to cinema is because of the
number of patents which were filed and the rivalry they produced.
At the climax of the race, the number of patents taken out in
England, France and Germany in connection with moving pictures, according to R. W. Paul, went from 63 in the five years
1890–5 to 566 in the years 1896–1900 (see Paul in Barker, Paul
and Hepworth.)

*

The origin of the patents laws lies in the Statute of Monopolies
of the English Parliament in 1624. Until this time, it was the
Crown which had exercised a right to grant Letters Patent of
Monopoly for any type of production. According to one authority,
'While originally designed to encourage the setting up of new
industries' – at any rate, industries which flourished abroad but
not at home, and which therefore needed protection if they were
to get off the ground – 'it is notorious that it became in fact a
method of farming out the powers of the Crown' (Falconer et al.,
ch. 1). This had adverse economic effects, for example, where
monopolies were granted for common but necessary commodities,
enabling the producer to keep prices up artificially. 'The abuses
of the monopoly system finally became so scandalous that the
agents most concerned in enforcing certain patents were im-
peached' (ibid.). This led Parliament to abolish the system in the
1624 Act, but at the same time they recognized the need for

some kind of system of protection. The Act therefore provided for patents to be granted to persons developing new branches of production or inventions, but only for a limited period of fourteen years. There is no doubt that the new system helped to give British industrial development an enormous advantage in the period which followed, and indeed it worked pretty efficiently without any major new legislation until the 1850s.

Sometime before 1800, however, it became established that the grant of a patent was conditional on filing specifications within six months. To improve the system, the 1852 Patents Act set up a Patent Office and a Register of Patents, and made it a requirement that the specification of a patent be filed on application; but it allowed that this specification need only be provisional and complete specification was still permitted a six months' delay. In 1883 another Act delayed the actual grant of the patent until both specifications had been filed. These changes obviously reflect the increasing importance of the patents system to the growth of the productive forces and in particular the growing competition between inventors. And yet it was not until the Patents Act of 1907 that an official search for novelty was introduced in Britain; in other words, the patent would not be granted until the Patent Office itself was satisfied, by inspecting its own records, etc., that the subject of the patent was indeed novel. Quite likely many of the patents filed in connection with moving pictures would not have been granted if this provision had been in operation earlier.

There are several important effects of the system which enter into the history of the invention of film. First, the patent was granted to the person who filed it. There was no kind of safeguard against the fact that this was not always the person who had made the invention. Already earlier in the century an invention by an individual workman was often patented by his employer. Now, as the century drew on and invention became more and more of a business, it often happened that the inventor employed an assistant, and it was sometimes the assistant who really made the invention. The question has been raised, for example, whether it was Friese-Greene or his assistant, Mortimer Evans, who really invented the moving picture camera they patented together in 1889. We know it was Dickson, not Edison himself, who did the real work on the kinetoscope.

The second thing is that a patent is a piece of property, like a parcel of land, which attracts capital for its development. With the growing complexity of the technology involved, this business aspect of attracting capital became increasingly important during the actual development of the invention, and not just after the invention had been completed. Either the inventor had to set up shop with all the facilities that were needed, or else the money had to be found to go outside for some of them. Christopher Rawlence has recently shown (1991) that the mysterious Augustin Le Prince was originally financed by his father-in-law, a Leeds businessman, but he failed to produce a working prototype after the family business collapsed and he ended up in debt. In Friese-Greene's case, he began by financing himself from the earnings of his highly profitable portrait photography business. In due course, however, this money ran out – indeed, he seems to have neglected the studios to work at times almost exclusively on his various inventions – and he set about selling shares in his patents or in companies formed for their exploitation. He does not seem to have been a very scrupulous businessman. It even seems that he sometimes sold the same share twice over, or sold more shares than actually existed! In the end, he went bankrupt (more than once). Edison, on the other hand, was a successful inventor because he was a very good businessman, a fact well known to his contemporaries. As the English journal *Photographic Work* said on 9 November 1894:

> The exhibition of Mr Edison's kinetoscope in London is disappointing, as when it is announced that Mr Edison has 'invented' something, we at least expect that he will carry refinement, completeness and perfection of construction a long way beyond what has previously been done. Mr Edison should, perhaps, rather rank as a careful and laborious constructor than as an inventor – that is to say, if a man may be called a constructor of articles which are made by others under his control.
>
> (Vol. 3, no. 132, p. 534)

The difficulties which occur in seeking financial support for the development of an invention are nowhere more apparent than in the case of another, almost forgotten figure, Wordsworth Donisthorpe, a barrister by profession and one of the gentlemen amateurs, who as already noted was granted a patent as early as 1876 for a device 'for taking a succession of photographic pictures and for exhibiting such pictures'. In 1897, eight years after a second patent which introduced a number of improvements, he wrote to the *British Photographic Journal* about its exploitation – or rather, non-exploitation:

> One or two millionaires were ... approached with a view to the commercial development of the patent. Amongst others, Mr Crofts and myself submitted the matter to two 'experts' selected by Sir George Newnes, to pronounce on its merits. One (I afterwards learnt) was an artist, a painter who was as ignorant of the physical sciences as Noah's grandmother, and the other was, I believe, a magic-lantern maker. I need hardly tell you that both these 'experts' reported adversely. They agreed that the idea was wild, visionary and ridiculous, and that the only result of attempting to photograph motion would be an indescribable blur. What could Sir George Newnes do in the face of such 'expert' testimony?

(Quoted in Coe, 1961)

But perhaps the most poignant testimony comes from William Friese-Greene himself. Friese-Greene came to moving pictures via the magic lantern and photography. It seems that around 1880, soon after setting up as a photographer in Bath, he met J. A. R. Rudge, who since about 1874 had been working on improvements in the projection of animated slides. Rudge's experiments did not depend on intermittent projection (and hence on persistence of vision as it was then understood) Instead they involved the use of two or more projection lenses, and the idea was a combination of the simple 'dissolving view' principle – merging one picture into a second – with the rapid change of a series of pictures arranged in appropriate succession behind the different lenses to produce a smooth moving picture without interrupting the projection. Brian Coe, who has researched Friese-Greene's claims very thoroughly, suggests that what Friese-Greene first got interested in was the problem of producing photographs which could be used in Rudge's apparatus (Coe, 1962).

Coe draws this conclusion from examining the published descriptions of the various demonstrations which Friese-Greene gave to technical meetings of the Photographic Society in 1886, 1887 and January 1889. The emphasis of Coe's examination differs in various ways from that of the account which Friese-Greene himself gave in an affidavit dating from 1910. In this account

Friese-Greene suggests that his interests progressed more rapidly than Coe allows. Even if he was trying to portray his work in the best possible light, and even given that his memory probably wasn't altogether accurate, it is still quite reasonable to accept many of Friese-Greene's own claims, since it seems quite likely that by the time he was able to demonstrate each piece of work to the Photographic Society he would already have become aware himself of at least some of the limitations, and to have begun trying to find improvements. The pieces of apparatus which Friese-Greene demonstrated at these meetings employed a variety of methods. The piece he exhibited on the first occasion had four lenses converging on a single point, with a revolving diaphragm in front of them, so that the images could be thrown on the screen in quick succession. On the second occasion he showed 'A disc . . . made to revolve in front of some negatives taken of suspended consecutive movements, so that one image appearing after another with a certain rapidity, the persistence of vision assisted the effect, and the result was an apparent continuous motion.' (The report adds, 'A conversation upon what might be done with such an instrument, then took place.') On the third occasion,

The apparatus consisted of a pair of lanterns furnished with a series of portraits of the same person with varying expressions. These portraits were mounted in frames linked together in a sort of endless chain and the pair of chains were actuated by clockwork driven by a heavy weight. On setting the apparatus in motion the portrait in one of the lanterns was covered by a dissolver, and whilst the portrait was hidden, the slide was changed by a movement of the chain, so as to bring another portrait into place. The other lantern objective was then covered, and the portrait behind it changed in the same way. It thus became possible by using a series of gradually changing images to represent the movement of a person when bursting into a laugh, when winking, etc. An addition to the apparatus which it was proposed to use was to photograph the sitter in the act of speaking, showing the movements of the mouth, and at the same time to use a phonograph to record the utterance. The phonogram being fitted up in conjunction with the lantern, the image on the screen might be made to appear to talk. In order to get a perfect representation of motion, Mr Greene considered it would be necessary to take photographs at the rate of five in one second ... Mr G. Davidson did not think five photographs in one second was anything like sufficient frequency to secure proper images of any rapidly moving object.

(Quoted in Coe, 1962)

Mr G. Davidson was of course right, as Friese-Greene eventually discovered.

Friese-Greene was something of a dreamer, like so many of the inventors, but he wasn't the only one to have the idea of linking the phonograph to moving pictures. Probably it was an obvious enough idea. In any case, Edison himself instigated work on what became the kinetoscope with this very idea in mind: he thought it would improve the possibilities of the commercial exploitation of the phonograph.

There is no evidence that it was Friese-Greene himself who gave Edison the idea, even though many years later he claimed that this was why he wrote to Edison, in June 1889, with details of his new camera, immediately after filing the patent for it. (In fact, it may have been Muybridge who suggested the idea to Edison, at their meeting in February 1888. This was what Muybridge claimed in the preface to his *Animals in Motion* (1899), although Edison denied it. But as Hendricks shows, Edison denied a lot of things, and falsified others, to suit himself.) The camera Friese-Greene referred to in the letter was the version which he patented jointly with his assistant Mortimer Evans on 21 June 1889. This patent contained many of the features of the future movie camera proper. It used a 'roll of any convenient length of sensitized paper or the like', which was driven intermittently (although Coe says the design of the intermittent movement was somewhat impractical). The driving roller had serrated edges to grip the roll more firmly – to be substituted subsequently by perforations and sprockets. According to Coe it would have been incapable of a speed of more than four or five frames per second, the same speed which at the beginning of the year Friese-Greene thought sufficient.

Until recently there was in fact no known evidence that Friese-Greene ever wrote to Edison at all apart from Friese-Greene's own sworn statement – an affidavit made before the New York courts in 1910 and published in full in the *Moving Picture News*, no. 49, 3 December 1910. Now, however, Gordon Hendricks has published a letter from Friese-Greene which he found in the Edison archives (Hendricks, pp. 11–12). This letter is dated 18 March 1890, and reads:

> Dear Sir,
> Have sent you by same post a paper with description of Machine Camera for taking 10 a second which may be of interest to you.
>     Yours faithfully,
>     Friese-Greene.

A note on the letter (made by one of Edison's assistants) indicates that it was answered on 15 April 1890, but a copy of the reply states that the paper itself had 'not yet come to hand'. Hendricks believes that Friese-Greene did not write to Edison in 1889, and that his biographer confused the dates.

The affidavit of 1910 was sworn when Friese-Greene went to the United States at the invitation of two American independents, Tom Cochrane and Edwin Thanhouser. Thanhouser was involved in a lawsuit with the Motion Pictures Patents Company, the trust formed by ten leading film companies, including Edison, in an attempt to establish monopoly control over the growing film industry in the United States. The legal basis of the trust was the set of patents held by Edison, but a good deal of its real power came from an agreement with Eastman, who held a monopoly on the production of celluloid-coated film, to the effect that raw film would not be supplied to anyone who had not paid the trust a licence fee. The full story of how the trust was eventually broken belongs to American rather than British film history, but Friese-Greene became involved because some of the American independents fighting the trust thought that by invoking Friese-Greene's 1889 camera and patent, Edison's patents could be invalidated. (In the event, after making his affidavit, Friese-Greene wasn't called upon to give evidence. In May 1911, a court of appeal reversed an earlier decision granting an injunction to the Patents Company against one of the independents which, it claimed, had infringed its patent rights. The Patents Company dropped the case, no doubt fearful of being prosecuted as a monopoly under the US anti-trust laws – which in fact was what happened four years later.)

Friese-Greene's 1889 patent called for a 'roll of any convenient length of sensitized paper or the like'. The phrase is important. Would Friese-Greene have put it that way unless he had tried, or at least thought of using some material other than paper? He said in his affidavit that in a camera he had constructed in 1888 he used paper (treated with castor oil to make it transparent), but he was aware of its limitations – it wasn't properly transparent, it tended to tear – and he began searching for a substitute. He also said in the affidavit that the camera used perforated film and a sprocket wheel, and achieved a rate of seven or eight frames per second. Then, he said, working with Alfred Parker, he succeeded in producing a transparent celluloid film at the end of 1888, in strips of about sixty feet, which he pieced together to produce even longer lengths. This was the material he claimed to have used in the 1889 camera. The use of celluloid film was reported in the *British Journal of Photography* in April 1890, and again in the *Photographic Journal* a month later. If Friese-Greene made this film himself, it must be considered one of his most remarkable achievements. Edison's assistant Dickson did not attempt to do this, but obtained his film originally from Carbutt of Philadelphia and then from Eastman. Carbutt, who manufactured the first celluloid-base 'film' in 1888, obtained his celluloid from the Celluloid Manufacturing Company. However, it was not supplied as film in the modern sense, but in the form of plates, either 8 × 10 or 11 × 14. The word 'film' was at first used only to distinguish it from plates which used glass as a base. We know that the minimum thickness of the celluloid sheets manufactured at the time by the Celluloid Manufacturing Company was 1/200th of an inch, and that Dickson, using the film in his kinetoscope experiments, found it too thick. Eastman, who began to manufacture celluloid-base film in August 1889, promising a thickness of 3/1,000ths of an inch, but there is no evidence that he achieved this thickness at that time, even though he produced his own celluloid. Moreover, throughout 1889 and 1890, and probably beyond, the Eastman film was subject to frilling, cockling and static electricity markings.

We don't know how thick Friese-Greene's celluloid film was, but I publish here for the first time fresh evidence that he was using it. This is a letter from Alfred H. Saunders, editor of the New York journal *Moving Picture News*, to Claude Friese-Greene, the inventor's son, and now in the possession of the

Friese-Greene family. Unfortunately the first page, containing the date, has been lost, but the remaining portion reads:

> I still have in my possession, negatives on paper and on celluloid made by Friese-Greene, which he gave me when I interviewed him in 1889. It was this knowledge in my possession when I published and edited 'The Moving Picture News', and which I freely placed at the disposal of the Attorneys of the 'independents' when they were fighting the claims of the Motion Picture Patents Co., and through which the claims of the Edison Co. were defeated in the Supreme Court of the U.S.A.

Friese-Greene died dramatically on 5 May 1921 during a meeting in London which had been called to discuss the problems facing the British film industry – his identity was only discovered when someone went through the dead man's pockets. Also in the possession of his family are some pencilled notes of his, dated 4 May 1921. This is obviously what he planned to say at the meeting the following day. They are published here in full for the first time, and I reproduce them exactly as they were written down, in respect of punctuation, etc., including one or two indecipherable words.*

> When I read in 'The Daily Mail' just above the leading article of Sept. 8th 1919, all men are not made alike, Nature never makes anything alike, every man is a part of one great whole, a part in the divine purpose, To one is given one gift, to another a different gift. . . . When men with one gift quarrel with men of another gift, & imagine they can do without each other, the result must be misery. How words like that tell upon me. In the closing days of my life being the Inventor, & pioneer of Cinematography in black & white, & colour, now proved by my patents, 1889 22954 & 1893 (Black & White) 21649 of 1898 & 9465 of 1905 (Cinematography in colour) but what was you[r] Invention in connection with the Cinematograph[y?], simply a strip of transparent film with a sequence of pictures

---

* Ray Allister, Friese-Greene's biographer, quotes a short passage which would appear to be the same. If her source was the same one I had access to – and it seems unlikely there would be another, almost identical note – then she has misquoted; she also says the note was written on the back of an envelope, but this is not true of the small piece of paper which I saw. But this kind of imprecision, and the absence of sources, is characteristic of the whole book.

taken at a rapid rate from one point of view & passed between a lens & light intermittently from roller to roller Can anyone today show the Cinematograph[y?] black & white or colour without using that Invention? No Well that is an English inception patented and proved, & nobody can show the Cinematograph[y?] today without using that Invention hence without any presumption I feel proud but no one appreciates the workers who has brought the Invention to such a wonderfully Industry all over the world creating Industries & employment to 1000s (more than I) a universal Tongue & Language of a far reaching future. Shall we have a film produced of the truth of the history of the Cinematograph[y?]. I flatter myself I am the only one that could help to produce [it] truthfully, there is plenty of Romance with all the vicissitudes relative to the phase of time we live – but would it be commercial they say, my humble opinion is, it will always be commercial if well produced, you can see the inventor coming from the country opening a business in Bond St 1885 having his business of photography in Bath Clifton & Plymouth helping him to open not only Bond Street but Piccadilly Oxford Street Westbourne Grove, Sloane St having success creating industry giving employment and starting wholesale the first picture post cards (call them Opal Cards 1889) the expense and enthusiasm of the Inception & proving the possibilities of Cinematography ended my business career, one man cannot compete, the [...?...] of jealousy of an Inventor which is not believe[d] at the time as the Inventor goes through the stages, 1st rubbish 2nd Impossible, 3rd possible & probable, 4th yes possible but is there any money in it 5th yes there is money in it (that is the stage of worry) 6th plenty of money in it 7th Oh I have heard of this invention long ago so the ebb and flow of invention like the ebb and flow of reason will always flow from generation to generation now the amazing part If I stood up in a picture hall & said I was the inventor I should even at this time, [be] turned out called a madman by the very ones who are making money over my brains, I can only return a smile, like the smile when the old lady first saw the cinematograph at a penny reading show, waited afterwards to feel the sheet to see for herself there was not living people there –

# Chapter 7

# Celluloid muse

> This invention by Eastman of continuous roll film support deserves to rank with Fleming's invention of the thermionic valve as one of the major events in man's social history. Without it the sound film, one of the most potent instruments for propaganda in the widest sense of the word, would have been impossible, and it owed its success initially to the remarkable physical properties of the plastic, celluloid.
>
> E. G. Couzens and V. E. Yarsley, *Plastics*

Like so many other inventions of the nineteenth century, before the era of corporate capitalism and the systematic application of massive funds to research and development, the invention of cinematography was a hit-and-miss process. Moreover, its technical gestation was a long-drawn-out affair, because it brought together uneven developments in a variety of fields, separate products of the growth of the forces of production under nineteenth-century capitalism. While the evolution of many of these elements has been studied in considerable detail, one of them, celluloid, has been somewhat neglected. This neglect is surprising when you realize that celluloid played such a particular role. It was the final catalyst, as it were, in the dialectic of invention of cinematography. Its appearance in the requisite form (as a thin strip) stimulated the almost immediate solution of all the essential problems which the inventors had been working on for so long.

The reason for the importance of celluloid, the first synthetic plastic material to enter industrial production, is not difficult to discover. It was not merely the only material able to carry the photographic emulsion which was properly transparent. It also promised to combine the other essential properties of being suf-

ficiently strong, thin and pliable to permit the intermittent movement of the film strip past the lens at considerable speed and
under great tension without tearing and in constant registration.
(It is not just a question of the speed of movement; since the
movement is intermittent, the film is subjected to rates of acceler-
ation and deceleration from one frame to the next which are
enormous, so that the material requires especially great strength
to withstand them.) And finally, celluloid film can be rolled up
into a convenient size.

Perhaps the neglect of celluloid as a subject for historical study
came about precisely because, of all the elements which came
together in the invention of cinematography, celluloid had the
least to do with the needs of film itself; although ironically it
became a synonym for the word 'film' as one of the common
names for the medium. However, celluloid developed quite separately and was already being produced industrially before its
moving picture uses were discovered. It was hardly even envisaged by most of the inventors of moving pictures. Even its introduction into photography as a base for roll film had nothing to
do with the search for cinematography. Yet it constituted the first
permanent monopoly which operated in the cinema, a monopoly
with extremely serious but so far largely unstudied consequences.
Indeed, Peter Bachlin states categorically that the dual technical
bases of film production are the manufacture of raw film and
of equipment, and that an examination of both is necessary to
understand fully the economic character of the film industry
(Bachlin, p. 85).

The history of the invention of celluloid begins with the discovery by C. F. Schonbein in 1846 of a substance known as
cellulose nitrate, produced in the form of a film which can be
stripped away from the casting surface after solidifying.* This
property led to its early use in medical treatment as a protective
covering for wounds. Schonbein himself thought of another,
rather more curious use. Impressed by its toughness and resistance to water, he thought it would make a good material for the
manufacture of banknotes. He sent a sample to the English scientist Faraday, who put him in touch with the paper manufacturer
John Dickinson. Dickinson rejected the idea because unfort-

---

* The account which follows here is based on a reading of several sources:
  Derry and Williams; Brockmann; Thiesen in Fielding, ed.; T. I. Williams; and
  *Chambers's Encyclopaedia*, 1874 edn vol. VI, pp. 778–9.

unately Schonbein had overlooked one rather vital property of the material: it was highly inflammable. Nevertheless, Schonbein persisted and came to England to set up manufacture with John Hall of Faversham. A disastrous explosion quickly put a stop to the enterprise.

But explosives have their uses, and Schonbein's discovery was quickly employed in the form of collodion, or gun-cotton, the first substitute for gunpowder. Indeed, writing of the development of the chemicals industry in the nineteenth century, Bernal has said that 'the first big independent development came with the discovery of the explosive properties of nitrated cotton and glycerine' (Bernal, p. 32). In view of the development, in our own times, of tighter and tighter links between production for warfare and regular peacetime production, no one should overlook the fact that the two were chemically linked at the moment when the seeds of modern technology were being sown. In fact, of course, the entire history of the development of the forces of production shows very clear cross-fertilizations between the development of armaments and of regular industrial production.

Film is in any case linked to the chemicals industry through the manufacture of photographic emulsions and developing materials. From 1851 these included collodion, which was used at first to bind the emulsion to the glass plates then in use, to create the wet-plate process. This represented a major advance in photography because it reduced exposure times to only a few seconds, but it also carried certain disadvantages, chief among them the fact that the plates had to be prepared by photographers themselves immediately before taking the photograph. An alternative dry-plate process was later developed using gelatin as a binding material. Although this reduced the speed of the emulsion and increased exposure time again, it nevertheless permitted George Eastman in the United States to begin the commercial manufacture of photographic plates, the original business which laid the foundations for his future monopoly. But the invention of celluloid answered to economic imperatives which lay outside photography.

In 1855 an English chemist, Alexander Parkes, was granted a patent for a substance called Parkesine, in which collodion was one of the raw materials. Parkesine was the first synthetic material of its kind. But a safe and therefore satisfactory basis for the manufacture of collodion was not discovered until 1866, when

Frederick Abel showed that its stability depended on removing all traces of the acids used in its preparation. The discovery of celluloid itself, a variant on the Parkesine process again using collodion as a raw material, followed almost immediately, in 1868. The inventors were the Hyatt brothers of Newark, New Jersey. They were printers, and were looking for a substance capable of withstanding variations in atmospheric conditions from which to make printers' rollers. This was one of many improvements to the technology of printing which were becoming daily more imperative with the extension of a popular consumer market for reading matter. Other uses for celluloid became obvious immediately, however, and the Hyatts were granted several patents. Celluloid was used as a substitute for ivory in the manufacture of billiard balls, and was also employed in false teeth, drumsticks, combs, collars and cuffs, and other small consumer items, as well as components like tubes, valves, taps and pistons. The original name which the Hyatts used was pyroxylin. The word 'celluloid' was first used in 1872 when the brothers assigned their patents to their new company, the Celluloid Manufacturing Company.

Celluloid is made by combining collodion with camphor. Up to 1904 the industry depended entirely on natural camphor, which was controlled by a Japanese government monopoly. This was gradually replaced by a synthetic material developed in Germany, the country which was also to present Eastman with some of his stiffest competition. Camphor, however, was not the only substance involved for which there was a unique source of supply. The same thing applied effectively both to the nitric acid and to some extent also to the cellulose required for the manufacture of collodion.

Let's take cellulose first. Cellulose is a vegetable constituent, highly resistant to most chemical reagents. The major source of pure cellulose is cotton (although it can also be prepared from flax or hemp fibres, wood pulp or even from pure, unsized paper). This helps to explain why the alternative name for collodion is gun-cotton, and also why the manufacture of collodion was centred on the United States – the world's major cotton producer. This development of a synthetic use for cotton occurred just when the American Civil War was playing havoc with the supply of cotton to its traditional markets, and the Northern victory opened up the South to industrial exploitation by Yankee capital.

Second, nitric acid. Collodion is made by a process known as the nitration of cellulose, which is achieved by the action of nitric acid and sulphuric acid on cellulose. There was no problem with obtaining sulphuric acid. The growth of the manufacture of sulphuric acid, a basic requirement for many processes, was one of the first developments of the chemicals industry in the course of the Industrial Revolution. Nitric acid was more of a problem. The nitration process was an old one, and originally nitric acid was derived from the action of sulphuric acid on salts of potash. But this only applied to small quantities. It was quite impractical for the larger quantities which were now becoming necessary.

It was the development of fertilizers in the second half of the nineteenth century, a necessity brought about by new methods of industrialized agriculture, which also provided a new source for nitric acid, thereby also supporting the munitions industry as well as allowing the production of synthetic plastics to get under way. The growth of the fertilizer industry was based on the exploitation of the sodium nitrate fields on the Pacific coast of Latin America, known as Chile nitrates. This was the world's only source of sodium nitrate, and it happened to contain 9 per cent more nitric acid than nitrate of potash. The name of the game is economic imperialism.

During the course of the nineteenth century, Britain had developed an unrivalled position of domination in world trade. It was through control of trade and commerce that British capital first penetrated Chile: it had cornered 49 per cent of Chile's foreign trade by 1875, and this led to the indirect control of domestic production. As the Chilean historian Hernan Ramirez put it, 'This means that no sooner did we cease being a colony of Spain than we became a dependency exploited by English capitalism' (quoted in Frank, p. 97). The development of marine transport technology, which began well before the mid-century, led to a fall in the price of raw materials and improved Britain's competitive position, and the victory of the free trade doctrine in Britain in the 1840s enabled British capital to extract the maximum advantage from these falling costs. Chile was only one of the countries which was subjected as a result to the domination of British capital interests over its economy.

In the early 1870s, however, the British economy encountered serious problems, the repercussions of which were felt around the world. The return on British capital investment in Europe and the United States began to fall off with the growing industrial capacity of these countries, which also led them to challenge British supremacy in the export of manufactured goods. A fall in world prices for manufactured goods began in 1873 and reduced British export values, without creating room for increased exports or reducing dependency on imports. This produced a real adverse balance of trade in Britain which had to be covered from the surplus capital previously available for foreign investment and reinvestment. But the same fall in prices weakened the position of raw-material producers, including the Chileans. The British began withdrawing capital from their industrial competitors and instead redirecting it towards countries like Chile.

This process involved more than simple capital interests. As Cole and Postgate put it:

> a new intimacy sprang up between the financiers concerned with overseas investment and the politicians to whom they looked to safeguard the interests of British capital. Foreign investment was no longer a means of helping Frenchmen and Americans to buy railways or machinery which they would then take over and work for themselves, paying back the loan in due course out of the profits of the undertaking. More and more it came to involve permanent ownership and management by British companies and investment agencies of indus trial undertakings carried on abroad; so that British investors acquired a permanent interest in the preservation of order and the protection of property rights in the areas in which their money was being used. Political interference went hand in hand with economic penetration.
>
> (Cole and Postgate, pp. 446 7)

This process was nowhere more transparent than in Chile. It led first of all to the War of the Pacific fought by Chile against Peru and Bolivia in 1879–83, of which James Blaine, US Secretary of State at the time, said 'One shouldn't speak of a Chilean/Peruvian War, but rather of an English war against Peru with Chile as an instrument.'

The territory which Chile won from its neighbours in the course of this war was rich in several minerals, but particularly sodium nitrates. Exploitation of these nitrates was already led by Chilean capital, and now, spurred on by the growing market, Chilean industrialists were in no mood to pay royalties to their neighbours. Whoever was responsible actually for instigating the war, its

object was clear: to achieve a single country monopoly over these
vital resources. The British were soon able to gain direct control
over the nitrate mines. A few years later they played the same
role in the Chilean civil war of 1891 that the United States
played behind the scenes of the coup d'état of 1973. The British
contributed funds directly to the overthrow of the then President,
Balmaceda, a nationalist committed to the repudiation of foreign
control and supported by, among others, most of the nitrate
workers, and who was finally forced, so it is said, to commit
suicide. Before his final overthrow, *The Times* reported, on 28
April 1891, 'There is in Chile a communist government, a despot
or various despots who under the false name of Executive power
have overturned all the peace, all the prosperity and all the
education of the preceding eighty years.' There is a poetic – or
filmic – irony in the fact, given this history, and the economic
role of Chile nitrates in the birth of the film industry, that revolutionary Chilean film makers have used cinema in recent years
to speak about the conditions of exploitation in the British-owned
Chilean nitrate mines at the beginning of this century. As part
of the rediscovery of Chilean history from the point of view of
working-class struggle – the height of the nitrate trade was the
period when the Chilean working class first organized itself –
Helvio Soto made *Caliche Sangriente* ('Bloody Saltpetre') in 1969
about the War of the Pacific; Claudio Sapiain made a documentary during the period of the Popular Unity government about
the massacre at Santa Maria de Iquique; and Miguel Littin,
working in exile in Mexico after the coup of 1972, made *Actas
de Marusia* ('Letters from Marusia') about another massacre
which took place in another British-owned nitrate mine shortly
after the one at Santa Maria de Iquique.

Another ironic twist: at the beginning of the First World War
the British cut off German supplies of Chile nitrates in order to
impede the manufacture of explosives in Germany. The Germans,
who by that time had developed a far superior chemicals industry
to Britain's, responded by developing a synthetic process known
as the ammonia oxidation process which does away with the need
for nitrate salts as a raw material, using nitrogen gas instead.
As for nitro-cellulose film stock, Eastman began to develop
modern safety stock, that is, acetate cellulose, in the period before
the First World War, partly because of the threat of competition
from Germany and partly to get round the problems caused by

the inflammability of nitro-cellulose (although safety stock didn't generally replace nitrate stock till some time later).

The first roll film was on paper and it was introduced in 1884 (or possibly 1885). It was designed to fit any camera, and in itself the idea wasn't new (Spencer and Melhuish had patented the idea of a roll of calotype paper as early as 1854). The revolutionary part of the business was that Eastman also provided a service for developing and printing the exposed film, and in 1885, to support the huge growth in business which he expected, he introduced new large-scale methods of coating the film which reduced labour costs by 95 per cent and materials by 50 per cent!

In developing and printing the film the emulsion had to be stripped from the paper; hence it was known as 'paper stripping' film. This was a delicate operation, certainly not one which could be accomplished easily by people new to photography, so it was equally necessary for Eastman to provide a developing and printing service for the project to succeed. Three years later, in the search for improvements, he produced the first Kodak camera, a simple box device which was advertised with the slogan 'You press the button, we do the rest.' In fact, on the first models the entire camera was sent back to the factory; the film was removed, processed and printed, and returned with the camera loaded with new film. Probably the first example of mass consumer mail order.

Eastman knew he was entering a growing market. The popularity of photography was firmly established. Large businesses had grown up in photographic calling cards which quickly spread beyond the middle classes; street corner photographers had appeared in the poorest districts of the cities as early as the 1850s. Meanwhile professional photographers, trying to earn themselves a respectable place among the arts, had already grown conservative, and much of the initiative had passed to the growing ranks of amateurs who formed the bulk of the membership of the photographic societies. But, as Hendricks has pointed out, 'nearly all amateur photographers were men of social position, more than common education, and – of necessity – considerable financial resources' (Hendricks, p. 54). Eastman knew that there was a new consumer market if the techniques of photography could be simplified and the costs drastically reduced; his genius lay in the way he reached this market. The name Kodak was devised especially so as to be easily pronounceable in as many languages as possible. Initially Eastman was aiming in this way at the growing numbers of fresh immigrants to the United States among whom he knew there would obviously be a huge demand for photographs to send back home. But the limit to the market was obviously nothing short of the world. And the photographs which the immigrants sent overseas not only carried their own sentimental messages but also advertised the wonders of the New World, which included the Kodak itself.

Nevertheless, the large-scale production methods he introduced in 1885 involved such a huge increase in the organic composition of capital – that is, an increase in the ratio of the costs of machinery and raw materials to the costs of labour, which results in an increase in productivity – that we can be left in no doubt about the basis of his future expansion. The introduction of celluloid-base roll film was simply the next logical step because it involved a cost reduction in the processing of the film. Once again it was not exactly an original idea of Eastman; he merely adapted it to his own requirements. He picked it up from his rival, Carbutt of Philadelphia, who first introduced it not for roll film but as an alternative base to glass in the manufacture of photographic plates.

With the development of moving pictures as a new market for celluloid roll film it was still a few years before Eastman or anyone else produced ready-perforated film stock. One reason for this delay was the effect of early competition in preventing standardization. The structure of the market during the first few years allowed direct competition in the supply of celluloid by small-scale producers who did not have the means, the expertise or the reason to supply the finished product – raw film ready to go straight into the camera or the printer. As long as the manufacture of equipment still lay in the hands of the same small entrepreneurs who had been involved in the *bricolage*-like process of invention in the first place, and each producer of the means of production of film – cameras, projectors and other items like perforators – was in direct competition with every other, and therefore jealous of his own techniques, then standardization could not take effect. One of the factors which contributed to this situation, at any rate in Britain, was the state of patents legislation. It was not until the Patents Act of 1907 that, as a direct result of increasing technological innovation in general and the many ensuing wrangles across wide swathes of industry, an official search for novelty was introduced on the part of the

Patent Office before a patent could be granted. But not before standardization was forced on the growing film industry anyway, by a whole range of developments. One of the most crucial was Eastman's introduction in 1899 of continuous casting of the film strip.

Since, during the early years of the cinema, the producers of films had to perforate their own stock, a few of them went further and, instead of buying it from an established supplier, bought celluloid sheets and cut and coated it themselves. This only testifies again to the relatively unsophisticated nature of the types of knowledge which served for the invention of cinematography. It seems the only commercial supplier of coated celluloid film in England in 1895 was the European Blair Camera Co., with a parent company in Nova Scotia. According to Birt Acres, an early associate of R. W. Paul, it was they who at his own request supplied the first film for moving pictures in England, although Paul said that he also used Eastman film. Of course, at the very beginning the only market for moving pictures was the one provided by the kinetoscope, of which Paul was manufacturing replicas and for which he was beginning to make his own films. Edison, unable to prevent Paul copying the kinetoscope because he hadn't patented it in England, tried instead to cut off the supply of films. Paul responded to this by studying the problem of the camera and producing one of his own (with Acres's help). It was not an especially difficult task for Paul to accomplish, given his skills as a precision instrument maker. Indeed, this enabled him to incorporate a number of very important innovations in so doing, including the use of the Maltese cross in the drive mechanism which Edison had passed over.

Apparently Acres approached the Eastman company in England at the end of 1896 with the suggestion that there was a growing market for film for moving pictures, but they said they didn't think it was worth their while. Since this seems an unlikely response from a company like Eastman, one wonders if they didn't already have some kind of agreement with Edison not to supply Edison's competitors. We know that such an agreement was in operation only a few years later. And while the Motion Picture Patents Company relied for its legal basis on Edison's patents, a good deal of its real power came from an arrangement with Eastman not to supply raw film to anyone who had not paid the Patents Trust licence fee.

In any event, by the middle of 1897 the *British Photographic News* was able to report that Eastman were experiencing considerable demand for cinematograph film. But they weren't the only ones. Several companies were either importing or manufacturing cinematograph film. Among the latter we find Birt Acres, who had split with Paul and set up in business on his own. The demise of this early competitive situation came in 1899 when the new process of continuous casting on rotating drums was developed. The evidence leaves it unclear as to whether priority here belongs to Eastman or to the Celluloid Manufacturing Company, but it was Eastman who cornered the market. The method gave much greater lengths and a uniform thickness. It also eliminated the static electricity markings which sometimes resulted from casting on a flat surface, and it was operable twenty-four hours a day. The result of this development was finally to force manufacturers of equipment to accept standardization, for the audience had by then grown sufficiently that it was no longer in anyone's interests to hold back, otherwise they would be unnecessarily limiting their access to the market.

As far as the story in England is concerned, Eastman in due course bought out his main surviving English rival, Blair. By 1916 there were nearly 1,500 British shareholders in Eastman Kodak, holding shares with a market value of £3.3 million and receiving dividends of nearly £300,000. The company had 1,466 British employees, 800 of them engaged in manufacturing operations.

The full and proper history of the production of raw film and its effects on the film industry remains to be written. Eastman Kodak is still one of North America's largest companies, although today a major part of its business comes from its incorporation within the latest developments in the telecommunications industry, such as the supply of photo resist for the photo-lithographic process by which microelectronic components are produced, and the development of new products such as infra-red film for military customers and satellite surveillance. But it still shares with only a handful of other companies a monopoly on both the production of movie film and the knowledge which is involved. A few years ago, when the Chinese wanted to establish their own colour film laboratory and did not wish to call on the expertise of the Soviet bloc, it was Eastman they called on instead. But Eastman was involved, as we have seen, in shaping the industry right from the start. His relationship with the Motion Picture

Patents Company has already been noted. Shortly after the First
World War, one of Eastman's main competitors, Charles Pathé
(who had connections with the Du Pont company, Eastman's
principal rival within the USA), wrote: 'I do not know ... of a
single company outside North America which only makes negative film, which has been able, even to a modest extent, to show
a return on capital invested.' Pathé said he was able to compete
with Eastman in the production of film stock only because he
was able to produce it more cheaply, but he was feeling the pinch
(see Sadoul, vol. 3, p. 416). Very little of this history is recorded
in the history books. Nor is it a monopoly which has been subjected to investigation by those government offices responsible
from time to time for investigating those monopolies which are
deemed to be against the public interest. The art of film has been
graced with the name 'the celluloid muse'. Muse we may over its
production. Meanwhile the powers exercised by the producers of
raw film are as clouded in secrecy as the sources whence the
Greek goddesses derived theirs.

# Part 3

# Culture and economics

# Chapter 8

# The production of consumption

Hunger is hunger, but the hunger gratified by cooked meat eaten with a knife and fork is a different hunger from that which bolts down raw meat with the aid of hand, nail and tooth. Production thus produces not only the object but also the manner of consumption, not only objectively but also subjectively. Production thus creates the consumer.

Karl Marx

Who was it, then, who invented cinematography? The answer is, of course, that no one person invented it. Not Marey, not Edison, not Friese-Greene, not Lumière, not any of the others. None of them. But at the same time, all of them.

According to C. W. Ceram, in a book called *Archeology of the Cinema*, 'It is a mistake to ask when the cinema was invented. Only cinematography was invented. The cinema is far more than an apparatus, and it was not invented; it "growed" – like Alice.'

Deslandes, who also holds that the technical importance of any individual contribution was not decisive, considers that the importance of Edison's kinetoscope was commercial and economic more than technical:

The essential act, the point of departure which finally led to the practical realization of animated projections, was the nickel which the American viewer dropped into the slot of the Edison Kinetoscope, the 25 centimes which the Parisian stroller paid . . . to glue his eye to the viewer of the Kinetoscope. . . .

This is what explains the birth of the cinema show in France, in England, in Germany, in the United States. . . . Moving pictures were no longer just a laboratory experiment, a scientific curiosity, from now on they could be considered a commercially viable public spectacle.

(Deslandes, pp. 213–14)

However, these two writers have different attitudes towards the prehistory of the invention, for, unlike Deslandes, Ceram goes on to discount the importance to the technical gestation of cinema of forms like the shadow play, the marionette theatre, phantasmagoria and other popular nineteenth-century visual entertainments, because he thinks they had no direct bearing on the technical problem of moving pictures. However, he cannot deny that there is an obvious affinity. He acknowledges that Felicien Trewey, who presented the Lumière's cinematograph in London, was a shadow showman and illusionist, while Méliès himself, more than anyone else responsible for carrying into film the fantasy tradition of the European shadow play, was the magician proprietor of the Robert Houdin Theatre in Paris. (Other names can be added too, like the magician David Devant, the first purchaser of a projector from R. W. Paul; Paul made a number of films of his stage acts, including *Devant's Hand Shadows*.) He notes that this affinity is not limited to European culture. For example, the exotic stories enacted by Javanese puppets, 'taken from the great national epics, have much in common with the chaotic, mythological films made earlier this century by the Shadra Film Company, Bombay'. (But why choose such an exotic example as the Shadra films when our own films in the West often display the same quasi-mythological elements?)

Whatever the relation of the European shadow play to its Eastern cousins, the examples which Ceram mentions, only to put aside, serve to remind us of the breadth of popular culture surrounding the birth of cinema, and the sheer diversity of popular entertainment at the end of the nineteenth century. Confronted with the anarchy of early film culture, the heteroglot welter of images so rapidly unleashed, we are bound to ask what these other forms contributed to the sensibilities which stimulated the invention of the cinema apparatus. Writers like Ceram and Deslandes have investigated technical aspects of the gestation of cinema with a fair amount of rigour, but accounts of the hotchpotch of cultural influences remain at an impressionistic level. The influences they suggest therefore seem like arbitrary hangovers of a pre-industrial age rather than active elements in the culture of the time. Many commentators ignore them altogether. This cannot produce an even half-way satisfactory account of the dialectic of invention. The technical and non-technical aspects do not separate out like that.

In the same way, the model of organic growth, if taken too narrowly, can also become misleading: if, for example, it is taken to imply a single act of fertilization, which progresses from egg to chicken. In order to get such a determinate result you have to start with a genetic blueprint. But what we're dealing with here is a generative process which had neither a single starting point nor any clear idea where it was going. It is a mistake to go searching for a linear progression instead of registering the real movement of cause and effect, in which any one cause might have several effects and any effect might have several causes. As Marx put it, 'The concrete is concrete because it is the concentration of many determinations, hence unity in the diverse' (Marx, 1973, p. 101).

In short, now that we know the shape of the technical gestation of cinematography, we should review the period over again to see how the various devices which fed the process of invention also shaped the sensibilities of the public from whom the first audience for cinema would be drawn. In this way we will also be able to unpick the idealist account of the invention advanced by Bazin, who put forward the notion that the conditions for the invention of cinematography existed long before it was achieved.

Bazin poses the problem of its invention as that of explaining its delay. He holds this idea so strongly that he stands Sadoul's history of the invention on its head:

> Paradoxically enough, the impression left on the reader by Georges Sadoul's admirable book on the origins of cinema is of a reversal, in spite of the author's Marxist views, of the relations between an economic and technical evolution and the imagination of those carrying on the search. The way things happened seems to call for a reversal of the historical order of causality, which goes from the economic infrastructure to the ideological superstructure, and for us to consider the basic technical discoveries as fortunate accidents but essentially second in importance to the preconceived ideas of the inventors. The cinema is an idealistic phenomenon. The concept men had of it existed so to speak fully armed in their minds,

as if in some platonic heaven, and what strikes us most of all is the obstinate resistance of matter to ideas rather than of any help offered by techniques to the imagination of the researchers.

(Bazin, p. 17)

However, unable to ignore the fact that photography provided the essential precondition for cinema, he comments awkwardly:

It might be of some use to point out that although the two were not necessarily connected scientifically, the efforts of Plateau are pretty well contemporary with those of Nicéphore Niepce, as if the attention of researchers had waited to concern itself with synthesising movement until chemistry quite independently of optics had become concerned, on its part, with the automatic fixing of the image.

(ibid., p. 19)

Commolli remarks on this difficulty. Wishing to avoid a mechanistic (or what he calls 'technicist') approach, he accepts Bazin's notion of delay and declines to look for an explanation of the contemporaneity of work on photography and 'movement' in the respective states of the sciences concerned: 'We must look rather at the crack which photography forced in the system of representation of the world, at the new questioning which it provoked of the central role of the human eye.' This leads him to suggest that the sudden interest of science in optical illusions can be seen as a symptom of a crisis of confidence in the eye, because its supremacy had been challenged by the ability of a mechanical process to do what the eye was supposed to do, only better. But this is questionable history, which misreads the chronology. The investigations into optical phenomena did not follow the discovery of photography but coincided with its gestation; if anything, they preceded it. Sadoul, for his part, does not see any problem here. He regards the investigations of the scientists as part of the whole array of technical and mechanical advances which, through feeding off each other, became so rapid around this period that they seemed to assure humanity's total possession of nature.

There are two issues here. First, Bazin claims that the historical coincidence of Plateau on the one hand and Niepce on the other

can apparently in no way be explained on grounds of scientific, economic or industrial evolution. The photographic cinema could just as well have grafted itself onto a phenakistiscope foreseen as long ago as the sixteenth century. The delay in the invention of the latter is as disturbing a phenomenon as the existence of the precursors of the former.

(Bazin, p. 19)

This becomes his excuse for regarding the inventors more as prophets than as precursors. The historian, however, cannot accept this kind of sleight of hand. As we have seen in the preceding chapters, proper attention to historical detail condemns the notion of delay as mistaken. Cinematography is a determinate product precisely of scientific, economic and industrial evolution. Its realization was a function of the development of the forces of production of nineteenth-century capitalism. There was no delay. Film was invented as soon as the technical conditions added up.

The second issue is the question of the mythical idea of a complete and perfect illusion which Bazin ascribes to the 'real' inventors of cinema, everyone else being somehow marginal. There is no denying that many of the inventors had great visions of what they might achieve. This is no more than to be expected – as Marx observed, what distinguishes the worst of architects from the best of bees is that the architect first constructs in his imagination what he aims to build in reality. But to make the desire to realize this myth an explanation for the invention of cinematography is unhistorical, because it is something which itself needs explanation.

Sadoul locates what for Bazin are the mythical origins of cinema in the dreams of Romanticism. Goethe, he reminds us, combined the ancient myth of Prometheus with the medieval Faust legend, where one of the principal episodes concerns the search for the materialization of the Homunculus, a man-made manikin, still unborn and encased in a womb-like glass enclosure, seeking to give birth to himself. Goethe had been dead for scarcely more than fifty years, Sadoul remarks, when screens in dark halls saw the first movements of beings of light, at the same time material and immaterial, relatives of his Homunculus (Sadoul, vol. 1).

The truth is that this highly masculine, even misogynist, symbol served the creative aspirations of the age and occurs in several variants. Mary Shelley's *Frankenstein* was to become the source book for a seemingly endless chain of films. A variation on the theme is found in the German writer and musician E. T. A. Hoffman, who evoked the mechanical automata constructed by the French inventor Vaucanson. In Hoffman's story *Automata*, the protagonist reflects on an example exhibited with the title 'The Talking Turk'. This automaton, he says,

> is really one of the most extraordinary phenomena ever beheld ... whoever controls and directs it has at his command higher powers than is supposed by those who go there simply to gape at things, and do no more than wonder at what is wonderful. The figure is nothing more than the outward form of the communication; but that form has been cleverly selected. Its shape, appearance, and movements are well adapted to occupy our attention in such a manner that its secrets are preserved and to give us a favourable opinion of the intelligence which gives the answers. There cannot be any human being concealed inside the figure; that is as good as proved, so it is clearly the result of some acoustic deception that we think the answers come from the Turk's mouth. But how this is accomplished – how the being who gives the answers is placed in a position to hear the questions and see the questioners, and at the same time to be audible to them – certainly remains a complete mystery to me. Of course all this merely implies great acoustic and mechanical skill on the part of the inventor, and remarkable acuteness – or, I might say, systematic craftiness – in overlooking nothing in the process of deceiving us.
>
> Still, this part of the riddle does not interest me too much, since it is completely overshadowed by the circumstance that the Turk often reads the very soul of the questioner. That is what I find remarkable. Does this being which answers our questions acquire, by some process unknown to us, a psychic influence over us, and does it place itself in spiritual rapport with us? How can it comprehend and read our minds and thoughts, and more than that, know our whole inner being?

If this too can be read as a prophecy, then it also forces on our attention the converse of Bazin's myth of total cinema – that the film is not just a magical and entrancing illusion, but exercises a terrible power: the figures on the screen are no more than outward forms of communication, which command our attention in such a manner that their secrets are preserved, while they gain a psychic influence over us.

Bazin's myth is an idealization born of hindsight, for there is no preconfigured logic in the story. The truth is that film, like every medium of artistic expression, is the product of a fusion of diverse factors and influences, with diverse relationships to each other, both technical and aesthetic, as well as economic and ideological. With this now in mind, let us look again at some of the formative instances.

*

Take the case of photography, whose invention is the essential precondition for the cinema. As Walter Benjamin reminds us, in his 'Small History of Photography', the time was ripe for the invention and the same objective was sensed by more than one inventor: 'to capture the images of the camera obscura, which had been known at least since Leonardo's time' (Benjamin, 1979, p. 240). Nevertheless, the inventors came to the idea from different directions. Joseph Nicéphore Niepce, a provincial gentleman amateur and veteran of the revolutionary campaign in Italy with a private income to devote to his researches, was interested in lithography (itself a new technique, discovered in 1796 by Alois Senenfelder). Louis Daguerre was a Parisian scene painter who had gone in for painting panoramas, and then devised a more sophisticated form of indoor visual spectacle which he called the diorama, which drew him into studies on the effects of light. Bazin describes Niepce and similar inventors as 'monomaniacs, men driven by an impulse, *bricoleurs*, or at best ingenious industrialists', but he ignores his own insight into the process of invention.

The panorama was devised by a painter called Robert Barker, who patented his first small circular view of Edinburgh under this name in 1788, when Daguerre was one year old. The object of the device was to give a group of spectators, surrounded by a 360° painting, the sensation of being present within the scene depicted, using *trompe-l'oeil* effects to do so. Barker's first panorama in Edinburgh had room for only half a dozen spectators standing a mere ten feet from the canvas, but the size of the spectacle quickly grew. By the turn of the century, Barker had opened his own building in London, a rotunda housing a circular canvas of 10,000 square feet, portraying *The Grand Fleet at Spit-*

*head*. Within a few years, cities throughout Europe and America had their own rotundas. Crowds queued to witness *The Battle of the Nile* in London, *The Battle of Navarino* in Paris, *The Battle of Alexandria* in Philadelphia. Two centuries later, the site of Barker's London panorama, Leicester Square, remains the capital's centre of cinema.

Daguerre was apprenticed to an architect at the age of thirteen, and three years later became a pupil of Degotti, a master scene painter at the Paris Opéra. He worked in the theatre and then became engaged on the production of panorama canvases. By this time the panorama was becoming more elaborate, and the canvases were carried on rollers to the accompaniment of a commentary and effects. As Christopher Rawlence puts it, in his intriguing book on the most mysterious of the inventors of cinematography, Augustin Le Prince:

> The subjects of early panoramas were predominantly landscapes and cityscapes. Stillness was inherent to these scenes and they therefore felt natural. But as soon as the subjects took on a narrative, they became more dynamic, and the lack of movement began to undermine the credibility of the illusion.
>
> (Rawlence, p. 144)

Daguerre and his then associate, Charles Bouton, embarked on a new venture, which they called the diorama, in 1822. Here, instead of being surrounded by the image, the spectators faced a changing proscenium incorporating a skilful combination of transparent canvases, silks and subtle lighting changes. When the first tableau had completed its cycle, the auditorium rotated, revealing another scene.

One of the popular dioramas which Daguerre presented in Paris was *A Midnight Mass at St Etienne-du-Mont*:

> At first it is daylight; we see the nave with its chairs; little by little the light wanes and the candles are lighted. At the back of the choir, the church is illuminated and the congregation arriving, take their places in front of the chairs, not suddenly, as if the scenes were shifted, but gradually, quickly enough to astonish one, yet without causing too much surprise. The midnight mass begins. In this reverent stillness the organ peals out from under distant vaults.
>
> (Quoted in H. and A. Gernsheim, p. 65)

Then the daylight slowly returns, the congregation disperses, the candles are extinguished and the church with its chairs appears as at the beginning. The effect was magical.

The photographic historians Helmut and Alison Gernsheim explain:

> The 'magic' was achieved by fairly simple though very ingenious means. The picture was painted on both sides of a transparent screen, and the change of effect was produced by controlling the windows and skylights so that sometimes the picture was seen by light from behind, or by a combination of both. In this particular tableau the empty church was painted on the front of the screen in transparent colours, and on the verso in the opaque colours of the figures of people. In reflected light the empty church alone was visible; the front of the screen was then gradually darkened by closing the skylights, and on opening those at the back the altar light and 'candles' were lit up and the congregation seemed gradually to fill the church.
>
> (ibid., pp. 65–6)

The diorama pictures measured about fifteen yards high by twenty-three yards wide at about fourteen yards from the audience. In later years, actual objects were added to the foreground. A view of Mont Blanc, for example, included a chalet as well as fir-trees (real) and goats (live) accompanied by cowbells, alphorns and folk songs; the sound effects were another important dimension. Following the success of the diorama in Paris, Daguerre and Bouton opened a diorama in London in 1823 in a building specially designed by Morgan and Pugin, which was turned into a Baptist chapel in 1855. But before the dioramas were outmoded, imitators followed in Breslau, Berlin, Stockholm and elsewhere, and indeed there were several others in London apart from the original.

The diorama at the Polytechnic in Regent Street used a sophisticated system of dissolving magic lantern slides, in scenes like *The Water Mill*. The image fades in on a mill, the wheels turning. Snow begins to fall, and the scene fades out and back into the mill covered with snow, the wheel stilled. Night falls and lights appear in the upstairs window of the mill building. Clouds float past the moon, and ripples appear on the surface of the pond. Then the thaw comes, and there is a fade to the mill as it was in the beginning, except for the addition of a swan gliding past in the foreground. To compete with these dioramas, panoramas grew in scale and were presented outdoors at places like the Surrey Gardens, where it was possible to see Vesuvius erupting, London burning, Gibraltar under attack, Badajoz stormed and Sebastopol raided. Indoor displays introduced live music as well as the lecturer and sound effects. Subjects included lengthy journeys through remote parts of the world. In the United States the panoramas were transportable, and in the 1840s a showman called John Banvard toured his *Mississippi* the length and breadth of the country. One chronicler told the story of 'the Yankee visiting a playhouse for the first time. He sat in the pit looking at the act drop before the performance commenced, and at the end of ten minutes rose and made his exit, remarking, "This is the slowest, darnedest panorama I've ever seen" ' (Rendle, p. 134).

The panorama and its successors are a peculiarly urban form of entertainment which responded largely to the cultural attitudes of the rising urban middle class. In the words of Walter Benjamin, 'Tireless efforts had been made to render the dioramas, by means of technical artifice, the locus of a perfect imitation of nature. People sought to copy the changing time of day in the countryside, the rising of the moon, or the rushing of the waterfall' (Benjamin, 1973, p. 161). It became in the process an expression of the town dweller's feeling of superiority over the countryside. It not only attempted to bring the countryside into the city, but also showed the city as a landscape and thus gave city dwellers a new means of taking pride in their environment. At the same time, Benjamin associates the diorama with the new literary form found in the French newspapers, the *feuilleton*, which consisted, he said, 'of individual sketches whose anecdotal form corresponded to the plastically arranged foreground of the dioramas, and whose documentary content corresponded to their painted background' (ibid.).

Thus the pride in the image of city which took shape in the diorama was a sentiment carefully fashioned. The bourgeois image of the city suppressed a host of unpleasant aspects which the diorama consequently failed to reproduce, such as the seething underlife which novelists like Dickens forced on the attention, for the diorama was a way of not showing them. In terms of Benjamin's comparison between the diorama and the *feuilleton*, the 'real' city was in the 'scape of the buildings; the incidental arrangements of particular features within it which changed from day to day could be disregarded as accidents. As if, instead of seeing people's lives shaped by the material conditions of the city, their lives were seen as merely the city's decoration. But part of the audience for the diorama took a sceptical attitude. As a music hall song of the time commented ironically:

> There's a model of Rome; and as round it one struts,
> One sinks the remembrance of Newington Butts:
> And, having one shilling laid down at the portal,
> One fancies oneself in the City Immortal.

*

Daguerre at first found it no easier than Niepce to attract financial backing for the development of the new invention of photography. However, as a showman, he was more successful in publicizing it and it soon became a favourite topic of conversation in scientific salons, with the result that in 1839 a group of Deputies persuaded the French government to purchase the rights of the invention for the nation and make it public (though in practical terms the gesture meant little: the process was so simple it would have been difficult to protect by patent anyway). Photography was thus in inspiration a product of the aesthetics of illusion, but made its public debut as an object of scientific curiosity. Benjamin comments that in the address which the physicist Arago made to the Chamber of Deputies on behalf of the invention, its dubious connection with painting seemed beside the point. It was the extraordinary role which photography promised to play in the development of the sciences which he emphasized. Indeed, he argued that the scope of the invention opened new vistas, for 'when inventors of a new instrument apply it to the observation of nature, what they expect of it always turns out to be a trifle compared with the succession of subsequent discoveries of which the instrument was the origin'.

The same is true in the domain of aesthetics. Photography did not displace the diorama as a public form of spectacular entertainment, but discovered its own vocation for the creation of images which satisfied nineteenth-century susceptibilities in new ways, many of which, at the end of the century, it bequeathed to cinema. But if photography taught the eye different ways of looking and of seeing, these new modes of vision led in different directions, for while it was widely taken up, on the one hand, by scientific amateurs, on the other, Arago was correct in prophesying that the daguerreotype would democratize art. It was not long, as we saw, before industry made its first real inroads into photography in the form of the photographic visiting card. Later in the century would come new commercial and industrial trends, especially after the introduction of the halftone process in 1880, which brought photography into print, and the Kodak in 1888, the first popular push-button camera, which popularized the snapshot. In its scientific usage, the medium was employed as a method of investigating what is normally too fleeting or too small to be fully visible. According to Marey, for example, whose contribution to the invention of cinematography Bazin considers incidental, 'Animated photographs have permanently fixed essentially fleeting movements but what they show, the eye could have seen directly; they add nothing to the power of our eyes, remove none of the illusion. The real value of a scientific method is the way it compensates for the inadequacy of our senses and corrects their errors.'

If Benjamin would want to qualify this assessment, it is because he too is concerned with the ability of the camera to reveal what goes on beneath the surface of vision, but in psychological, not physiological terms. Explaining how this 'most precise technology can give its products a magical value, such as a painted picture can never again have for us', he draws attention to the way that the camera addresses the unconscious:

> It is possible, for example, however roughly, to describe the way somebody walks, but it is impossible to say anything about that fraction of a second when a person starts to walk. Photography . . . can reveal this moment. Photography makes aware for the first time the optical unconscious, just as psychoanalysis discloses the instinctual unconscious . . . photography uncovers . . . aspects of pictorial worlds which live in the smallest things, perceptible yet covert enough to find shelter in daydreams, but which, once enlarged and capable of formulation, show the difference between technology and magic to be entirely a matter of historical variables.
>
> (Benjamin, 'Short History of Photography', in *Screen*)

Not just the difference between technology and magic, however, but also between science and art, a separation which has not yet become complete in figures like Niepce and Daguerre, but imposes itself over the next half-century. In the process, photography forced painting, and painters, into a temporary retreat (as Baudelaire testified in the third quarter of the nineteenth century) until they successfully challenged the supremacy of the photographic mode of vision.

A split had grown up between different modes of knowledge of the world, which photography exacerbated. It was first posited in the rationalizations of the philosophers who, in the course of reinterpreting the post-Renaissance world in the light of the new science, elevated the empirical and degraded the imagination, reducing it to a series of fanciful tricks in the cranium. The processes of perception were thus reduced, in the understanding of many of the philosophers of the Enlightenment, to the mechanisms whereby the organs of perception reconstructed inside the brain the picture of the outside world which was transmitted through the senses. Imagination and fancy were held to be separate and subsidiary processes which operated not on reality itself but on the images of reality constructed by the process of perception. The classic form of this concept of imagination is given by Voltaire in his *Philosophical Dictionary*: 'Active imagination . . . seems to create, while in fact it merely arranges: for it has not been given to man to make ideas, he is only able to modify them.' Within a generation or two, artists responded by insisting on the primacy of imagination, not merely as an active but a creative power, and an integral part of the process of perception. In short, the Romantics reacted against the devaluation of art consequent upon the downgrading of imagination by claiming that artistic production was the highest form of perception *because* of its engagement in imagination. In Coleridge's famous definition in his *Biographia Literaria*, the 'primary imagination' is 'the living Power and Prime Agent of all human Perception' and 'The rules of the Imagination are themselves the very powers of growth and production.'

Photography was to enter this arena as a paradoxical force which would completely reshape the inner workings of the visual imagination. Perception was thrown on the mercy of the automatic reproduction of a semblance of the perceptual object, in a form which lent to it the promise of industrialization. It is no accident that, as Benjamin mentions, the first manufacturer of the photographic visiting card became a millionaire. Distributed as a keepsake, the commercial photograph rapidly extended its range from personal portraits to celebrities and then to views, curios, and a whole variety of other themes, thereby asserting its presence – once again – at heart of urban culture. As G. H. Martin and David Francis explain, these prints

> are most literally the city-dweller's view of the world. They familiarised an urban public, avid for instruction, amusement, and discreet reassurance, with the wonders of the great exhibitions, with exotic scenery, with the triumphs of civil engineering, with the architecture and the living patterns of British and foreign towns. They showed a world complex and diverse, now subdued and even imprisoned, captured on pasteboard by the powerful devices of man. The photograph was a means of education, not just by virtue of what it depicted, but also in itself: it was part of the process by which men could persuade themselves of their mastery of material things.
>
> (Martin and Francis in Dyos and Wolff, eds, p. 234)

The photograph, says Benjamin, brings together transience and reproducibility. The object is stripped bare, and divested of its unique existence – by means of its reproduction. Bourgeois sensibility then finishes the job by placing it outside and beyond the domain of the social reality that gives birth to it, on the one hand idealizing the image it carries and, on the other, placing it within the privacy of individual consumption. Even the starkest images of which photography is capable are thus offered up as images of a pristine and objective beauty, made up of textured surfaces and patterns of light and shade, which ends up isolating the individual from their social formation – whether the one within the photograph or the one looking at it. It is no accident that the consumption of the photograph as an aesthetic object is originally located within the domain of the private individual and their family.

The photograph is a most peculiar commodity. The camera is what we nowadays call a piece of hardware, which belongs to the class of durable goods. The unexposed film becomes a commodity belonging to the class of perishable goods which nowadays come with a sell-by date. But except when taken by a professional, the photograph which results when it's exposed is not a commodity at all, but is transformed into a purely cultural object. It is this discovery of a mass amateur market which stimulated the growth of the photographic industry at the end of the nineteenth century.

The process is kind of analogous to the account of the economic process according to the classical bourgeois economists, like Smith and Ricardo, for whom acts of consumption lay outside the realm of study of political economy. But this is misleading. It was one of the limitations Marx found in the classical economists that if consumption indeed lay outside the economic process as they maintained, they then had no way of explaining how it was able to develop new branches, create and satisfy new needs. For Marx, consumption lay *within* the economic process because it 'produces production by creating the necessity for new production, i.e. by providing the ideal, inward, impelling cause which constitutes the prerequisite of production' (Marx, 1973, pp. 88ff.).

The way the classical economists understood consumption was this. Production, they said, creates objects which correspond to given needs. Distribution then divides them up according to social laws. Exchange further parcels them out in accordance with individual desires. Finally, in consumption, the products become direct objects of individual gratification. Consumption, in this way of looking at it, appears to be the end at which production aims, indeed an end in itself. This is why, in the eyes of the political economists, it lay outside their sphere of interest. It took place only after the economic transactions involved had been completed.

What they failed to grasp, according to Marx, is that production is also consumption. Each arbitrates the other, or, in Marx's own word, each mediates the other, and to speak of one therefore implies the other. Raw materials are consumed in the process of producing manufactured goods; human beings transform the food they consume into energy which is consumed in the activity of production. This replenishment, says Marx, 'is also true for every kind of consumption which in one way or another produces human beings in some particular aspect' (ibid.). Art, which is a means of enjoying the growth of our imagination and sensibilities, is one of these aspects.

In short, new forms of production create new forms of consumption by making possible new forms of response, that is, new possibilities for consumption. 'Production mediates consumption; it creates the latter's material; without it, consumption would lack an object. But consumption also mediates production, in that it alone creates for the products the subject for whom they are products' (ibid). The paradigm which Marx repeatedly offers for this process is art, aesthetic production. He constantly refers to art in order to explain how production creates consumption, because it is the same as the way works of art create aesthetic tastes: 'The object of art – like every other product – creates a public which is sensitive to art and enjoys beauty. Production thus not only creates an object for the subject, but also a subject for the object' (ibid.). Photography and the cinema are prime examples of the process.

The capitalist knows well how to prey on the consumer. As Marx wrote in the *1844 Manuscripts*, long before he analysed the inner workings of the capitalist economy:

> Private property does not know how to change crude need into human need. Its idealism is fantasy, caprice and whim; and no eunuch flatters his despot more basely or uses more despicable means to stimulate his dulled capacity for pleasure in order to sneak a favour for himself than does the industrial eunuch – the producer – in order to sneak for himself a few pennies – in order to charm the golden birds out of the pockets of his Christianly beloved neighbours. He puts himself at the service of the other's most depraved fancies, plays the pimp between him and his need, excites in him morbid appetites, lies in wait for each of his weaknesses – all so that he can then demand the cash for this service of love. Every product is a bait with which to seduce away the other's very being, his money; every real and possible need is a weakness which will lead the fly to the gluepot. General exploitation of communal human nature, just as every imperfection in man, is a bond with heaven – an avenue giving the priest access to his heart; every need is an opportunity to approach one's neighbour under the guise of the utmost amiability and to say to him: Dear friend, I give you what you need, but you know the conditio sine qua non: in providing for your pleasure, I fleece you.
>
> (Marx, 1963)

No novelist could have put it better.

There is nothing in this passage from Marx – or anywhere else in his work – to suggest that there is any essential economic distinction between the satisfaction of aesthetic pleasure, or of fancy, and any other kind of human need. From an economic point of view it doesn't matter whether a need to be satisfied is a physical need or a need of a 'mental' kind: both are needs of human nature, and therefore equally material, satisfied through the senses if not by physical consumption. It does not matter whether the need is profound or trivial, or whether it should be satisfied in a profound or trivial manner. The only issue is matching a material need with a material way of satisfying it. Or matching a new material way of satisfying a need with a need it can satisfy.

Even societies with the lowest level of development of the forces of production still find the resources for aesthetic production. At the most primitive level it can still be difficult to distinguish between activities which function directly for subsistence and biological reproduction, and those which serve some kind of distinct and 'purposeless' cultural purpose. When human beings engage in material production they do not just produce their means of existence, but at the same time they produce the instruments of a culture, the means through which experience is given shape and relationships are engendered (relationships between individuals and groups, and between the species and nature). Capitalism itself makes no distinction between 'necessary' and 'unnecessary' production as it reaches out to expand the market and increase consumption. It is in the mode of production that it brings something new into play. Under capitalism, the production of culture comes increasingly to be mediated by the production of commodities: objects to be sold in a market place. Indeed, capitalism can only recognize needs through the commodity form; that is the only way they can become 'real' needs under capitalism.

The photograph found its industrial market in the arena of domestic consumption. Its animated version, cinematography, was to take a collective form, which harks back to the diorama but locates itself in the music hall, in which the model is public spectacle and exchange value comes through the box office. The commercialization of music hall, which began in the middle of the nineteenth century, had considerably intensified by the time that moving pictures came along. In the last quarter of the century, the number of independent theatres fell as management companies took them over. As a result, artistes were increasingly booked not for appearances in individual theatres but for tours which included several. Agents consequently grew more powerful. On the one hand they negotiated with the management companies on the artistes' behalf; on the other they dealt with the song publishers because the song was associated with the artiste who sang it. Publishers were most interested in the songs which received the greatest exposure, because – until the record industry took off at the turn of the century – there was little else to serve as a measure of the likely success of a song. Artistes were therefore pressured to work over the same material again and again, and in developing new material, to keep it as close as possible to the stuff which had already proved successful. The logical outcome of these conditions was Tin Pan Alley, a nickname for the street in New York where the new commercial music publishers of the 1890s had their offices, which has long been identified with the practice of 'manufacturing' songs by assembling ready-made parts in new permutations.

Film fell in with the process with alacrity, eagerly adopting the same mechanism of the repetition of formulae with a proven success rate. Early film production became the manufacture of a standard product under several different brand names, known from the very outset as genres. For a good many years, the product was sold at a standard price, calculated in feet. The method of pricing would change as soon as the peculiarities of the film as a commodity became evident. And as we shall later see, it is no accident that in the process the milieu of the early film shifted from music hall, fairground and the penny gaff to the first dedicated venues, and moving pictures turned into cinema.

# Chapter 9

# Music hall and popular culture

You may disguise a music-hall with pretty names, decorate it in silver and gold, turn the wooden benches into tip-up seats, install electric lights, run it with companies or syndicates, but it is always a music-hall.

T. McDonald Rendle, *Swings and Roundabouts*, 1919

Until the growth of proper cinemas from about 1904 onwards, music hall and vaudeville were a primary focus of commercial attention for the film pioneers. The two first film shows which were given in London, early in 1896, were both immediately snapped up by music halls. These were the Lumière show, presented by Félicien Trewey to a paying audience at the Regent Street Polytechnic on 20 February, and the show which Robert Paul presented privately, coincidentally on the same day, at Finsbury Technical College. The Lumière show was taken up by the Empire, Leicester Square, where it entered the company of such acts as Mademoiselle Marthe Marthy, Eccentric Comedienne, and Belloni and the Bicycling Cockatoo. According to an account which appeared in the magazine *Entracte* on 7 March 1896, Trewey had been asking £30 an evening. On 14 March, the same magazine reported that the Empire was paying him £150 per week, and a week later they reported that owing to the show's success matinées would be given as well. By this time the Alhambra, across the road from the Empire, was anxious to find its own moving picture entertainment. Morton, the director of the Alhambra, had missed the boat with Trewey, although he'd previously engaged him several times as a juggler and illusionist. He therefore engaged Paul, who had meanwhile been persuaded to present his show, under the name Theatrograph, at Olympia, by the impresario Sir Augustus Harris.

Paul had produced sixty Edison-type kinetoscopes the previous year, after discovering that the kinetoscope wasn't covered by a British patent (a question I shall investigate in a later chapter). He had installed fifteen of them,

> in conjunction with business friends . . . at Earls Court, London, showing some of the first of our British films, including one of the boat race and derby of 1895. The sight of queues of people, waiting their turn to view them, first caused me to consider the possibility of throwing the pictures upon a screen.
>
> (Paul in Barker, Paul and Hepworth)

Harris's wife had seen Paul's film show at the Royal Institution a week after the one in Finsbury. Paul himself reported:

> Next morning, Sir Augustus Harris telegraphed me to meet him at breakfast, and proposed that a projector be installed at Olympia on sharing terms. He added that he had recently seen animated photographs at Paris, and prompt action was necessary as he was sure that the popular interest would die out in a few weeks. Though I knew nothing of the entertainment business I agreed to install the machine in a small hall at Olympia in March, 1896, and was surprised to find my small selection of films received with great enthusiasm by the public, who paid sixpence to view them.
>
> (ibid.)

Moul engaged Paul at the Alhambra at a rate of £11 per performance, which Paul said was 'far more than I expected'. Music hall rates later fell, to about £4 or £5 per week. Later still, when theatre electricians learnt to operate the projector, they took on the job as a perk which earned them an extra ten shillings or so above their regular wage. This perfectly suited music hall management: they no longer had to 'engage an act', but instead rented their films from one of the agencies. Paul's initial engagement was for only two weeks, but he stayed much longer. (Some accounts say that he stayed for two years. John Barnes has shown, however, that Paul's show was replaced in June 1897 by a programme presented by Wrench. This was the result of a dispute between Paul and the theatre over terms for showing the films

of Queen Victoria's Diamond Jubilee, and a court case was
involved.)

Moving pictures spread to music halls throughout London and
then wider afield within an amazingly short time. Paul reports
that there was a considerable market of individual purchasers for
his equipment. They included conjurors and music hall proprietors, and had to be taught how to use the machinery:

> Though we did our best to train lanternists and limelight oper-
> ators to use the machine properly, their results were sometimes
> indifferent. Therefore, I attended in the evenings at many of
> the London music halls, the times of showing being carefully
> arranged in advance. This helped to maintain the reputation
> of the projector. I drove, with an assistant, from one hall to
> another in a one-horse brougham, rewinding the films during
> the drive.
>
> (ibid.)

Not everyone, however, was prepared to join this scheme – like
Maskelyne of the Egyptian Hall, for instance, who engaged David
Devant, Paul's first purchaser, to perform twice daily at a salary.
Others set up their own circuit of music hall clients in the same
manner in which proprietors of individual acts sub-contracted to
the music hall agents and syndicates. We shall see later how the
economic development of cinema exhibition was built up partly
on the basis of this pre-existing model, even as it began to drive
these music hall acts out of business.

The milieu of the music hall had several effects on the kinds
of film that got made. Paul, for example, says that some of the
leading performers were quite willing to appear in films, often
without payment. They saw it as good publicity. But these were
not in the first instance films of the music hall turns themselves.
They were more like actualities taken in expectation of audience
pleasure at seeing shots of the stars. For example, Warwick Trading Company's 1898 film, *Animated Portrait – Miss Marie Lloyd*,
for which the catalogue description reads:

> Taken at the entrance of the Alhambra Theatre of Varieties,
> Brighton. Miss Lloyd comes out of the theatre towards the
> road, and a friend, driving past in a dog-cart, returns and
> comes to meet her, when they go in to the theatre together.

Marie Lloyd was not sympathetic to the moving pictures, judging from an incident reported by Albany Ward:

> At that time ... we showed [films] from behind through a transparent screen ... which was thoroughly damped with water and glycerine. ... I well remember ... getting fearfully ticked off by Marie Lloyd, who was the Turn following us, as we wetted the stage rather badly, to which she took very strong and forcible objection, particularly as far as language was concerned.
>
> (Quoted in Low, vol. 1, p. 115)

Here, two years after its introduction, moving pictures occupied a billing second only to the leading stage artistes. (The attitudes of the artistes to film is something I shall take up again later.)

Paul says that Moul, manager of the Alhambra, 'wisely saw the need for adding interest to wonder', and so they staged a short comic scene, *The Soldier's Courtship*, on the theatre roof, 'which caused great merriment' (Paul): a courting couple on a park bench are interrupted by the arrival of an old lady, who sits down and begins to edge them off the seat. The couple get up suddenly and tip the seat over, so the old lady topples to the ground underneath the upturned seat. Taken from pantomime traditions, this kind of one-shot film came easily and multiplied rapidly.

Music hall is commonly and correctly thought of as the dominant form of popular urban entertainment in Britain in the second half of the nineteenth century. Its roots lay in a variety of traditions and it was formed by a series of influences which were common or comparable across much of Europe. The case of pantomime is representative, and of special relevance to early film culture since mime was the natural mode of acting on the silent screen. Pantomime had given rise to a certain type of theatrical clowning which was later carried to a very high level of perfection in the cinema by such artistes as Chaplin (while acrobatic clowning like Buster Keaton's evolved rather more from circus traditions). During the height of music hall, many of the greatest stars of the halls appeared in that peculiar English version of the tradition, the Christmas pantomime, which dated back to the previous century, with its roots even earlier, in the *commedia dell'arte* of sixteenth-century Italy.

Those who remembered the great clown Grimaldi (Dickens

had edited his memoirs a year after his death in 1837) bemoaned the introduction of music hall artistes to the pantomime stage. They regarded them as coarse and vulgar and accused them of transforming the old pantomime characters beyond recognition, because instead of serving the old art they used the stock characters for their own ends, as a vehicle for their own self-projection. This is probably true, as the old tradition was already in demise, and the music hall stars were brought into pantomime by commercial interests in an attempt to give it a fresh lease of life.

The evolution of pantomime out of *commedia dell'arte* is a prime example of a capacity for adaptation which is deeply characteristic of popular culture, a capacity to take disruptions of the tradition in its stride. The *commedia* was a form of improvised professional comedy performed by travelling players, built up around a cast of stock characters – Pantalone, the Spanish Capitano, Pulcinella and so forth. These characters over the years had developed variants; the Spanish Capitano, for instance, had evolved into Scaramouche, the cowardly and foolish boaster, constantly cudgelled by Harlequin. In due course, the *commedia* began to exert a huge influence on higher-class forms of theatre throughout Europe. The Neapolitan Toberia Fiorelli, probably the most famous Scaramouche of all time, played before European royalty, and created a sensation when he brought a troupe with him to London in 1673, the inspiration for Edward Ravenscroft's comedy *Scaramouch* four years later. But in France, where the travelling *commedia* players had joined up with fairground entertainers, *commedia* turned into pantomime when authority imposed a restriction on speech in the fairground theatres. As Samuel McKechnie puts it, in his *Popular Entertainments through the Ages* (p. 70):

> The actors of the fairs ... were irrepressible. When they were forbidden ... to speak in their comedies they acted in pantomime, and let down from the ceiling of the stage scrolls of verses which explained the salient parts of the story. They could not very well have got nearer to the form of the silent film, with its pantomimic acting and its explanatory captions.

The transition from live to filmed performance re-enacted the process, though the driving force was now commercial promise, not political repression. The film apparatus was mute, and the pantomimic exercised a natural attraction.

The catalogues contain a considerable variety of one-shot pantomimic music hall sketches, and later we shall take note of some
of the more interesting. But catalogues give limited insight into
the full effects of the music hall milieu upon the early development of cinema. The influences are complex and extensive, both
direct and indirect, and have aesthetic, ideological and economic
aspects. Aesthetically the screen is significantly shaped by discoveries about the medium which were made in the context of
filming the simple stories of popular sketches – and the differences which thereby soon began to appear between the film
medium and the music hall traditions. In economic terms, there
was the influence of the commercial patterns of the music hall
business – performers selling their acts through agents to impresarios and circuits – which the film business transformed into the
different sectors of production, distribution and exhibition, as we
shall later see in some detail. Finally, on the ideological level,
film inherited many of the issues of representation and identification in a society dominated by class interests already found in
music hall as the principal form of popular culture, but it gave
them a new slant. To appreciate these various and parallel
changes, we need to review salient aspects in the history of music
hall. The story will have to be told in some detail, because it
remains shrouded in sentimentality and nostalgia.

*

From the time of the separation of England from the Church of
Rome in the 1530s through the period of the so-called Glorious
Revolution of 1688 a series of controls and sometimes open acts
of censorship operated on the free expression of heretical ideas.
Throughout this period, religious heresies provided a forum for
the conduct of political rivalries. With the French Revolution,
such ideas took on a more directly political flavour. As these new
political ideas emerged, authority felt the necessity of demarcat-
ing clearly between 'respectable' art, which could be controlled
with relative ease and officially sanctioned, and popular forms
which remained anarchic. A separation was necessary not only
because popular forms were increasingly regarded as vulgar, raucous, and offensive to refined aesthetic (and moral) susceptibilities, but also because from time to time these rowdy and often
unbridled satirical tones threatened to engulf the more formal

theatre and turn it into a political forum. According to the historian Elie Halévy, the middle classes began to withdraw from the theatres because their rigid Puritan codes became increasingly intolerant towards the stage. In particular, the growth of strait-laced evangelical beliefs, he says, no longer found acceptable the kind of wit extracted in Reformation comedy at the expense of minority religious movements (Halévy, vol. 1, pp. 500–5).

The restrictions which guarded the theatre and inhibited its artistic development had less effect on the popular stage, in spite of the intolerance and censorship of the period. The main forms of control over the theatre were the legal requirement of licensed premises and the Lord Chamberlain's powers of censorship. These controls derived from the Theatres Act of 1737 and the Disorderly Houses Act of 1757. The first of these reinforced the monopoly held by the Covent Garden and Drury Lane theatres, known as the Royal Patent theatres, because of the Letters Patent granted to them by Charles II for the performance of straight plays. Prevented from presenting straight drama, the other theatres went over to the popular musical stage, so successfully that the Royal Patent theatres themselves were forced to adopt the popular forms and bid for the leading position in the presentation of pantomime.

By the early 1790s, and especially, as E. P. Thompson pointed out, in the provinces, theatres became a forum where rival political factions of Loyalists and Radicals confronted each other, and provoked each other by 'calling the tunes' in the intervals (Thompson, p. 808). The Royal Patent theatres came under considerable pressure, caught between jealousy of the huge popularity of the 'illegitimate' theatres on the one hand, and authority's disapproval of the ebullience of the popular audience on the other. The popular audience was sufficiently demonstrative to force Covent Garden itself to close for two months in 1809 following riots against the raising of seat prices, and there were further riots there in 1813 and 1815. Added to this was the fact that the popular audiences were making new cultural demands. For example, various kinds of subterfuge were being employed for the performance of straight drama, including especially Shakespeare, under non-licensed conditions. *Othello* was staged in the East End of London with a musician playing a chord on a piano every few minutes, so softly it could hardly be heard, but it was a way of getting round the law. Also in the East End, John Palmer quite brazenly opened a theatre in 1787 with a performance of *As You Like It*, telling the audience that 'tumblers and dancing dogs might appear unmolested before you, but other performers and myself standing forward to exhibit a moral play is deemed a crime' (Farson, pp. 18–21). Palmer was arrested, under an Elizabethan statute, as 'a rogue, vagabond or sturdy begger'. Shakespeare was also played by the travelling theatre companies, though generally abridged, sometimes heavily. Orthodox historians of British theatre tend to overlook these connections between popular theatre and the Shakespeare revival of the early nineteenth century. When it comes to the great Shakespearian actors, they forget that Kemble took private lessons from Grimaldi, and that Keen started Shakespeare recitals when he was playing in pantomime and melodrama with one of the most successful fairground companies, Richardson's.

In due course the popular demand became too great to resist. Another East End theatre proprietor, Sam Lane, led a march on Westminster when he lost his licence for staging a straight play; banners in the procession proclaimed 'Workers Want Theatres' and 'Freedom for the People's Amusement'. In the 1830s, Bulwer Lytton campaigned in Parliament against the monopoly, which, he said, 'condemns the masterpieces of Shakespeare, whose very nature scorns all petty bounds, fetters and limitations, to be performed at only two theatres, the only place above all others, where they can least intelligently be heard' (quoted in Farson). Finally, the royal monopoly was broken by Act of Parliament in 1843. Lane celebrated by re-opening his theatre, the 'Brit' at Hoxton, with a Shakespeare festival; he told his audience, 'I am proud to have helped this success in obtaining freedom for the people's amusement. Never again will you be deprived of a free theatre. It has come to stay' (quoted ibid.). The 'Brit' (Britannia), which is still standing, later became a music hall.

The Shakespeare revival played an important role in the movement to liberate theatre from its eighteenth-century middle-class confines, but then formed only a small part of the new lower-class theatre that now emerged. A number of new playhouses were opened which mainly produced melodrama, comedy and farce. Melodrama, according to Michael Booth, was

the form in closest touch with the needs and dreams of the

urban masses. . . . By the 1840s melodrama had already become
a crude theatre of social protest and had taken up such matters
as slavery, industrialization, class conflicts, game-laws, and
other problems of contemporary society. As for London, melodrama was full of its homeless poor, and of their crime, drunk-
enness, and nostalgia for the lost life of the village.

(Booth in Dyos and Wolff, eds, p. 217)

Of course, these plays were subject to a strong moralizing trend
as producers succumbed to the ideologues of the establishment,
a stance which was passed on when their subject matter was
taken up by cinema, especially during the years of maturity of
the silent film.

Ironically it was the Act of 1843 which created the music hall
properly speaking. The Act determined that straight plays could
now be given under licence, but the terms of the licence pro-
hibited the sale of food and drink in the auditorium. Contrariwise,
the sale of refreshment in the auditorium entailed a prohibition
on the performance of straight plays, but not of musical entertainment. Naturally those taverns giving straight plays in order to
satisfy the demand forbidden to theatres went over to music,
since their primary business was the sale of drink. In short, the
1843 Act was a game of musical chairs, a last-ditch attempt by
authority to retain some kind of social control over theatre and
to keep the two strands – the popular tradition and officially
approved art – separate. If the attempt largely succeeded, the
effect would last until the rise of cinema, which would radically
change the rules of the game.

*

The idea of the origins of music hall found in standard histories
like Mander and Mitchenson (1974) is in crucial respects mistaken, claiming as they do that music hall developed out of the
Catch and Glee Clubs and Song and Supper Rooms of the early
nineteenth century, and ignoring the roots of music hall in
working-class culture.

The Catch and Glee Clubs were in fact of upper-middle-class
origin, going back to The Madrigal Society, founded in 1741, and
the Noblemen's and Gentlemen's Catch Club twenty years later,
whose membership included seven earls, five dukes and numerous
viscounts, generals and lords, as well as George IV when Prince

of Wales and William IV when Duke of Gloucester. The Glee Club itself was founded in 1783 as a series of private entertainments in which gentlemen sang motets, madrigals, glees, canons and catches together after dinner. Although its first public meeting was held in a coffee house and it afterwards moved to a tavern, its musical character can be judged from the fact that its guests over the years, until it was dissolved in 1857, included the composers Samuel Wesley, Moscheles and Mendelssohn. The Catch and Glee Clubs should therefore rather be thought of as forerunners of Victorian drawing-room music.

The Song and Supper Rooms, on the other hand, were a kind of superior tavern or forerunner of cabaret, much frequented by members of the upper middle classes going slumming. It is said that one of them, the Cave of Harmony, filled with a rush of MPs and peers when Parliament rose for the night. The entertainment was both sophisticated and lewd – this was something altogether different from the styles of pantomime and fairground clowning and other popular forms which reached a highly developed stage in the popular theatre of the day and strongly influenced music hall traditions. It was also marked by the absence of women, who were not, however, excluded from the working-class equivalent, the penny gaff. There was a certain overlap. Many of the Song and Supper Room singers found their way into the halls, and many of them came from the variety theatres in the first place – the Song and Supper Rooms provided them with supplementary employment. The repertoire in venues like the Cave of Harmony thus included a good number of popular items, which were liable to offend the more genteel clientele. In dealing with contemporary accounts it is therefore necessary to distinguish the kind of environment they portray and pay suitable attention to the personality and class position of the author. Mayhew, for example, in his vivid description of an East End penny gaff, still voices the moralizing horror which colours even the most liberal of bourgeois Victorian views of working-class culture.

The penny gaffs were so called because of the usual admission price, although the better seats up front might cost twopence or even threepence. Like the cinematic penny gaffs which inherited their name, they were often shops. Sometimes the first floor had been removed to make way for a gallery. In the one which Mayhew visited, the clientele were young and more than half of

them female, and their raucous behaviour 'presented a mad scene
of frightful enjoyment' which spilled out on to the pavement.
Inside,

> An old grand piano, whose canvas-covered top extended the
> entire length of the stage, sent forth its wiry notes under
> the beringed fingers of a 'professor Wilkinsini', while another
> professional, with his head resting on his violin, played vigor-
> ously, as he stared unconcernedly at the noisy audience.
> Singing and dancing formed the whole of the hour's per-
> formance, and, of the two, the singing was preferred. A young
> girl, of about fourteen years of age, danced with more energy
> than grace, and seemed to be well-known to the spectators,
> who cheered her on by her Christian name. . . . The 'comic
> singer' in a battered hat and a huge bow to his cravat, was
> received with deafening shouts. Several songs were named by
> the costers, but the 'funny gentleman' merely requested them
> to 'hold their jaws', and putting on a knowing look, sang a
> song, the whole point of which consisted in the mere utterance
> of some filthy word at the end of each stanza. Nothing, how-
> ever, could have been more successful. The lads stamped their
> feet with delight; the girls screamed with enjoyment. . . . There
> were three or four of these songs sung in the course of the
> evening, each one being encored. . . .
> There was one scene yet to come, that was perfect in its
> wickedness. A ballet began between a man dressed up as a
> woman, and a country clown. The most disgusting attitudes
> were struck, the most immoral acts represented, without one
> dissenting voice . . . here were two ruffians degrading them-
> selves each time they stirred a limb, and forcing into the
> brains of the childish audience before them thoughts that must
> embitter a lifetime.
>
> (Mayhew, pp. 86–90)

But if standard histories of theatre are typically prejudiced against
what they call the 'lewd and racy' lower types of popular entertainment, which they consider too hybrid and 'artistically negligible', these popular origins are often downplayed by labour
historians too, for reasons of their own. As E. P. Thompson has
warned:

> Those who have wished to emphasise the sober constitutional

ancestry of the working class movement have sometimes mini-
mised its more robust and rowdy features. All that we can do
here is bear the warning in mind. We need more studies of the
social attitudes of criminals, of soldiers and sailors, of tavern
life; and we should look at the evidence, not with a moralising
eye ('Christ's poor' were not always pretty), but with an eye
for Brechtian values – the fatalism, the irony in the face of
establishment homilies, the tenacity of self-preservation. And
we must also remember the 'underground' of the ballad singer
and the fairground which handed on traditions to the nineteenth century (to the music-hall, or Dickens' circus folk, or
Hardy's pedlars and showmen); for in these ways the 'inarticulate' conserved certain values – a spontaneity and capacity for
enjoyment and mutual loyalties – despite the inhibiting pressures of magistrates, mill-owners and Methodists.

(Thompson, pp. 63–4)

(The film historian reading this passage can hardly avoid thinking
of the role played in the 1930s by the Methodist mill-owner
J. Arthur Rank.)

Raymond Williams, in his classic study *Culture and Society*,
drew a distinction which is pertinent here, between the different
idea of the nature of social relations to be found in bourgeois
culture, which is individualist, and working-class culture, which is
one of community: 'what is properly meant by "working class
culture" . . . is the basic collective idea, and the institutions, man-
ners, habits of thought, and intentions which proceed from this'
(R. Williams, 1968, p. 313). E. P. Thompson follows Williams's
distinction but changes the emphasis. According to Thompson,
the institutions etc. did not proceed from the ideas: both the
ideas and the institutions arose in response to certain common
experiences. For example, the friendly society, says Thompson,
can be seen 'as crystallising an ethos of mutuality' which is widely
diffused 'in the "dense" and "concrete" particulars of the personal relations of working people, at home and at work. Every
kind of witness in the first half of the nineteenth century –
clergymen, factory inspectors, Radical publicists – remarked upon
the extent of mutual aid in the poorer districts' (Thompson,
pp. 462–3). But in that case music halls, the taverns they grew
out of, the penny gaffs which sprouted up in the localities –
these were types of gatherings which directly satisfied the same

working-class sense of community. As Marx observed in the *1844
Manuscripts* (where he based himself on experiences in France),
when workers gather together, what they express is a need for
social intercourse in order directly to counter the increasing fragmentation of society and the increasing alienation of the individual forced on the worker by the progress of capitalist forms
of production: 'Smoking, eating and drinking are no longer simply
means of bringing people together. Society, association, entertainment which also has society as its aim, is sufficient for them'
(Marx, 1963, p. 176). This is not unlike the 'feast crowds' which
Elias Canetti describes in *Crowds and Power*: 'Nothing and no-
one threatens and there is nothing to flee from; for the time
being, life and pleasure are secure. . . . For the individual the
atmosphere is one of loosening, not discharge. There is no
common identical goal which people have to try and attain
together. The feast is the goal and they are there.'

This proves helpful in explaining several things. First, it throws
into relief the content of bourgeois moralism; the middle classes
were uneasy and suspicious about this kind of gathering to which
no purpose could be attached, because the Puritan heritage
required that entertainment be viewed in utilitarian terms. Theatre should teach moral lessons; visual entertainments like the
magic lantern should be educational. Even music was seen in this
light, as a means of disciplined socialization of the individual
(this, and not beneficence, is why miners and mill-owners supported brass bands and choirs among their workers). Second, it
explains why organized radicalism too, as Thompson points out,
similarly frowned upon music hall for its dissipation of energies
and funds, both of which it felt could be put to better uses. In
comparison, the culture of the music hall is not only anarchic but
inarticulate.

*

The roots of these inarticulate traditions, which Thompson calls
'robust and rowdy', are found in part in the annual cycle of fairs
which go back to the middle ages and which began to be eclipsed
by the development of industrialized agriculture after the mid-
century, dwindling as a result of the destruction of the old patterns of rural life. This process of industrialization destroyed the
economic functions of the fair – annual hirings, horse and cattle
dealing, sale of miscellaneous commodities, and so forth – but

according to Thompson, 'Until late in the nineteenth century there was still a network of fairs held throughout the country (many of which authority tried in vain to limit or proscribe), at which a fraternity of pedlars, cardsharpers, real or pretended gypsies, ballad-mongers and hawkers were in attendance' (Thompson, p. 444). Films spread as quickly through the fairs as they did through the music halls. They first reached Hull Fair, for example, in October 1896, brought there by one of the original fairground showmen of cinema, Randall Williams. Indeed, for several years it was the fairground showmen who set the pace outside the music halls, although their operations ranged in size from the very large to the very small. A. C. Bromhead said of them:

> a certain directness characterised their methods, but they were full of good hard common sense and were shrewd hands at a bargain. Sometimes it was difficult to collect accounts from them. A representative meeting a showman who was behind with his account was immediately invited to 'come and collect it yourself'. That representative spent a couple of days on the roundabouts collecting the amount due, in tuppences. It was not at all unusual to wait all day until the money for the film just sold had been collected and to stay in the pay box or round the show while it was coming in.

At the same time as the penny gaffs were opening up in disused shops in the towns, the biggest fairground showmen were touring the country with powerful electric generators in tow, erecting huge tents, often with a capacity of several hundred seats, and with magnificent fairground organs (instruments by Chiappi or Garroli costing up to £1,000 each) to provide the music – and to try and drown their competitors, for there were often as many as four or five travelling film shows alongside each other in the same fair. They established an atmosphere for seeing films which had a lasting influence.

In the cities, the 'more rowdy' elements of working-class culture which Thompson speaks of entered into music hall, while the organized workers' movement, with its brass bands and choirs, amateur theatricals and reading circles, fostered a more orderly style in its hymns and anthems, with their agitational content and elated feeling. During the course of its creation and growth, music hall drew on the creations and performances of a host of semiprofessional and amateur entertainers, who joined the ranks of the professionals already working in the variety theatres and the song and supper rooms. Some of the recruits were well-known local talents. Others were strollers who wandered from place to place and performed for just a few pence or their drinks; many of them came from the fairgrounds. At the midpoint of the century, when Mayhew undertook his survey of London life and labour, there was still a thriving business for street ballad singers and patterers and a host of other street and popular entertainers who followed the popular mood in the songs and entertainments they offered. Mayhew's informants include an astonishing number of different types of such entertainers: the Punch man; the Fantocini (marionette) man; the exhibitor of mechanical figures; the telescope exhibitor; the peep-show man; the street acrobat; the strong man; the juggler; the conjuror; the snake, sword and knife swallower; the street clown, the circus clown, the penny gaff clown; the stilt vaulter; the tightrope walker; street musicians and singers of more than a dozen different varieties; exhibitors of trained animals; and street artists of several varieties, among whom Mayhew counted the street photographer, who had only just appeared.

Obviously some of these entertainers depended on more specific and highly developed talents than others: the Punch man (another descendant of the *commedia dell'arte*) and the Fantocini man, for example, were particularly proud of their respective traditions. (They sometimes gave private shows in respectable houses, a habit practised by some of the early film people: Paul mentions the case of David Devant, who used to charge twenty-five guineas for a private show.) Other street entertainments evidently required no particular talents at all; they could be taken up by anyone wanting to make a few pence on the streets. Although these entertainers began to disappear from the streets soon after the mid-century, many of them took their place naturally in the music halls. This tradition helps to explain why many of the early film people thought of themselves as performers of some kind – many of them were, especially conjurors, who according to Paul saw film as an extension of their illusion acts. This self-image persisted long enough that some of the early projectionists even applied for membership of the Variety Artists' Association when it was founded in 1902, although they were turned down on the grounds that their work wasn't 'comparable'.

Not least, the popular tradition also reinforced a lack of aesthetic pretensions among those early film pioneers who had links with it, and thus helped to determine the general shape of early film culture.

There were some highly organized networks among traditional entertainers. The patterers, for example, formed according to Mayhew a close-knit fraternity: 'It would be a mistake', he says, 'to suppose that the patterers, although a vagrant, are a disorganised class. There is a telegraphic dispatch between them, through the length and breadth of the land' (Mayhew, p. 147). (Notice the metaphor: 'telegraphic dispatch' – a very recent invention in Mayhew's day.) Patterers, he says, recognized each other through their special cant (slang) and, like tinkers, left chalked signs to indicate the lie of the land. They were basically sellers of street literature of all sorts, 'pattering' their contents to attract a likely crowd of buyers. The range of their literature included almanacs (which contained lists of criminal cases committed for trial), the dying speeches of condemned men and women (often apocryphal and ready for sale before the execution), chap-books (cheap tracts) and so forth; and between 1816 and 1820 and at periods thereafter, the 'unstamped press' and radical journals.

In other words, there was never a total separation between popular entertainment and popular politics. The radical journals represented a market for politics which was shared by the broadside ballads, and it was sustained by the surviving ballad printers even after the patterers had begun to die out. Along with the unstamped press, says Martha Vicinus, broadsides 'were the poor man's newspaper until the rise of the popular press in the 1850s':

> The unstamped contained more news, political analysis and factual information, but did not reach as wide an audience as the broadsides, which printed headline news without too much concern for factual accuracy. They covered every conceivable event from the supposed rows between members of the royal family, peccadilloes of MPs, fashions, and various battles fought by the British overseas. The treatment of subjects was dramatic – grandiose gestures of patriotism, moral indignation or comic dismay invariably found favour among buyers.
>
> (Vicinus, p. 10)

If the unstamped press was politically more radical than the ballads, nevertheless a good many songs survive from the early part of the nineteenth century, not all of them printed ballads, which express the deepest class consciousness. However, according to Victor Neuberg, 'There is no evidence to suggest that any of those concerned in the street trade ever set himself the task of forming attitudes. Events were followed, seized upon, and exploited' (Neuburg in Dyos and Wolff, eds, p. 201). Even so, there was sometimes enough sense of irony in the way these themes were treated for this to be an influence on early film culture too, though it did not survive much beyond the artisanal period of early cinema.

Both music hall and the rise of the popular press undermined the broadside ballad. The writer in the *National Review* in 1861 said:

> The decay of the street ballad singer, which is a fact beyond question, and which we attribute more to the establishment of such places of amusement as Canterbury Hall and the Oxford, and the sale of penny song books, than to the advance of education or the interference of the police, will probably be followed by the disappearance of the broadsheet, and may silence the class of authors who write the street ballads.

The economics of this process are pretty clear: not only did music hall directly offer greater financial rewards, especially now that it was undergoing commercialization, but the changing pattern of song publishing eclipsed the old broadside publishers because their resources were too limited. Their editions were often huge – 30,000 or 40,000 at a time was quite normal – but they were printed on cheap old wooden presses. They could not match the style of presentation of publishers whose more expensive format often included colour lithographic covers aimed at the more prosperous sector of the market, as the lower middle classes bought the sheet music of the songs the crowds were listening to in the halls, in order to sing them at home in their parlours.

There is nonetheless a certain continuity between the old-style patterer and the new stars of the halls. According to Mayhew, the art of 'working a catechism or a litany', that is, pattering politics, represented the 'higher exercises of professional skill' among the patterers and 'is sometimes followed by a street patterer as much from the promptings of the pride of art as from hope of gain' (Mayhew, p. 149). The same pride is found in the class of music hall artistes represented by, say, Dan Leno. The

ironic style of the humour of the halls may be judged from Leno's
typical patter. In 'The Midnight March', for example, he takes
on the character of 'one of the unemployed' and you get the
following:

> It is my intention to hold a meeting here to-day and say a few
> speaks. Working men of England, you must rally round me.
> Working men, you don't seem to understand yourselves. You
> must rouse yourselves, get behind yourselves, and push yourself
> forward. Don't stand about the place and stand about just for
> the sake of standing. No! Now is the time and the only time.
> When time is time you can't get away from facts. What did
> Mr. Gladstone say the other day? I again ask you, working
> men of England, what did he say? You know some people see
> things when they look at 'em; you can't eat soap and wash
> with it. Well, that proves what I have just said, that the working
> men of England at the present day are nothing more or less
> than, than – than working men! You can't get away from facts!
> Again, is the working man going to be scrunched into the
> earth? No; why should he be scrunched? No more scrunching,
> and down with the scruncher! . . . My dear people, what I've
> suffered for the working man no-one knows. I've had black
> eyes, broken noses, smashed heads and torn clothes.
> And all through joining in the midnight march.
>    With the pals of order and friends of Arch;
> You've read it through in Lloyd's,
>    The so-called unemployeds.
> Hard rare hard work to do the midnight march.
>
> (Quoted in Vicinus, p. 277)

The loss on the silent screen of that most ironic dimension,
speech, was obviously a serious inhibition which prevented the
more caustic parts of music hall humour from being carried over
to the new medium. But the loss of speech was far more serious
for straight actors than music hall artistes, with the result that
very few of them appeared in early films. Straight theatre was
governed by literary principles, and since words had become the
principal means of the actors' exposition, without them they were
exposed. Perhaps, by reproducing only its outward appearance,
the camera deformed the rendition of the actor. At any rate, to
a later generation, re-educated by film, the literariness of nineteenth-century theatre had shifted acting away from its proper

physical basis. Antonin Artaud argued that the theatre had been impoverished by the grotesque prejudices of the literary mind, which reduced to an illustrative, incidental or contingent level everything which, he held, was truly theatrical. But on the popular stage it was words which were, in an important sense, contingent: they were situated in the characters and their business, rather than the business and the characters being situated in and by words. There is a pertinent story about Marie Lloyd, one of the greatest exponents of *double entendre* on the music hall stage, who was summoned before a London County Council committee to answer unfavourable reports of her rendition of songs like 'What Did She Know About Railways?', about an 'innocent' country lass coming to town for the first time:

> She arrived at Euston by the midnight train,
> But when she got to the wicket there, someone wanted
> to punch her ticket.

> The guards and porters came round her by the score,
> And she told them all she'd never had a ticket punched
> before.

However, she thwarted the committee by singing them her own songs perfectly straight and then, complaining that the sort of poetry *they* liked was far more reprehensible, reciting Tennyson's 'Come into the Garden, Maud' in a manner so loaded with innuendo that the poem's invitation to Maud to join the speaker at the garden gate where he waited alone became highly suspect indeed.

*

Music hall is conventionally said to have been properly born in 1852, when Charles Morton opened the Canterbury in Lambeth. Morton was certainly an innovator. He was born in Hackney, and began his career as the licensee of a tavern in Pimlico where he ran a 'Free and Easy' for 'Gentlemen only'. When he took over the Canterbury Arms he embarked on a series of improvements designed to take advantage of the comparatively favourable location of the place, which led in due course to the erection of a new hall at the back of the tavern which was further improved over the years as he went from success to success. The new hall was decked out in crystal and gilt and plush upholstery. Its programmes reflected the social facelift of the building by ranging widely from popular comic hits to operetta excerpts, presented with great panache under the direction of a chairman, a feature adopted from the Song and Supper Rooms. Also taken over from the Song and Supper Rooms were the chairs and tables on the floor; but Morton introduced innovations from popular sources too, including the admission of women.

Morton did more than just add splendour to the halls, or even set in motion the process of full-scale commercialization, inevitable at the moment when working-class real incomes were beginning to rise. He set the general tone for the affair, and his cultural pretensions were integral to his whole approach. He not only included operetta excerpts in the programmes but once even put on a straight opera – Gounod's *Faust*. And in 1858 he opened a picture gallery in the Promenade. In all this he was playing on the moral susceptibilities of the Victorian bourgeoisie and clearly succeeded in appealing to their desire for 'good intentions'. When the picture gallery was opened, a contemporary journal, *The Builder*, commented:

> Although almost every other class of the community is represented at the Canterbury Hall, his chief supporters are to be found among the working classes. If, then, while providing for them the innocent and enlivening enjoyment of music in the hall, the fine-arts gallery can be made the medium for raising in their minds ennobling and refining thoughts, and of creating and fostering a taste for the beautiful, the proprietor feels that his establishment can prefer a fresh claim to public support.

> (6 November 1858)

If Morton's aim was to widen the audience by broadening the class appeal of the entertainment offered, then according to one commentator writing of the 1840s some twenty years later, 'in those days, cellars and shades and caves were the chosen resorts of roystering spirits of all degrees... whither knowing young gentlemen of fortune from Oxford and Cambridge would occasionally repair to show friends how very acute and penetrating they were' (Blanchard Jerrold, quoted in Cheshire). It was this audience Morton wished to expand. Mander and Mitchenson say that he 'was certain he could capture for the halls the "Man About Town" and "the sporting fraternity", luring them away from the less respectable haunts and the song and supper rooms. He saw music hall as a form of entertainment for a mixture of both Bohemian and working-class audience' (Mander and Mitchenson, p. 24). But this endeavour, in which he succeeded, was not as moral as it sounds: the upper-class sectors of the audience at both the Canterbury and other new halls were drawn largely by the gambling and sexual underworld which soon kept business there, for betting houses were suppressed by Act of Parliament in 1853 and the bookmakers moved into the halls. As one historian of the halls, D. F. Cheshire, has commented: 'the subsequent presence of bookmakers shouting the odds during the performance at the Canterbury where many of their customers congregated emphasises the close connection between the turf, the ring and theatre in Regency and Victorian England' (Cheshire, p. 24). Prostitution likewise was quite blatant at certain halls. The Empire, Leicester Square, in particular was firmly established as a 'club' for colonial officials on leave, soldiers, civil servants, 'advanced' clergymen, aristocrats, young bloods and Bohemians. In 1894 (two years before the cinematograph was presented there), the Empire was forced to close down temporarily as a result of a scandal when a couple of unsuspecting North Americans were accosted. At one point a screen was erected at the back of the circle between the seating and the promenade area where such business was carried on. A group of young bloods invaded the place and tore it down. One of them was Winston Churchill (*My Early Life*, 1930). Although there was considerable pressure from certain quarters to close the Empire permanently, by that time the workers in the halls were beginning to be unionized, and a protest meeting of the Theatrical and Music Hall Operatives' Union opposed the withdrawal of the Empire's licence on the grounds that 140 union men employed backstage would be thrown out of work and a total of 670 employees in the theatre would be threatened with loss of jobs. These figures indicated just how big music hall business had become by then.

In the 1850s, Morton's example had led to the first wave of commercialization of music hall business – the reconstruction of old halls and the opening of new ones, all of them appealing one way or another to the all-important elevation of the moral tone of popular entertainment as a respectable sheen for their less salubrious aspects. An integral part of this process was the differentiation of seat prices, which led to the separation of different social classes within the same hall and to the different class composition of audiences in different types of hall. The process continued over a long period. In 1890, a writer in Harper's *New Monthly Magazine* distinguished four main categories of hall: the 'aristocratic' variety theatres of the West End, chiefly around Leicester Square; the smaller, less 'aristocratic' West End halls; the large 'bourgeois' halls to be found in less fashionable middle-class districts and suburbs; and finally the minor halls in the poor and squalid working-class districts. The audiences, as might be expected, correspond to the social scale of the particular place of entertainment, but the differences in the performances provided by the four classes of music halls are far less strongly marked' (F. Anstey, quoted in Mander and Mitchenson, p. 51).

A large part of the audience at the suburban halls included clerks and shop assistants and other petty bourgeois types, and in due course these same people formed, together with the working class, a much more ready audience for the cinema than the stolid bourgeois, who scorned the halls. For this reason, when cinema started trying to appeal directly to the respectable bourgeoisie at the end of its first decade, through well-appointed 'bijou' cinemas, there was a definite change in the kinds of films that were made. These exhibitors favoured those genres which, following well-established magic lantern principles, appealed to the moral principle of film as an 'educational' medium, like actualities and travelogues. To these were now added, as the first attempts were made at more sustained narrative forms, the first efforts to adapt pieces from the legitimate stage.

The 1850s was also the period when the first music hall artistes' agents appeared, a decade or so in advance of agents catering for 'serious' concert artists. One of the indications of the general ethos of the halls can be found in the satire which artistes from this moment on directed against themselves, as the professionalization of popular entertainment picked on men and women who were entirely untrained – and knew it – raising them from the anonymity of indigenous entertainment to become the hirelings of managers and impresarios. In spite of the pretensions of the bigger and plusher houses, the managers too were forced to remain on the defensive. Their increased business, the extensive boozing and the seedy associations of even the 'best-run' halls gave continuing cause for concern among the respectable. Parliament did not feel that the licensing problems had been solved, and various Select Committees were appointed to investigate. And to add to the trouble, there were a number of more or less serious fires which broke out in both big and small houses.

These were among the factors which led in 1878 to a new Act of Parliament, known as the Suitability Act because it required certificates of suitability for music halls and variety theatres. This meant a proscenium wall dividing stage from auditorium, the installation of a safety curtain, and the sale of liquor being finally banished from the body of the hall. The smaller halls could not afford to pay for the necessary alterations, and closed down. Mander and Mitchenson point to the devious workings of this Act when they tell us that sometimes a hall was forced to close because when a proscenium was installed in an older building, the authorities then refused permission for a safety curtain on the grounds that the structure of the building would not take the weight of the iron curtain. Some 200 halls across the country were forced to put up shutters, though many just managed to struggle on until, with the arrival of cinema, they found a new lease of life. But even so, their problem was exacerbated by the big economic depression which began in the middle 1870s and restricted the availability of investment funds needed for rebuilding. As a result, big business, with readier access to such funds, found it all the easier to move in on the halls, and to form syndicates and chains which consolidated their controls. In due course, in the late 1880s and the 1890s, as the depression receded, the business interests which had entered the music hall business after the 1878 Act began to put up bigger and plushier halls. This extended control explains why the programmes in a great number of halls in the 1890s did not vary greatly although they catered for different classes of audience: the same acts were moved around the theatres of a syndicate. It also helps to explain the speed with which cinematographs penetrated the halls: not just through the process of free competition, but also because they were taken up by the syndicates as soon as their success was apparent.

The Act of 1878 can be seen as a precedent for the first piece of legislation concerning cinema, the 1909 Cinematograph Act. Like the Suitability Act, this was introduced ostensibly for reasons of safety. There had again been a number of fires and there was certainly a good deal of legitimate concern over the dangers stemming from the inflammability of celluloid. Pressure for new legislation began to mount as it turned out, with the growth of cinema exhibition, that under certain conditions the venues where films were shown did not come under the licensing powers of the local authorities. Fires were sometimes caused by the incompetence of projectionists. This was inevitable as exhibition grew so rapidly that skilled projectionists were in short supply. However, both the exhibitors and the recently founded National Association of Cinematograph Operators tried to remedy this by instigating training schemes and placing the projector in a fireproof booth. The trade press claimed accordingly that cinema shows were relatively safe, and they bemoaned the delight which the lay press seemed to find in headlining any slight fire that had some connection with film. There was considerable justification in this attitude, since it is also likely that in some cases disasters were due rather to panic in the audience. (In one incident, reported by Audrey Field in *Picture Palace*, the panic was compounded by the fact that an exit door had been locked. She also says that in the Barnsley disaster of January 1908, when sixteen children were crushed to death, there was neither fire nor panic, but only a failure in crowd control (Field, pp. 19–20).)

But it is also clear that what the legislation lobby was after was a means of social and moral control. After the bill had been passed, Walter Reynolds of the LCC, one of the strongest agitators in its favour, said:

> Will the power given to the council enable them to control the nature of the entertainments given? It is the duty of the police to stop any entertainments of a doubtful character, but certainly the council would have the power when the licence came up for renewal once in twelve months, to refuse to license places which had presented undesirable shows. The knowledge that they possessed that power would be another powerful factor in securing a high class of entertainment, to the general good of the trade.

(Quoted in Hunnings, p. 45)

Nor had the 1878 Act been introduced for purely altruistic reasons. Concern over safety was used then too as a cover for the extension of social control over the halls. In London in particular, nervousness about the music halls was grounded in a set of social changes which had been gathering pace over several decades, and which issued in the last quarter of the century in the growth of trade unionism and the labour movement and to this connection between music hall and the labour movement I shall now turn.

*

One of the indices of the working-class character of music hall around the time of the birth of cinema comes from the degree of trade unionism to be found in the halls and the variety theatres. Three unions were involved: the first to be established was the backstage workers' union, the National Association of Theatrical Employees, which was founded in 1891 as the United Kingdom Theatrical and Music Hall Operatives' Union; then came the Musicians' Union, which grew out of the London Orchestral Association formed, in 1891, and the Amalgamated Musicians' Union, a provincial organization formed in 1893; third was the Variety Artists' Association, formed in 1902. The formation of the backstage workers' union belongs to the aftermath of the great dock strike of 1889, which is conventionally regarded as the origin of the new unionism which increased trade union membership from 750,000 at the end of 1888 to 2,025,000 in 1901. But the example of the dock strike for the backstage worker was not merely an indirect one. Communities of workers are never totally isolated from each other. There is always a flow of workers from one area to another who carry their experiences with them, and this was particularly true of the entertainment business in relation to industrial labour in London. Traditional craftsmen among the backstage workers, such as carpenters, usually came to the theatre from other fields where they had originally learnt their craft. Casual workers like doorkeepers and baggagemen found employment in other casual sectors during the off-season. The largest group – including stagehands, flymen, propertymen, gas and limelightmen – included not only those whose families traditionally worked in the theatre but those coming from outside too. The influx was all the greater since theatre employment had expanded greatly during the period of its commercialization. Finally a sub-group must be included consisting of the 'nightmen' who (according to Booth) only came at night to shift scenes and properties during the performance. These may very well have been workers with other daytime jobs, forced to earn extra money.

It is evident from Booth's account in *Life and Labour of the*

*People in London* (1896) that backstage workers even among heads of departments could easily have come from outside. For example, the property-master 'must be a man of resource who can effect hasty repairs, and, if need be, himself make the simpler articles. There is no special course of training to be gone through for the post, but to have learnt some mechanical trade is a very good introduction to it' (Booth, p. 124). The property-master is in charge of one of the 'two great departments, the heads of which, like foremen in factories, have power to engage and discharge their subordinates, while they are themselves responsible directly to the stage manager. These are the stage-carpenter, and the property-master, to whom in large theatres may be added a third, the wardrobe-mistress' (ibid., p. 122).

In other words it was mostly only the heads of departments who were regular employees in the theatre. Booth explains that under the principal stage-carpenter, for example, were the

> jobbing carpenters who specially devote themselves to theatrical work, and who go from theatre to theatre wherever they hear that men are wanted. For such men work is very uncertain; for a few days, or perhaps a week or two, they have as much work as they can get through, and then, for weeks, they are without a job.
>
> (ibid., p. 123)

There was, in other words, a full-scale system of sub-contracting within the entertainment world which covered many of the same kinds of work in which large numbers of semi-skilled workers who were now undergoing proper unionization for the first time were also employed. As with all sub-contracting systems, since the bulk of the workers were not directly employed by the bosses, the theatre managements were long able to disclaim responsibility for the appalling conditions of labour and remuneration which prevailed. This sub-contracting system was the original evil which the backstage workers' union was formed to deal with. The origins of the union can be found among a group of stagehands whose approach to the master-carpenter under whom they worked for a wage increase had been rejected. And when the union called its first strike, it was to deal with the problem of the limelightmen, who also worked under the same system. They were called out to establish a minimum wage just at the start of the pantomime season in a move which was so well timed that the contractors were forced to give way after only four days. But the conditions of labour made for difficulties in organization which were not easy to overcome. Booth says that the Theatrical and Music Hall Operatives' Trade Union had only about 750 members out of a total of 1,500 who might belong, and that they had a rule to the effect that 'theatrical carpenters should be paid not less than the standard rate of the London Building Trades' Federation', but it was not strictly enforced (ibid.). This type of problem continued to plague the cinema unions in later years (see Chanan 1976b).

The origins of the Musicians' Union are rather different. Musicians were, of course, a highly skilled professional group (although standards differed), and had been organized once before, long ago, in the Worshipful Company of Musicians, although this had been unable to exert any power after the mid-eighteenth century. However, the revived need to organize for protection had been felt already in the 1870s; the London Musical Artists' Protective Association was formed in 1874, and another in Manchester, but both of these only lasted for two years. The Birmingham Orchestral Association was founded the same year, and managed to last till 1878. The union as it now exists goes back directly to the London Orchestral Association, formed in 1891, and the provincial bodies which began in Manchester and Birmingham in 1893 and spread quickly to Oldham, Leeds, Preston, Southport and other smaller centres, as well as Glasgow, Liverpool and Newcastle. This list makes it obvious that their strength lay among theatre musicians.

In spite of their more petit bourgeois character, in 1901 the musicians joined with the backstage workers in London in trying to get a 'fair-wage' clause included in the theatre licence which the local council now had command of (since the 1888 Local Government Act). The London County Council responded timidly, even when one of the unions' witnesses before the council was dismissed from his job; but we can surmise that the musicians' influence was a moderating one, and no strike action was called for.

The big music hall proprietors were certainly seen as the main enemy. In 1905, the *Stage Staff Journal* attacked one of the leading impresarios, Oswald Stoll, in pretty forthright terms, as 'an organiser of other people's talents' who takes 'from the profit they earn' and only 'pays a portion of it to those he hires':

Is there any reason why Mr Stoll should take 10,000 a year and the sceneshifters be content with 6d an hour? ... Labour is as necessary to work the stage of a theatre as it is to the cultivation of a grain of wheat.... Does not this fact show how little, in himself, the music hall magnate is? He depends on talent, he depends on labour, he depends on the public, and none of these depend on the individual music-hall magnate.

(Quoted in Mrs Syd Heath, p. 11)

But the talent – the artistes – were as yet hardly organized. In order to remedy this, the Variety Artists' Association was formed in 1902, on the initiative of Charles Coburn (of 'The Man Who Broke the Bank at Monte Carlo' fame). The most significant thing here is that there was no class division between the leading artistes and the less successful ones or between artistes and others. This is demonstrated particularly by the strike which the Variety Artists led at the end of 1906. Twenty-two leading London halls were involved, and picketing was led by several of the popular favourites, among them R. G. Knowles, George Robey and Marie Lloyd.

The top comedians did alright:
Two hundred a week so they say,
Two songs, a red nose,
And a suit of old clothes

(Quoted in Leeson, p. 48)

went one of the songs on the subject. But the lesser artistes were scarcely better off than the backstage workers. Fred Karno, for example (the man who later took a company to the United States which included Charles Chaplin and Stan Laurel), got paid £300 for one of his sketches. With a troupe of thirty in his company, top pay to the artistes would be £4 and many would only get between £1 and 30s. With two houses a night it wasn't much for a lot of hard work. Marie Lloyd sang a song about Karno during the strike, to the tune of 'Oh Mr Porter':

Oh Mr Karno, what are you trying to do,
Make more money from the sketches, if what they say is true,
All your lads are winners, not one's an also-ran,
Oh Mr Karno, don't be a silly man.

(ibid.)

Her name also headed a list of eighteen which appeared on a Variety Artists' Federation strike handbill bearing the following inscription:

Twinkle, twinkle, brilliant star!
Oh, I wonder where you are.
With the V.A.F. so bright
You will not show here to-night.
artists not appearing at Payne & Gibbons' Halls till dispute settled: Marie Lloyd, etc.

I am not, of course, claiming that there was much political consciousness involved in all this. But class solidarity? Of that there can be no question. The significance of this for early film culture should not escape us. It establishes beyond a doubt that film made its appearance in an entertainment world whose values were structured in several respects – behind the scenes and in front of them – according to a strong sense of social class.

# Chapter 10

# Culture and politics in the middle classes

The Goody Good Time

A magic lantern show will be considered very fast,
Sing hey for the good time coming!
And folks will say, 'How nice to have a moral show at last',
Sing hey for the good time coming!
The Ballet, too, will be a real credit to our stage,
Decorum and Propriety of course will be the rage,
You'll never see a dancer under fifty years of age,
In the very, very good time coming.

Albert Chevalier

William Friese-Greene's early career was that of a successful portrait photographer with a provincial petit bourgeois background. Backed by studios which he opened in various towns in the south of the country, he came to London in 1885 and opened a fashionable studio in New Bond Street which he shared with Esme Collings, who later became known as one of the so-called Brighton School of early film makers (a term introduced by the French film historian Sadoul). Others in this loose-knit group included G. A. Smith, a keen astronomer and Fellow of the Royal Astronomical Society; James Williamson, a chemist; and Alfred Darling, a technician who supplied these two with equipment and went to work with the firm of Wrench in 1897. It was entirely natural that film drew in men from such technically related trades, easily able to adapt their skills to the needs of cinematography. At the same time, along with figures like the precision instrument maker R. W. Paul and his associate Acres, another professional photographer, these men form a distinct petit bourgeois layer among the film pioneers, and should be distinguished from those of more popular origins like the fairground showmen.

There was a marked difference between the two groups. The showmen represented the robust features of independent popular culture, and their contributions to early British film culture owed a great deal to their close contact with popular sensibility, as in the figure of, say, William Haggar (of whom, more later); but their type was under attack from several sides. The professional technicians, on the other hand, were not only socially removed from working-class culture, but were hardly any closer to the world of high culture, and certainly totally removed from the ferment which had come to grip the avant-garde in the closing years of the century, in the struggle against the restrictions of the late Victorian bourgeois mentality. Men like these would have been dutifully horrified not only by what they saw as the excesses of working-class cultural behaviour but also by the deviations of the Bohemians. For them, artistic culture was essentially decorative and inoffensive.

In 1951, the British film industry decided that its contribution to the Festival of Britain would be a film, called *The Magic Box*, about the life of William Friese-Greene, intended as a long-due recognition of his much-debated claim to hold the prior patent in the world on a working film camera. The film was based on Ray Allister's then recently published biography, a book which is poorly researched and full of errors and romanticized accounts of various episodes in Friese-Greene's life. In the typical manner of the commercial cinema, the film treated its source book in thoroughly cavalier fashion, so the film is even less historically accurate than the book. There is one scene, however, introduced into the film on the basis of a casual remark in the book, which deserves our attention here. It shows the Friese-Greenes as members of an amateur chorus, rehearsing and performing a work by Sir Arthur Sullivan. It captures the cultural milieu perfectly, the milieu of established petit bourgeois cultural values in musical shape, in the tradition of harmonic societies, low-status classical concerts and church music. A complete contrast with the world of music hall, it is precisely the kind of milieu which governed the evolution of the moral and aesthetic attitudes of the lower middle classes during the nineteenth century.

The contrasts within nineteenth-century musical culture are extremely revealing: they say a great deal about the sociological tendencies and even political proclivities of different classes, especially because musical life underwent considerable changes in the middle decades of the century when a new breed of commercial concert promoter appeared on the scene. Until then, the bourgeoisie had largely followed the models of aristocratic musical life. In imitation, for example, of the salons common in the town and country houses of the nobility, semi-public gatherings had started up in London in the taverns and coffee houses frequented by professionals and entrepreneurs. Around 1680, a self-made coal merchant, Thomas Britton, known to history as 'the musical small coal man', who ran a series of concerts in a room above his business premises, hit upon the idea of a subscription; payment of admission at the door soon followed and the institution of the concert was born.

The growth of concert life during the course of the eighteenth century involved a good deal of social mixing between the aristocracy and the upper middle class. Meanwhile, the growing musical life in the Pleasure Gardens, such as London's Vauxhall, anticipated the style of the commercial concerts which developed in the 1830s and 1840s. Known as promenade concerts, these soon began to displace the musical function of the Pleasure Gardens (though they represent only one factor in the Gardens' decline). At the same time, the upper echelons of the bourgeoisie found themselves engaged in a battle with the aristocracy for social prestige and control of the elite concerts, a musical battle which paralleled the political battles they were locked in over the issue of Reform, in which rival upper- and middle-class groupings cultivated aesthetic interests as a guise for continuing social and political battles.

Inevitably, lower-middle-class groups found that musical life offered them, too, a means of social and even political self-assertion. Hence the emergence in the 1830s of large-scale choral organizations, especially in the City and East End of London, where they had strong roots among the religious dissenters. These organizations dramatized mass involvement in social and political life. Control of the choral societies therefore became a politically volatile issue. In 1834, for instance, the Crown put on a festival of Handel oratorios in Westminster Abbey to commemorate the seventy-fifth anniversary of the composer's death. As the musicologist William Weber recounts: 'it had the obvious purpose of dramatising royal leadership after the bitter dispute of electoral

reform. Its administrators not only restricted admission to a carefully chosen list, but also excluded local church choirs from the
chorus, inviting only singers from Anglican churches and predominantly upper-middle-class provincial choruses' (W. Weber,
p. 102). This policy of discrimination caused a bitter outcry among
the new London choirs; they responded by presenting their own
amateur music festival of Handel's oratorios, and later formed
the important Sacred Harmonic Society. Symbolically, this society
became in due course the proud owners of the bust of Handel
which used to stand in the Vauxhall Gardens. (Ironically, and as
if to demonstrate the ultimate victory of the development of the
consumer market in art over political or social pride, the same
bust now adorns the offices of the music publishers Novellos,
which became part of the Granada group of companies a few
years ago.)

The promenade concerts conquered the growing middle-class
musical audience. They were the most important means by which
the heritage of informal musical entertainment, derived largely
from the Pleasure Gardens, was turned into large-scale commercial enterprise in the general middle-class public, and it was here
that the professional musicians first took command and introduced a new repertoire. As one reviewer of the time put it, 'Lords
spiritual and temporal are useful in their proper places, but they
are sorry managers of a concert' (ibid., p. 98). The alternative
was readily available: a growing middle-class audience with
enough money to make public concerts a paying proposition. The
success of the promenade concerts provided a model for the
commercial developments which later took place among the
working classes, in a different setting – the music hall – and with
a different musical repertoire.

By the 1850s, when the commercialization of music hall began,
middle-class musical life had already established a firm pattern
with a definite scale of aesthetic values, which placed the concert
hall on a higher moral level than the stage. This explains why it
was acceptable for Charles Morton to try and 'raise the level' of
the music presented in the music halls by including the 'light
classical' repertoire, but on the other hand, why music written
for the theatre was not so acceptable in the concert hall. One
composer who was caught up in this contradiction of musical
values was Arthur Sullivan. The Savoy operettas were his most
popular (and best) music, but they were theatre music, and

damaged his reputation as a 'serious' composer of symphonic and sacred music before his partnership with W. S. Gilbert began. While the operettas stormed from success to success, well-intentioned friends bemoaned the waste of his talents in a frivolous and unworthy manner. Tormented by these criticisms, he gambled away some quarter of a million pounds which he earned from the operettas, and tried continually to escape from the commercial bandwagon back to the more 'exalted' world of the concert hall. The Sullivan portrayed in the scene with the Friese-Greenes in *The Magic Box* is the 'serious' composer of sacred anthems and secular cantatas, not the composer of such popular masterpieces as *Iolanthe* and *The Gondoliers*.

*

Other art forms suffered a similar process to music as taste was marshalled into its various social levels. The process not only involved a growing secularization of art, but also the creation of a whole new set of cultural institutions in order to establish new standards of cultural behaviour and attitudes. For example, museums and art galleries not only enshrined the works of the European tradition, but also became the depositories for cultural relics from other societies, brought to the metropolis as the spoils of imperial conquest. Expropriating the riches of history, museums served to proclaim the historical ascendancy of the new imperialism.

At the same time, with the growth of entrepreneurial society, the bourgeoisie itself constituted a new market for cultural products, and painting became more and more of a professional business. As William Gaunt puts it in *The Aesthetic Adventure*, painters were becoming 'a recognised and esteemed type of professional, ranking equally with such other esteemed professionals as barristers and doctors. They were, likewise, conservative and conventional as well-to-do people thoroughly identified with the society in which they live, must be' (Gaunt, p. 41). This conservatism and identification with their clients allowed them to accept a select number of respectable amateurs among their ranks – such as their professional counterparts engaged in the creation of the modern civil service – but for the most part the Academy, in spite of its name, was a professional institute, not an academic institution; and most of the professional artists of the Victorian age who were trained in the Academy schools went there because that was the accepted form of apprenticeship. As for the source of their business and their respectability, this was the steady demand of the prosperous bourgeoisie for paintings to hang among the drapes on their drawing-room walls, the salons where their wives and daughters conducted musical evenings.

The rising entrepreneurial class naturally demanded portraits in imitation of their aristocratic predecessors, but they also developed a taste for a certain type of painting known as the 'subject picture' – which became a more central part of the painters' output as the century wore on and portraits were increasingly supplied by means of photography. This is how one art historian has described the genre: the painter

> selected from his reading or his imagination a subject which was elevating, pathetic or romantic, and proceeded to realize this upon his canvas with as near an approach to photographic exactitude as his abilities allowed. The subject-matter of his picture thus assumed a primary importance, and the picture as such had a merely secondary significance. It became a thing not to be looked at, but through, a window behind which was presented a tableau vivant with a moral.
>
> (Montmorency, p. 189)

This is the part of nineteenth-century painting, not the experimental practice of the painter whom photography liberated from verisimilitude, which passes to early cinema. The cinema screen, at the moment when the illusion of reality is at its strongest, behaves in this way too. It disappears; we no longer seem to see images set upon a screen; it is as if the screen has become transparent, not a screen but a window. And this illusion links the cinema, via the *tableau vivant*, to the very birth of modern European painting in the Italian Renaissance, when the idea of the picture surface as a window first arose with the invention of artificial perspective.

According to art historian John White, the invention of artificial perspective was not a neutral tool, but an instrument for the expression of a certain world view, loosely called Renaissance humanism, which established the central position of the human observer as the judge of Nature's order:

> Man's central position as observer of a pictorial world of which he himself is the measure, together with the new reality to

which that world aspires, is shown immediately Alberti describes his actual method of perspective composition, beginning with a suitably large square which, he says, 'I consider to be an open window through which I view that which will be painted there.'

(White, p. 122)

This connection is enough for a number of film theorists to see the camera, which supposedly reproduces Renaissance perspective, as a kind of repetition of the original sin of the Renaissance in the invention of perspective. According to Pleynet, for example:

The film camera is an ideological instrument in its own right, it expresses bourgeois ideology before expressing anything else. . . . It produces a directly inherited code of perspective, built on the model of the scientific perspective of the Quattrocento. What needs to be shown is the meticulous way in which the construction of the camera is geared to 'rectify' any anomalies in perspective in order to reproduce in all its authority the visual code laid down by Renaissance humanism.

(Pleynet in *Cinéthique*, no. 3, p. 10)

Commolli criticizes this view, quite rightly in my opinion, by pointing out that to make the camera itself the object of complaint is to reproduce on the level of theory the same division between the visible and the invisible which film itself tends to create. For as Serge Daney puts it, the cinema is in partnership with the Western metaphysical tradition and its vested interest in seeing and sight which film as an optical system is called upon to concretize. Cinema, says Daney,

postulates that from the 'real' to the visual and from the visual to its reproduction on film, the same truth is reflected infinitely and without any distortion or loss. And in a world where 'I see' is automatically said for 'I understand' such a fantasy has probably not come about by chance. The dominant ideology which equates the real to the visible has every interest in encouraging it.

(Daney in *Cahiers du Cinéma*, no. 222)

What this suggests, however, is that the operation of ideology in the cinema does not come simply from the structuring properties of the lens, the reproduction of illusory appearances, or even the distortion of reality, but rather from the exclusion of what is not directly or easily visible. The reality which film represents may be real enough, but it is marked by a constant absence: the absence of elements which do not take on a convenient and straightforward visual form. (Including, necessarily, the process of production of the film itself.)

*

Let us go back for one last time to photography. 'Earlier', wrote Walter Benjamin, 'much futile thought had been devoted to the question of whether photography is an art. The primary question whether the very invention of photography had not transformed the entire nature of art – was not raised' (Benjamin, 1969, p. 227). Today, said Benjamin (he was writing in the 1930s), the dispute seems devious and confused, but this did not diminish its importance; if anything, it underlined it. It was a distinctive characteristic of early photography that making a photograph was just as studied a process as executing a painting. You could not, in the early days, 'take' a photograph as you could later, in the age of the snapshot. There was nothing instantaneous about photography at the beginning. As Benjamin explains in his 'Small History of Photography':

> Many of Hill's portraits were taken in the Greyfriars cemetery of Edinburgh and nothing is more characteristic of this period than the extent to which his models seemed at home there. Indeed, in one of Hill's pictures the cemetery looks like an interior, a secluded, enclosed space in which the tombstones, set against partition-walls, rise up from the grass, hollowed out like chimney-pieces with inscriptions taking the place of flames. Nevertheless, this location could never have achieved its effect had there not been good technical reasons for choosing it. The earlier plates were far less sensitive to light and this necessitated long exposures in the open. This in turn made it desirable to place the subject in as secluded a spot as possible where nothing could disturb concentration. 'The synthesis of expression brought about by the length of time that a model has to stand still', says Orlik of early photography, 'is the main reason why these pictures, apart from their simplicity, resemble well-drawn or painted portraits and have a more penetrating and lasting effect on the spectator than more recent pho-

tography'. The procedure itself taught the models to live inside rather than outside the moment. During the long duration of these shots they grew as it were into the picture and in this way presented an extreme opposite to the figures on a snapshot.

(Benjamin, 1979)

The very look that photography therefore aimed at, tied up with the social role it accepted by adopting portraiture and so allying itself to the leisured classes, encouraged photographers to seek the sanction of aesthetic approval from above. In France in 1856, Nadar proposed that photography should be admitted to the exhibitions of the Académie des Beaux Arts. A committee was formed to investigate which included Delacroix (who made considerable use of photography as an aid in painting) and Théophile Gautier, both strong supporters of the initiative. The result was a photographic section in the Salon of 1859 – the occasion of Baudelaire's famous attack on photography, or rather on commercial photography, as 'the refuge of every would-be painter, every painter too ill-endowed or too lazy to complete his studies'. But by this time legions of portrait miniaturists had become photographers, at first merely as a sideline and then exclusively so, using their knowledge as painters to touch up the photographs and remove imperfections – imperfections which may have been technical but which were also those of reality, previously excluded by the painter wishing to flatter the subject, captured now by the camera's scrutiny.

In Britain, the Royal Academy was far too conservative for such an initiative as Nadar's even to have been conceivable. And yet the photograph had been adopted readily enough by painters, first as an aid, and then as a whole new means of production of works of saleable art. Already in 1843 David Octavius Hill used a large number of portrait photographs for his fresco of the general synod of the Church of Scotland. Before very long William Lake Price, a water-colourist-turned-photographer, was producing a series of illustrations for *Robinson Crusoe* and monumental tableaux like *Don Quixote in his Study* with the aid of photography. These were not simple photographs but collages, in which posed photographic figures were cut out and placed in position on the traditional model of a painting. Indeed, Oscar Gustave Rejlander, a Swede who came to work in Britain, created similar large allegorical compositions in a *tableau-vivant* style (sometimes with a pseudo-erotic content of reclining semi-nude figures and the like), which were explicitly inspired by his earlier study of the Old Masters while he was in Rome. Rejlander influenced Henry Peach Robinson, perhaps the most successful of this group. Robinson was an amateur artist who had exhibited at the Royal Academy in 1852, and then opened a photographic studio in Leamington Spa in 1857. His large exhibition pieces have been described as 'wholly artificial compositions' by the historians of photography Helmut and Alison Gernsheim. They included items like *The Lady of Shalott*, an illustration to Tennyson, and *Bringing Home the May*, after a poem by Spenser. His sketches show us how he worked. He worked up his compositions, in composite fashion, by building them around the individual photographic figures. He charged twenty guineas for a final exhibition print, 49 × 15 inches; but he was soon inundated by so many orders that he laboured to produce a half size version which he sold for one guinea.

The *tableau-vivant* style adopted by the 'composite' photographers was a form of ideological closure, the imposition of a fixed point of view on a subject, which subdues instead of stimulating the imagination of the beholder. This should be clearly distinguished from the necessary material closure of aesthetic forms which results from the physical characteristics of the medium in question. It is a material necessity in the case of photography that images should take on one fixed form or another; but this is different from the deliberate (if in certain ways unconscious) business of arranging the pattern of images within a frame to correspond to certain accepted aesthetic canons. Photography itself produces this difference. A painting also takes the form of a frozen image, but an image which is necessarily composed, since the painting has to be painted. As the techniques of photography developed, however, and exposure times became shorter, the quality of studied composition came to be displaced. The frozen form of the image now becomes increasingly accidental, and we recognize it as such, as arrested motion. That is why there are some photographs we tend to pick out and say of them 'But that's posed.' Or as Benjamin put it:

> However skilful the photographer, however carefully he poses his model, the spectator feels an irresistible compulsion to look for the tiny spark of chance, of the here and now, with which

reality has, as it were, seared the character in the picture; to find that imperceptible point at which, in the immediacy of that long-past moment, the future so persuasively inserts itself that, looking back, we may rediscover it.

(Benjamin, 1979)

The essence of the tableau is in this respect precisely the opposite of photography: it copies not reality, but art. Here the classical ideals of composition are subsumed into the crystallization of ideal meanings. As Diderot defined it:

> A well-composed picture [tableau] is a whole contained under a single point-of-view, in which the parts work together to one end and form by their mutual correspondence a unity as real as that of the body of an animal; so that a piece of a painting made up of a large number of figures thrown at random onto the canvas, with neither proportion, intelligence nor unity, no more deserves to be called a true composition than scattered studies of legs, nose and eyes on the same cartoon deserves to be called a portrait or even a human figure.

It was this highly reified notion of visual form which dominated institutional aesthetics, and perforce the visual imagination of the Victorian petit bourgeoisie, at the moment of the birth of the film. At the same time that the closed aesthetic of the academy was undergoing increasingly well-concerted attacks by the avant-garde, the first film makers were confronted with the properties of the moving camera. Everything about the film camera contradicted the static visual ideas enshrined by the establishment. The camera recorded movement within the scene in front of it, which immediately threatened to dissolve the tableau. More than that, the camera itself soon became mobile, turning as it went. It became an active agent. In the process, established notions of composition were radically attacked: as the camera moves, it immediately, frame by frame, negates every composition that it throws up. This potential visual anarchy was unsettling, aesthetically, psychologically, ideologically. Before the film camera could be recognized as an artistic instrument, it would have to be tamed and subdued.

\*

The genres of the visual illustration were greatly expanded in

Victorian Britain by the publishing trade, with an increasing number of illustrated editions of literary works, including the magazines which published novels in serialized form, and the use of lithography for the covers of sheet music editions. Here we find that moralism gives way somewhat to anecdotalism: for example, the image of a train-load of excursionists passing under Shakespeare Cliff at Dover on a South Eastern Railway train, used on the cover of the 'Excursion Train Gallop' in the 1840s. Mackerness remarks that 'The design of covers for songs and instrumental pieces developed as a lucrative branch of commercial art, especially after the introduction of chromolithography in the early 1840s' (Mackerness, p. 177). The illustrator's art was to anticipate the audience's selection of this essential icon in order to promote the sale of the work.

The illustrative paradigm, with its anecdotal content, represented such a dominant influence over the visual imagination of the nineteenth century that it even took hold of theatre. It first took shape in the development, beginning in the 1830s, of the box set: a boxed-in setting of three walls with real doors instead of a backdrop and wings, as if the audience in the auditorium were all cramped up against the missing fourth wall. The stage thus ceases to be simply a playing space and becomes a room, the domestic room of the bourgeois household: the 'natural' setting of dramatic action in bourgeois society. For example:

Handsome suite of rooms in featherstone's house. Decorations blue and white, profusely relieved by gilt work. Furniture rich, and elegant mirrors adorn the walls, so as to multiply the reflection of the vases and statuettes placed about; chandelier hangs from ceiling of inner room. The two rooms open into each other by a broad arch, surmounted by a handsome cornice, from which fall velvet curtains, drawn up at sides so as to show table spread with refreshments, wines, fruits, &.c.&.c., the whole giving idea of elegant but prodigal luxury. Music and laughter as guests (all in full toilet) came crowding from inner room.

(Watts Phillips, *Lost in London* (1867) (quoted by M. Booth in Dyos and Wolff, eds, p. 220))

At the same time, the improvement of lighting and stage mechanics permitted the application of surface naturalism to exterior locations as well. Gas lighting played a crucial role in the process:

detailed surface naturalism in the theatre before gas lighting was pointless anyway; it could hardly be seen. Nor could a sufficient range of contrast in lighting levels be achieved. According to Michael Booth, 'A rather shocked Clement Scott described the last-act setting of George Sims's *The Lights o' London* (1881), the Borough market on a Saturday night':

> It is a marvellous example of stage realism, complete in every possible detail. . . . If anything, it is all too real, too painful, too smeared with the dirt and degradation of London life, where drunkenness, debauchery, and depravity are shown in all their naked hideousness. Amidst buying and selling, the hoarse roar of costermongers, the jingle of the piano-organ, the screams of the dissolute, fathers teach their children to cheat and lie, drabs swarm in and out of the public house, and the hunted Harold, with his devoted wife, await the inevitable capture in an upper garret of a house which is surrounded by police.
>
> (ibid., p. 221)

In a sense, says Booth, this kind of drama was true to life – at least enough for character and situation to carry sufficient conviction. 'The fact that the basic content of such drama was in many respects notably unreal, the dream world of the popular melodrama or the middle-class "drama", was an added reason for enjoyment rather than the reverse; a taste for the real and an indulgence in the illusory could be satisfied simultaneously. Such a duality lies at the heart of Victorian drama' (ibid., p. 219).

Raymond Williams goes further. The introduction of the box set, he argues, was not aimed at realism:

> If you look at when the first 'box sets' with reproduced rooms were put on the stage in England (the English and French theatres moving at about the same rate in this respect), you will find that the rooms are there not to give any impression of recognition or demonstration of environment, but simply to display a certain kind of luxury. They are 'society' plays of a consciously displayed kind – of a fashionable kind, as we would now say – and most of the technology of the box set and the subsequent adaptation of theatres to the fully-framed box set, which was not complete until the 1870s, was more conditioned by this 'furnishing display' than by . . . other intentions.
>
> (R. Williams, 1977)

The same illustrative aesthetic entered music hall with the Act of 1878 and the installation of the proscenium arch according to the new legal requirements. The artist's act now acquired a scenario which incorporated painted backcloths. Here, for example, is Samuel McKechnie's description of Charles Godfrey's 'On Guard':

> It represents the fate of a British soldier who, after fighting and bleeding for his Queen and his country, is left by the latter to die in the streets of misery and want. The first scene is laid in the trenches before Sebastopol, where a solitary soldier stands valiantly 'on guard' until a chance bullet from the enemy lays him low. The exterior of a village churchyard forms scene II, with a dimly lit church in the background, from which issues the music of the organ and the choir in more or less luminous strains. The old Crimean hero, enfeebled with age and work, now enters, and after bewailing the neglect of his country whose foes he fought so well, sinks down on a convenient gravestone, where he dies to the accompaniment of slow music and a fall of snow.
>
> (McKechnie, p. 153)

The effect is clearly to sentimentalize what began as a protest song, and indeed certain verses were cut when it was played in the West End. But there were cases where this kind of tableau setting was used to original effect. 'My Old Dutch', for example, is remembered today as one of the most sentimental of all music hall numbers – 'We've been together now for forty years, and it don't seem a day too much' – yet originally it was set against a backdrop of a workhouse, with separate entrances for men and women, to which the ageing couple have been condemned: poverty destroys the companionship of old age in front of an iconographic representation of economic reality.

The highest achievements of theatrical realism – to be found in the work of late-nineteenth-century dramatists such as Ibsen or Chekhov – depend on a much more organic understanding of space, which sees an indissoluble relationship between character and environment, and where a room becomes a character in its own right because (as Raymond Williams put it) 'it was a specific environment created by and radically affecting, radically displaying, the nature of the characters who lived in it' (R. Williams, 1977). But this is far removed from the surface realism which dominated the melodramatic stage. In the year moving pictures

arrived in Britain, a writer in the journal *Engineering* on 'Modern
Theatre Stages' worried about the 'stage reform' movement for
aiming at 'the possible imitation of nature in the mise en scène
of our opera and drama':

> This is . . . practically only due to the public having associated
> the movement with the encouragement of that crude realism
> which has of late met with such general appreciation in all
> branches of arts and letters. There has been no outcry against
> the non-descript mounting of a play, and the realism of a
> spectacle has been generally more appreciated by audiences
> than its merits as a work of art. Stage reform in this country
> is still associated with the sensational shipwreck, the bona fide
> race, or other realistic items of a programme, and its popularity
> is practically due to the successful rendering of such scenes.

We can safely say that the naturalism of stage spectacle was a
stronger influence on early cinema than the realism of high dramatic art, which will remain a paradigm beyond the grasp of
early film for reasons both aesthetic and technical. Aesthetically,
the site of early film is distant from the arenas of high art,
and the fictional genres of early cinema – from comedy to crime
– were initially derived from the popular stage. The film was
mute, projection was accompanied by music; these subjects trans-
ferred easily. Technically, early film was limited to daylight filming,
or else required the use of bulky lights, which precluded the use
of real indoor locations, even if anyone had thought of it. The
camera generally assumed the view of a spectator in front of a
scene; since fiction takes place in a theatrical setting, this setting,
and not the real instance of what it imitates, is what was placed
in front of the camera. The effect was a crucial perceptual tension,
for the means which in the theatre produce a naturalistic illusion
are rendered on the film screen as exactly what they are: theatrical. In order to produce a new and integral screen realism, film
would have to overcome this contradiction by a route quite different from stage drama. Not only because it was mute but also
because it would have to free the camera from the fixed position
of the spectator which reproduced this theatricality, and learn to
penetrate the space in which the fiction unfolds. When this is
accomplished, and film acquires the plasticity of montage and the
altering frame, the spectator assumes the vision of the ubiquitous
camera, and the period of early cinema comes to a close.

# Part 4

# The early years

# Chapter 11

# Market competition and industrial growth

The cinema is a branch of the economy without any tradition; it has developed sometimes in an autonomous way and sometimes by assuming forms of organization from other sectors. In a very short time, this industry has been through almost all the forms of capitalism which were born before cinema itself, from personal enterprise to trustification. The very considerable risks it entails and the arrangements made to remove or reduce them give to its production, distribution and exploitation a very peculiar character.

Peter Bachlin

The final birth-pangs of cinema in Britain began on 17 October 1894 with the English debut of Edison's kinetoscope, in a parlour opened at 70 Oxford Street, London, by Frank Z. Maguire and Joseph D. Baucus of the Continental Commerce Company of New York. As in other countries, the kinetoscope stimulated imitators and improvers. The order of events in Britain was roughly: first, the appearance of copies of the kinetoscope machine using the same mechanism and the same films; second, the re-invention of the camera, to produce more films to meet the demand caused by the spread of the kinetoscope; and third, the invention of the projector which turned Edison's peep-show into cinema proper. Other associated pieces of equipment were also invented in the process, such as machines for the perforation of film stock.

Edison neglected to patent the kinetoscope outside the United States. Was this merely an oversight? Or was it because he didn't think it worth the expense for something he didn't believe would be more than a short-term money-spinner? Some commentators suggest it was probably the latter, since he wasn't usually careless about patents. As early as 1881, the British *Electrical Review* described him as 'the young man who keeps the road to the Patent Office hot with his footsteps', and explained:

> His plan appears to be to patent all the ideas that occur to him, whether tried or untried, and to trust to future labours to select and combine those which prove themselves the fittest. The result is that the great bulk of his patents are valueless in point of practicability; but they serve to fence the ground in from other inventors.

But there might have been another reason. As the English pioneer Birt Acres said in a letter to the *British Journal of Photography* in 1896:

> I believe that no patents were taken out on the Edison machine, the Company relying on the difficulty of the successful making of films, and, as machines were of no use without films, they made it a stipulation with the sale of films that they were only to be used with their own machines.
>
> (Quoted in Barnes, p. 35)

This is more than plausible. Many of the early businessmen who owed the origins of their business to Edison's neglect practised more or less the same policy with the sale of their own films. In fact, the lack of standardization made this easier. For example, idiosyncratic perforation designs meant that not all films could be shown on all makes of projector.

Edison did not take out an English patent, as Paul discovered after the visit by the two Greeks who wanted him to copy the kinetoscope they'd brought from New York. So Paul decided to manufacture his own when he found there was nothing to stop him: not for the Greeks, however; he set up in business for himself. He sold his machines to travelling showmen, and 'in conjunction with business friends installed fifteen at the Exhibition at Earl's Court, London, showing', as he later recalled, 'some of the first of our British films, including the Boat Race and Derby of 1896' (Paul in Barker, Paul and Hepworth). As noted earlier, the success of this venture encouraged Paul to devise a method of projection to replace the money-in-the-slot peep-show in order to cater for a number of simultaneous viewers.

But Paul's recollections skip over an essential intermediate stage. He copied the kinetoscope easily enough, but before he could make his own films he had to devise a camera. He realized that this was necessary, first because 'a demand existed for a greater variety of subjects than at present available', as he himself explained in a letter to Edison (quoted in Barnes, p. 20); and second, because of his concern that, although the kinetoscope was unpatented in England, the films themselves were probably subject to copyright. Indeed, in the same letter to Edison, in which he proposed 'that our mutual interests would be served by an exchange of films', Paul added,

> In case you decide to entertain this proposal I shall be pleased to cooperate with you in stopping sundry attempts now being made here to copy your films – which, I take it, is an offence against the international Copyright Act.

In fact the condition of copyright throughout the early years of cinema was extremely fluid and uncertain, dependent upon a body of law devised to cover literary and musical publication and performance, which had not yet even recognized mechanical copyright in the form of sound recording, let alone a strip of photographs. Since originally films consisted of a single shot, they were registered for copyright purposes in the same way as a photograph. The principal fear was piracy, that is, the making of unauthorized copies, and some producers even took for a time to putting a small stamp in the corner of every frame of film. But throughout the early period films were freely copied in another sense, all the time: they were remade by the same and different film makers in direct imitation of the original. Even the very first Lumière films were remade several times not only by Lumière himself but also by others, initiating a practice which was rampant throughout the early years, of copying subjects and stories sometimes exactly and sometimes with added elaboration, thereby helping to establish the growing range of genres in early cinema. In the literary world this would be called plagiarism, but unlike the unauthorized duplication of copies, in cinema there was originally no form of legal retaliation possible. Nor would there be, until appropriate revisions had been made to the Berne Convention, and these had been adopted in the subscribing countries (which, to complicate matters, did not include the USA). This process of legal redefinition occurred over precisely the same period as the transformation of film from an international but artisanal trade into a vertically organized multinational industry with three sectors, comprising production, distribution and exhibition. This transitional period begins around the end of cinema's first decade, depending on the country; it is also the period in which films grow longer and begin to tell stories, and the basic principles of the narrative code of the film screen are adumbrated. These parallel developments can hardly be a matter of coincidence.

Early attempts to consolidate industrial power in the film business were based on patents, not copyright, and there continues to be a gap in historical studies in regard to copyright. Burch, who mentions that the first major trial in France concerning artistic property rights in the cinema dates from 1908, suggests that early film makers hardly considered the practice of plagiarism objectionable (Burch, 1990, p. 197). In that case it would make what he calls the prodigious circulation of signs which characterizes early cinema comparable to the domain of popular music, in which tunes and lyrics circulate freely and are freely adapted. André Gaudreault, who writes about court cases in America in 1902 and 1904, sees in the legal arguments wielded in these cases an attempt to grapple with the question of the definition of the film not just as a material object but also as an aesthetic one. In a deposition by Edison's manager James H. White in 1902, for example:

> In taking moving pictures photographically, great artistic skill may be used. As a rule the nature of the subject taken prevents the artist from grouping or draping the objects photographed. But on the other hand, artistic skill is required in placing the camera in such a position that the lights and shades of the picture, when taken, still have proper values.
>
> (Gaudreault in Elsaesser, p. 116)

The emphasis here, as Gaudreault observes, is squarely on the function which he calls monstration, the fact of displaying the profilmic scene which is the primary act of film making. Only a couple of years later, however, editing has entered the scene, and the function of monstration begins to give way to that of narration. The art, says Biograph in its defence in 1904, 'has advanced beyond the point of a single view of a single object', likening the succession of scenes to 'books written in ... the picture writing of the Indians and other early peoples, and ...

the picture-written books for children of today' (ibid., p. 120). A few months later, the judge sums up:

> I am unable to see why, if a series of pictures of a moving object taken by a pivoted camera may be copyrighted as a photograph, a series of pictures telling a single story like that of the complainant in this case, even though the camera be placed at different points, may not also be copyrighted as a photograph. . . . In that story, it is true, there are different scenes. But no one has ever suggested that a story told in written words may not be copyrighted merely because, in unfolding its incidents, the reader is carried from one scene to another.

As Gaudreault comments wryly, 'The theory of cinema was born much earlier than we generally believe' (ibid.).

\*

Because of his own lack of knowledge of photography, Paul found that he needed assistance. The man he turned to was Birt Acres. 'In Birt Acres', said Paul later (in Barker, Paul and Hepworth), 'I found a photographer willing to take up the photography and processing provided I could supply him with the necessary plant, which I did early in 1895.' Thus Acres became the first film cameraman in England. But the association didn't last long. A disagreement arose between the two men in 1896, probably over a patent which Acres filed on 27 March for a camera – claiming features which had already been incorporated in the camera they had made together, which had not been patented — for which Paul felt he largely deserved the credit himself.

The story is told in a correspondence in the trade press which is quoted by John Barnes in his book *The Beginnings of the Cinema in England*. Barnes remarks that information about the first camera which Paul made is difficult to come by, but that this isn't surprising:

> Cameras generally are the least documented of early cinematographic equipment, since it was usually the practice of the first film-makers to supply films exclusively for use in projectors of their own make. The camera was thus regarded as the fountainhead of their success and its details were kept secret. . . . The precedent had been set by Edison who, although

he marketed over 1,000 kinetoscopes, retained the camera –
the Kinetograph – as the sole source of film production.

(Barnes, p. 19)

Barnes himself has investigated the technical details of Paul's first
camera, and many other technical details of the first couple of
years of British cinema, so there's no need to go into such details
here. What I'm most interested in are the economic implications;
and in the next chapter, the aesthetic developments that became
interlocked with the economic, as the court cases quoted by
Gaudreault indicate.

Paul had in fact already been toying with the idea of projecting
pictures when he heard of Lumière's success. An article in the
*Strand Magazine* of August 1896 reported that Paul 'made and
exhibited ... kinetoscopes ... and noticing the rush for these marvellous machines, he wondered if their fascinating pictures could
be reproduced on a screen, so that thousands might see them at
one time'. In October he was awarded a provisional patent for
an idea which, mixing practicality and fantasy, adds to the evidence that the pioneers were dreamers. Here he spoke of presenting spectators with 'scenes which are supposed to occur in the
future or past'. In fact, this was very much more than a projector
and a screen. As he explained to *The Era*, it also consisted of an
arrangement of

seats to which a slight motion could be given. He would plunge
the apartment [in which the audience was seated] into Cimmer-
ian darkness, and introduce a wailing wind. Although the audience actually moved but a few inches, the sensation would be
that of travelling through space. From time to time the journey
would be stopped, and on the stage a wondrous picture would
be revealed – the Animatographe, combined with panoramic
effects.

(Quoted in Barnes, p. 37)

Something rather like this idea, although shorn of its science
fiction aspects, appeared a few years later, under the name of
Hale's Tours. But Paul's inspiration, as he told the magazine
interviewer, came from a 'weird romance': H. G. Wells's *The
Time Machine*. In effect he simply combined this with established
show traditions. It was indeed very much a fantasy of its time,
with family relationships to Jules Verne and to films like *The Trip*

*to the Moon*, which Méliès made within a few years. Nor did this streak of Paul's disappear – he was to become for some years Britain's most productive maker of trick films.

Paul's original scheme was highly ambitious and would have taken a long time to realize, but within two months he was stimulated into activity by the news of Lumière's Paris showing of the Cinématographe. He set to work immediately, and it says a good deal about his skills as an engineer that he was able to produce a working projector within the amazingly short period of two months. (This supports Paul's claims that he and not Acres played the decisive role in the development of the camera.) The next few months, after the machine had made its public debut, were spent in working up improvements. According to Barnes:

> The verdict of contemporary opinion was that Paul's first Theatrograph did not provide the quality of projection attained by the Cinématographe-Lumière. Paul himself later admitted that the results obtained with the Lumière machine were 'superior in steadiness and clearness' to his own. But in its defence it must now be admitted that Paul's machine was much superior in principle and provided the prototype for the modern film projector.
>
> (Barnes, p. 48)

Paul's work on the projector combines with the initial care taken to guard the camera's secrets to explain the course which his film business took. Although rival models quickly began to appear, often incorporating their own idiosyncrasies to get round patents problems, Paul developed a large business in the manufacture and sale of projectors and a secondary business in the manufacture and sale of films. He started by shooting actuality; he then joined with Moul, the manager of the Alhambra Theatre, to film short scenes on the theatre's roof; finally he opened the first film studio in Britain, in North London, which gave him the scope to make trick films. The scale of Paul's success was noted by Cecil Hepworth, in the regular column he was writing for *Amateur Photographer* at the time, in the issue of 7 May 1897:

> More than once I have aired the opinion in this column that animated photography is getting played out. That I was utterly and hopelessly wrong in so soliloquising is now proved – or nearly proved. A few days ago a new company was brought

out under the title of 'Paul's Animatographe, Limited', with a capital of £60,000. The profits on the business which the company have brought over from the period from March, 1896, to the same month in the present year were £12,838 15s. 4d. and the estimated profits for a similar period in the future are £15,000 per annum! So, you see, animated photography is *not* played out by any means.

Paul's experience was hardly unique. In several countries the first important companies in the film trade made both films and equipment, but the former were originally secondary to the latter. That is to say, they did not make equipment in order to be able to sell films; they made and sold films in order to promote their primary business of making equipment. Thus it would happen that in order to gain an edge over competitors, the maker of a projector would incorporate an idiosyncratic design, for example, in the perforations, corresponding to their own camera, requiring purchasers of the projector to purchase films from the same source. The object of this strategy was not to capture the market in films, but to support the market for what we would nowadays call the 'hardware'.

In many places these companies dominated the film business right up to the First World War, including Pathé and Gaumont in France, Edison, Biograph and Vitagraph in the United States, and Messter in Germany. Their situation may be likened to leading companies in radio broadcasting in the United States in the early 1920s, before the establishment of the commercial broadcasting system. The radio stations were initially set up by equipment manufacturers for the simple reason that without the transmission of programmes, the broadcast radio enterprise was pointless. Hence, on similar grounds, the importance but also the subsidiary role played at first in businesses like Paul's by the manufacture of films themselves.

In the beginning, films were treated as straightforward commodities which were sold on the open market like pieces of cloth at a uniform price of so much per foot, and different kinds of film were all treated in the same way – no distinction was made between lengths of different quality, or between the different types of subject matter. The price of films was determined primarily by the cost of raw film stock. This condition is reflected in the fact that film production at this stage was simply called 'manufacture'; and that, not unnaturally, the price of films fell during the first couple of years as the supply of ready-coated celluloid roll film increased.

But film is not an ordinary commodity: it has a number of peculiarities which lead to its behaving in unexpected ways. Since it took a certain time for the film business to discover what these peculiarities were, the history of the early development of cinema is in large part the history of this process of discovery. And the best way to understand these peculiarities, in short to understand why film is not an ordinary commodity, is to trace this history.

As films were sold on the open market, a brisk second-hand trade developed quickly. It was initiated by enterprising showmen prepared to exchange, rent or sell their mounting stocks. In Britain the pioneers in this development seem to have been J. D. Walker and E. G. Turner, whose company was called Walturdaw. They were already exploiting the Edison kinetoscope and phonograph early in 1896, and in July bought a film projector, the first manufactured by Wrench. They toured the country under the significant name North American Entertainment Company, using first Edison films and then films by Lumière. By the end of 1897 they had three machines in operation and an accumulating stock of films. Turner himself later explained what happened then:

The price of films quickly dropped from 1s. to 8d. per foot, and then became standard at 6d. per foot; this allowed us to increase our store, but it soon became evident that to have to provide new films every time we took a repeat engagement was too expensive. So we conceived the idea, first of all, of an interchange with other exhibitors, who experienced the same difficulty in regard to new supplies. From this we eventually evolved the renting of films to other people, because we found that we had by far a larger stock than any of the other men. By buying films regularly we could use them ourselves and hire them to the other people, and so in such small beginnings was evolved the great renting system as known today.... We would buy as many as ten and twelve prints of an interesting subject, and on one occasion we actually bought eighty prints of a film, which was entitled *Landing an Old Lady from a Small Boat....* We then extended operations to the entertainment bureaus, such as Whiteley's, Keith Prowse, Harrods, Gamage, Webster and Girling, H. L. Toms, Woods of Cheap-

side, Ashton and Mitchell, Army and Navy Stores, the Church
Mission Halls, Salvation Army, the Leysian Mission, City
Road, and many more.

(Quoted in Low, vol. 1, p. 34)

What was discovered here? In the first place, that a film is a
relatively durable commodity which is not used up in a single
act of consumption but continues to be available for further
exploitation. However, since there are various types of relatively
durable commodity (from clothes to washing machines), this in
itself does not account for the peculiarity of the film. The peculiarity discovered by the likes of Walker and Turner was the consequent rentability of the product. In other words, where goods
usually pass from the producer or manufacturer to the wholesaler,
from the wholesaler to the retailer, and thence to the consumer,
the terms 'producer', 'distributor', 'exhibitor' and 'audience'
which we now apply to the film industry do not signify quite
the same set of relations; and this difference already existed
embryonically even before the rationalization of the film industry
into its subsequent structure. The film, in short, is like a performing art in some regards but not in others – a synthetic performing
art which is marketed in multiple editions. It comes to depend
mainly on narrative forms and personalities, but thanks to its
photographic qualities and its reproducibility, it extends and
intensifies the exploitation of the actor's performance beyond the
reach of the individual stage. The means by which its prices are
fixed, and the manner in which market domination is achieved,
are therefore quite different. In short, film is different from regular commodities, including other cultural commodities like the
gramophone record and the book, whose sale removes the copy
from the marketplace. Each copy of a film remains within the
market until it has deteriorated physically from so many showings
that it is no longer viewable.

The conditions which governed the development of cinema in
the first few years can thus be summarized as follows. To begin
with the manufacturers of equipment are favoured as long as
they are able to hold back from the open sale of the means of
production, that is, the camera; this enables them to achieve a
dominant position in the production of films, although production
remains a smaller proportion of their business than the manufacture of equipment, because they are using the sale of films at a

low and uniform price to promote the hardware. At the same time, the monopoly of the manufacturers of film stock is advanced by the development of standardization in the production of ready-coated and perforated film; the equipment manufacturers accede because it is no longer in their interests to resist: for a manufacturer not to accept standardization at this point would limit his access to the market. The result is that the number of film producers quickly multiplies, and dealers emerge to whom they sell their films for distribution in territories beyond their reach, including foreign territories, for the film market is from the outset international. Some of these dealers begin to realize that film as a commodity is possessed of certain peculiarities; and a film that is rented instead of sold remains within the market and is able to produce a continuing exchange value.

*

Film production in Britain started more or less as a cottage industry, or a little more precisely, as a business you could run from your detached suburban house and garden. Paul opened a studio in the outer London suburb of New Southgate in 1899, attached to his manufacturing works. Hepworth built a studio in the back garden of a house which he rented slightly further out of London, at Walton-on-Thames, in 1900. Something of the class character of these ventures can be gleaned from these locations. Both of them were well served by low-fare suburban railway lines which catered for the petit bourgeoisie of middle managers, supervisors and better-paid clerks, who were trying to escape from the older, inner areas of the city to more attractive and more sanitary areas. The population of Southgate increased by 124 per cent between 1901 and 1911 (when it reached almost 34,000). But the district included larger industrial enterprises than Paul's – for example a gas works and a glass works. Walton-on-Thames was more congenial, and new housing developments appeared there later than in Southgate. This pattern developed further with the establishment of other studios in other outer London districts, such as Croydon, Ealing, Shepperton and Elstree.

Hepworth moved to Walton-on-Thames after leaving the Warwick Trading Company, which was run by Charles Urban. Urban was an American who first came to Britain to manage the London office of Maguire and Baucus – the original importers of Edison's kinetoscope. (He had a counterpart in the figure of Fred Gaisberg, who arrived in London a couple of years later to run the London office of Berliner's Gramophone Company, and who went on to become HMV's senior record producer.) According to Terry Ramsaye in *A Million and One Nights*:

> When Urban inspected conditions in London he found that competition was using anti-American propaganda against his concern. He decided to change the address and become British, for trade purposes at least. The business blossomed out anew under the very English name of the Warwick Trading Company, in Warwick Court, High Holborn. The Warwick concern prospered. In time Urban acquired the business and developed a large import and export trade.
>
> (Ramsaye, p. 363)

This is not quite accurate, however. In fact Urban quit Warwick to form his own Urban Trading Company, taking with him a number of patents and contracts he had signed personally with Lumière, Méliès, and the two Brighton pioneers, Williamson and Smith. He thus became a major figure in his own right, the very prototype of the producer-distributor of early cinema; I shall pick this up again later.

Before working for Urban, Hepworth had run a small shop (according to his own account unsuccessfully), selling cameras and dry-plates for still photography; but he had already begun to tinker with film. After his arc lamp, originally designed for magic lantern projection, which brought him into contact with Paul, he bought a film projector which he proceeded to modify. While working for Urban, Hepworth made his own first film, but he says that Urban employed him basically to process and print the films which the company handled: Hepworth had invented a semi-mechanical process in which the film was cranked through the developing baths in the same way as it was cranked through the camera and the projector. In fact, his first machine used parts taken from a projector. Without such a device, the strips of film had to be handled individually – one of the reasons why films were so short. According to Hepworth, Urban agreed to pay him a royalty of a farthing per foot for all films processed on the new machine, but evidently he soon found this an uneconomic proposition and he sacked Hepworth. Hepworth thereupon took his machine away with him and set up on his own, in the house at Walton-on-Thames. But he found there was not enough work to be had processing other people's films to sustain a business, so he decided he'd better make his own. That was when he built the stage in the back garden.

On the other hand, in 1900 Urban signed a two-year contract with G. A. Smith whereby Smith would print some fifty films per day for the Warwick Trading Company. Smith too had mechanized the printing process. A 1900 article in *Chambers's Journal*, 'The Humours of "Living Picture" Making', describes Smith's 'developing factory' at St Ann's Well and Wild Gardens in Brighton as having 'a number of great wooden wheels, not unlike mill wheels, standing higher than a tall man ... driven by an electric motor' with 'arrangements for supplying heat' to dry the film after it had passed through the developing bath.

Hepworth followed general practice and filmed a variety of public events, such as Edward VII's coronation. This was where his printing and developing machine paid off most handsomely (even if it wasn't as sophisticated as Smith's). Hepworth tells us that he and his staff spent a week solid, non-stop, trying to satisfy the demand for prints of the coronation film (one of the younger members of the staff actually fell asleep at the machine). This advantage in the manufacture of copies gave Hepworth a leading position in production, a lead he managed to maintain right through to the early 1920s. He was one of the few producers who managed to stay in business in Britain during the First World War, though he finally went bankrupt when he tried to float a public company in the middle of a highly apathetic money market, with the result that it was seriously undersubscribed. In the early 1900s, however, he was able to expand simply by building a large glass-covered studio, and seems to have been one of the first British producers to open his own distribution office in New York.

Exhibition was largely at first the business of itinerant showmen because, as Peter Bachlin comments in his pioneering economic study of cinema, that was effectively the only way it could be. 'The exhibitors were able, thanks to their continual change of location, to present their programmes until the films were totally used up, and in this way to amortise the cost price through numerous showings' (Bachlin, pp. 14–15). These itinerant shows were often, as Bachlin observes, family businesses. One of the outstanding examples in Britain was William Haggar, who ran an itinerant theatre troupe to which he added film exhibition as a sideline and then turned to making films himself, thus embodying the link between early film and the popular itinerant theatre.

Haggar, the illegitimate child of a maid who worked in a comfortable home in Essex, left home at the age of twelve with three friends – members of the local Salvation Army band – to seek a living as a travelling brass quartet, and in 1870 married the daughter of the owner of a travelling theatre company which he later inherited. Neither he nor his wife had much formal education, but his descendants claimed that he knew his Shakespeare intimately by the age of nineteen. The company produced a different play each day of the week and moved location every Sunday. Like other such companies they avoided the big towns. Their touring ground was South Wales, with venues in towns like Merthyr, Nantylgo, Blaenafon, Aberfan and Blaina. The repertory included Shakespeare, but otherwise mostly somewhat lewd melodramas with titles like *A Mother's Revenge*; *Llewelyn, The Last Prince of Wales*; *The Miser of Newport*; *The Druid's Curse and the Rocking Stone of Pontypridd* and *The Maid of Cefn Ydfa*, which he filmed. Such films were highly condensed versions of the principal scenes and actions of the play, differing very little from the stage versions and thus consisting simply of a series of tableaux; they consitute another of the distinctive genres of early cinema.

Haggar was drawn into film in the summer of 1897. He was playing a highly successful season in Aberafon to the hundreds of workers who formed the migrant labour force building the new docks at Margam. He bought a projector with some of the profits, having already been running a photographic business as a side-show. The following summer he handed the theatre over to his son and went on tour with the new projector. He opened on 5 April 1898 at the Aberafon fair, and collected £15 in two pences and threepences. The following week at Pontypridd he took nothing at all, owing to a combination of rain and a strike. Such were the tribulations of the itinerant film shows.

Competition, however, was considerable. Haggar decided to start making his own films when faced with a competitor, a firm called Wadbrooks, which scored a huge success in 1901 with their actuality of a Wales–England football international at Cardiff. One of his first films, *The Maid of Cefn Ydfa*, made in 1902, proved a great success. He took £40 at the ticket office on the first showing alone.

Naturally, travelling showmen like Haggar could shoot their own films, but they had no facilities for developing and printing them. Haggar made an agreement with the Gaumont company in London, who bore the costs of developing and printing the film in return for countrywide rights except for the area which Haggar himself covered. Bromhead, who ran the Gaumont London business, later thought he remembered also supplying Haggar with negative stock, but even then the deal was very much in Gaumont's favour. Some 480 prints were struck of Haggar's *The Poachers*, for example, of which well over 100 were exported to Europe.

Bromhead himself, who later became one of the leading figures in the British film industry, began as an urban showman, in partnership with T. A. Welsh. But like other early showmen he quickly developed interests in film dealing. He and Welsh were astonished, he recorded later, when A. D. Thomas bought 100 copies of a film made by Gaumont in Paris showing the Seaforth Highlanders marching through Cairo *en route* to the Battle of Omdurman in 1898 (again, an index of the internationalism of the early film trade). He then discovered that Thomas had bought them for the film dealers McGuire and Baucas, which at that time was still being run by Urban before he set up his own Warwick Trading Company. This discovery made Bromhead realize, he said, what business potential there was in importing films. He therefore simply went ahead and obtained British sales rights on films he and Welsh found out about from the catalogue of Gaumont in Paris, which listed films for sale made by people who had bought cameras from them. This was how Bromhead's association with Gaumont began. Some film histories record that Gaumont opened a London office in 1898. In effect it was Bromhead and Welsh who set themselves up in an office in Cecil Court as agents for Gaumont films. Within a short time, Cecil Court became the site of the first concentration of film businesses in one location, and came to be known as 'Flicker Alley'.

Bromhead also operated as an agency for film producers in Britain such as Haggar. He was also Hepworth's agent, for instance, until Hepworth opened his own office. Between 1902 and 1904, he began to expand into both production and exhibition, opening a studio in 1902 at Loughborough Junction for which he obtained Gaumont's backing, and then in 1904 what was probably the first permanent cinema in the country, the Daily Bioscope in Bishopsgate. Before this, urban showmen used to take over derelict shops or other suitable premises but only on a temporary basis, introducing films in new locales and then moving on. Again this was one of the results of the sale of films on the open market: these small-time operators could not afford to keep replenishing their stock, so they moved on to find new audiences instead. It was a satisfactory system only in the very early days while the thing was still a novelty.

The English equivalent of the American nickelodeon, Bromhead's Daily Bioscope was cousin to the local music halls known as penny gaffs, the term which in England was applied to the mushrooming high street picture houses. But Bromhead's operation contained the seeds of something else. The opposite to the line of development pursued by Walker and Turner, exhibitors who became dealers, this was the dealer turning exhibitor.

Over the next few years, Bromhead's most significant interventions lay in the organization of distribution. It was he, at any rate in Britain, who seems to have initiated the system of exclusive booking contracts whereby the highest bidder in each locality secured the sole rights for a particular film – a development which could only take place when fixed cinemas began to dominate the market. According to Bromhead's own account, he took this step in order to try and insert some order into the somewhat chaotic conditions which prevailed at the time. He was concerned not only that the same films came to be available on both open sale and rental simultaneously, but also with the sharp practices of certain exhibitors, who would take copies of films on approval and show them to audiences regardless, then return them without booking them. To rectify this common malpractice, Bromhead introduced the institution of the preview. We should not regard these malpractices as incidental traits of the primitive economy of early cinema. The history of the film industry is so riddled with them that they can only be understood as the inherent result of the peculiarity of film as a commodity, and the contradictions which this produces in the capitalist mode of production.

Peter Bachlin explained the broad rationale behind the appearance of rental in the first place, like this:

The distributor took the risk of purchasing films on his own account, while the exhibitor did no more than rent them; and the distributor's intervention improved economic conditions for the exhibitor by allowing more frequent programme changes. This created a growth in the market for the producer: films could reach the consumer in greater numbers and more rapidly; moreover the new system constituted a kind of sales guarantee for their films. In general, the distributor bought copies of one or several films from one or several producers and rented them to many exhibitors; by doing this it was possible to obtain for them a greater sum than their cost price. The old system of selling the individual copy, which meant ceding a piece of property, was replaced by the temporary concession of the right to exhibit.

It is undeniable that the birth of the branch of distribution accelerated the development of the film industry: the reduction in the price of films, their diffusion and more rapid distribution led to an increase in the number of cinemas.

(Bachlin, p. 21)

It may be that when Bromhead opened the Daily Bioscope he was simply taking advantage of his position as a dealer with a large and constantly changing stock of films. But as a result he made a vital discovery, of the same kind as that made by Walker and Turner, namely, that rental favoured the establishment of fixed cinemas because every fixed exhibitor would quickly see the advantages. Who wants to be lumbered with their own copies of films which they could only repeat a limited number of times? Initially, however, the introduction of rental had a chaotic effect because of the way it intensified competition. Exhibitors of the 'town hall' variety, for instance, who moved from one fixed location to another, were forced to purchase a greater number of new films for fear that someone else would already have shown them in the locality where they were about to play; this upset their habit of calculating their costs on the basis of a fixed pro-portion between money paid out for films and the rental paid for the location. Meanwhile fairground showmen spent more on doll-ing up their trailers and tents. Many of the developments in this period can hardly be thought of as anything but fads: for example, the famous Hale's Tours which opened up in Oxford Street, London, in 1906, in which (as Rachael Low puts it) 'for 6d. a time the would-be traveller could sit in a jolting railway carriage and watch the illusion of passing scenery' (Low, vol. 2, p. 13). Hale's Tours lasted for six years and gave rise to rival versions, but it was hardly a lasting proposition (though similar fads, like 3-D films and Cinerama, have appeared at intervals throughout the history of cinema).

Other fads of the period included 'efforts to link tea with living pictures', an idea which according to Rachael Low came from France and spread through London to the provinces. Bioscope Teas were particularly popular at the New Egyptian Hall in Piccadilly, 'where in 1908 the lady from the suburbs could pause in her afternoon's shopping, and for a shilling enjoy a "dainty cup of tea and an animated display" ' (ibid.). Of these developments, the one which had the most lasting importance was the competition to improve the attraction of cinema through the use of music – which is discussed from the point of view of aesthetics in the next chapter. As for the economics of music in the cinema, this belongs as much, if not more so, to the history of music in the age of mechanical reproduction as to cinema itself (see, for example, Ehrlich, 1985).

*

The crucial difficulty created by the introduction of film rental was the producers' loss of control over their product. The key to this problem takes us back to the peculiarities of film as a commodity and their effects – in a word, the new form of reproducibility and durability of the film, which means it can be seen simultaneously and successively by many audiences, and is not removed from the market by the process of consumption but remains in circulation until the copies have deteriorated physically.

Open sale encouraged the manufacture of large numbers of copies of successful films (in spite of the physical difficulty which this entailed, since the manufacture of copies was not yet automated). Fifty copies in a few weeks was not uncommon, while the biggest sellers, such as Hepworth's *Rescued by Rover* and Haggar's *The Poachers*, reached over 400 copies each and remained in circulation for four or five years. (Undoubtedly Hepworth was favoured in this by his own semi-mechanical printing process.) The result of this system was that as production increased, people began to fear a glut on the market which would drag the price of films downwards. A cry went up of

'Overproduction!' But the trouble was not overproduction in any ordinary sense. The trouble was largely that old films stayed on the market circulating second-hand while new films were only rented.

The situation around the end of the first decade of the cinema's existence was (to follow Peter Bachlin's analysis) as follows. As long as exhibition places remained small and films short, the possibilities of profit resided mainly in a correspondingly large number of daily showings. Frequent programme changes were therefore necessary, and this resulted in a large growth in demand for films and production was stimulated. Film 'factories', as studios were first called, only managed to satisfy this demand with difficulty. In every country the problem of the expansion of the market was necessarily solved by international trade. The number of cinemas began to mushroom, all the more because they were not yet very large. In Britain, venues in the first ten or twelve years were rarely bigger than 200–300 seats, with the exception of the biggest fairground tents, which were sometimes more than twice that size. Films in this period had an average length of 400–800 feet (5–10 minutes, the maximum length of what became the standard 35mm reel) and were still made crudely and in the shortest possible time. The first generation of purpose-built picture houses would be larger still, and in this setting films would grow longer – the standard length of the acted film in the middle of the second decade of cinema was two reels or around twenty minutes. The true picture palace and the introduction of long films of more than an hour lay in the post-war future.

The conditions of free competition, the absence of a commercial tradition or of any trade bodies to regulate it, necessarily contributed to chaos. Competition intensified on every level. The exhibitors, who paid a rental which was calculated according to a certain percentage of the purchase price of the copy in relation to the age of the film, were being forced to go for the newest films. The dealers, since they had to maintain relationships with several producers, and exclusive agreements did not yet exist, also had to purchase the newest films as soon as they became available, for immediate rental to the exhibitors. It may seem that this would have ranged the producers and the dealers equally against each other, but the production companies were increasingly obliged to go through the renters in order to sell their goods, because they were progressively less able to sell them directly to the growing number of exhibitors. The dealers who went over to rental and entered the import–export business built up an increasingly strong position: they had better control over the conditions of supply and demand than either producers or exhibitors. Although they were also liable to bear the brunt of the risks involved. But they were the ones best placed to determine prices.

As these contradictions gathered momentum, the industry was plunged into a variety of price wars and trade combinations characteristic of capitalist competition in a pre-monopoly stage. To begin with, the growing power of the dealers and renters made the manufacturers who didn't distribute their own films feel increasingly insecure. One result of this was the formation of the first producers' trade organization, the Kinematograph Manufacturers' Association (KMA), in the summer of 1906 – a few months before the formation of the industry's first trade union, the National Association of Cinematograph Operators (NACO).

The international conditions of the film trade meant the competition of foreign producers. Chief among these in Britain was the French firm of Pathé, who were then supplying 20 per cent of the films on the British market. In 1906 Pathé deemed that the time was ripe to embark on a major offensive, and they slashed the price of film by a third, from sixpence per foot to fourpence. As Rachael Low comments, the bogey of overproduction called forth its twin, undercharging; and since majestic wrath was useless against such a powerful competitor, within a month or two every British firm had perforce followed Pathé's example, although skirmishing continued for some time.

The conflict between the manufacturers and the dealers came to a head with the European Convention of Film Makers and Publishers held in Paris early in 1909, which resulted in an agreement to which the chief British firms were all signatories (Urban, Hepworth, Gaumont, Cricks and Martin, Wrench, Warwick, Clarendon, Williamson, Walturdaw and Paul). With this agreement, the manufacturers tried to impose conditions on the distributors which limited the life of individual films, set a minimum price, and obliged them not to obtain films from manufacturers who were not signatories to the convention. The agreement emerged from an attempt by a group of leading European film producers to combat the threat from America, where industry leaders had ganged together under the leadership of Edison and with the backing of Eastman, in the episode known as the Motion Picture Patents War. The European riposte was ineffective. In the first place, there was too much disagreement and jostling for places amongst the European companies concerned. In the second place, the conditions of the agreement were unacceptable ideologically. They flew in the face of the philosophy of laissez-faire to which the industry as a whole was firmly attached; especially in Britain, where the Tories had lost the election of 1906 partly on the issue of Tariff Reform. Indeed, in Britain the European Convention was accused of attempting to impose a monopoly and distributors went so far as to propose a boycott, which in the event proved unsuccessful. Its legacy was the formation of the Cinematograph Trade Protection Society, which posed as a grouping of exhibitors but crucially included a small number of renters, among them a few large companies, like Jury, which were both. This body did not, however, survive for long – the industry was still in too much of a state of flux – but it was the ancestor of the Cinematograph Exhibitors' Association, which still exists.

Although the resistance of the renters to the Convention was fierce, it was not the major reason for its failure. More important was the absence of Pathé, the largest single European producer of both film stock and films. Along with Méliès, Pathé had joined the Motion Picture Patents Company, Edison's North American Trust, whose formation heralded the explosive development of the North American film industry, which within a few years undermined the position of all European producers, large and small. Behind the growing power of the North American film industry were the facts of political geography. The rapid accumulation of capital in the early US film business followed from the very large size of the North American market. These circumstances encouraged the early entry of Wall Street, which had frequently backed Edison before, and finance capital brought the introduction of appropriate methods of production, which could yield proper accounting.

Edison's strategy was based on his patents. He was well experienced in this field – or rather the lawyers and financiers who presided over the affairs of his companies were. In October 1892, for example, the Edison camp had finally won a resounding victory concerning the validity of the basic electric lamp patent on which the General Electric Company was based – a case which had been initiated in 1885, four years before General Electric was formed. Nor by far was this the only suit for infringement. Edison companies already owned 345 lighting patents as early as 1887. The cost of defending these and further related patents in the courts between 1885 and 1901 was around $2 million, and the opponents in these cases must have spent nearly as much. Obviously this kind of money could only be forthcoming from big banking interests, which in Edison's case meant J. Pierpont Morgan. But the costs of this kind of legal action were often too great for the smaller companies to bear and, win or lose, led to liquidation or forced sale. In other words, bankers promoting trustification provided huge sums not because they believed in the legal validity of the patents they supported, but because, willy-nilly, it was a way of driving smaller competitors to the wall.

Edison's attempt to gain control of the new film industry has been compared to John D. Rockefeller's predominance over the oil industry, who promoted Standard Oil to monopoly power by leaving the task of discovering new oil wells to small independent companies while establishing control over refineries (Sadoul, vol. 2, ch. 1). Gilmore, who ran the Edison film interests, hoped to achieve something similar, Sadoul says, through control of film processing. The comparison is an apt one but only very general. Rockefeller's procedure was based on conditions which did not obtain in the film industry. The level of capitalization needed to set up operations in the film industry was in no way comparable, and the same problems of scale in transport and marketing were not involved. And a small operator in the film industry, producer or exhibitor, could always do what an oil well or a refinery cannot do: get up and move away, taking his film and his camera or projector with him. And thus, to escape the clutches of the Edison trust, the film makers shifted to the West Coast and established a colony near Los Angeles in a spot called Hollywood.

It took ten years for the situation to come to a head, time for substantial new companies to emerge, and the trust to grow in aggression, applying methods used against competitors by General Electric, the manufacturing company formed on the basis of Edison's electricity patents. According to Matthew Josephson's account in *The Robber Barons*, this was to engage alternately in waging war against adversaries and then coaxing them to enter into combination. The formation of the Edison Film Patents Trust depended on just such a rapprochement between Edison and his principal opponent, Biograph, which was financed by the Empire Trust Company. When Biograph encountered difficulties and began to lose money, Empire Trust placed it under the control of Jeremiah J. Kennedy, an outsider as far as the film industry was concerned but an expert in the restructuring of deficit businesses. The rapprochement between Edison and Biograph only came about after fierce battles between the two of them, which Sadoul interprets as an episode in the much bigger battle between the Morgan banking group, linked to Edison via the Electricity Trust, and Rockefeller, which was linked to Kennedy, via his reorganization of one of the railway companies which formed part of the Gould empire which had fallen under Rockefeller's control. At first, Kennedy responded to threats from Frank Dyer, Edison's legal adviser, with the claim that Biograph was in possession of alternative patents (those of Latham and Armat). Kennedy was bluffing. He had merely acquired a $3 million option on Armat's company, aimed at keeping out other bidders. The fact was that although Biograph was in serious trouble, Kennedy wanted neither to wind up the company nor to give in to Edison's demands. Josephson explains that one of the tactics perfected by Jay Gould – who had owned the Norfolk and Western Railway where Kennedy gained his first business experience – was a deliberate policy of 'mismanagement' designed to upset the knowledge and expectations of the real state of a business in the market and among competitors. Kennedy applied the lesson and appeared to the world as an anti-Edison campaigner, thus grouping independents behind him, while actually preparing to join with Edison but only on his own terms, not merely saving Biograph but establishing with Edison joint command of the industry. When the rapprochement finally materialised, and the Motion Picture Patents Company were formed as a result, representing something like 95 per cent of North American production, Eastman, the principal manufacturer of film stock, signed an agreement with them according to which he would only sell his film to producers agreed by the Edison Trust.

Not only Pathé but Gaumont too had been invited to join the Patents Company, but as Bromhead later recalled, 'Gaumont didn't sign. We had an agency agreement with a member, Klein, on the one hand, to protect us, and on the other, would not accept the implications with regard to patents. Rightly as time proved, considering that their strength lay less in their patents than in the arrangement with Mr Eastman.' The Paris Convention, says Bromhead, was actually called by Eastman; Sadoul says only that the Congress was seen as 'a way out of the crisis with Eastman's aid', and it was hoped that Eastman would grant to a European Trust the same kind of exclusive treatment as he had granted to the Edison Trust (see Sadoul, vol. 2, ch. 30). He also says that it was the British trade association, the KMA, that originally proposed the convention because they were the first to feel the North American threat. Either way, Eastman came to Europe for the convention, which was delayed until his arrival, in the belief that the Edison Trust would collapse if it came up against a cartel of European producers. At a meeting with Pathé, who was hoping to eliminate his own European competitors, Eastman persuaded him that the best way of doing this was to join the Patents Company. Dangling in front of Pathé the carrot of access to the North American market, he was able to create a split of interests among the European companies, which effectively sabotaged the convention.

But if Eastman created the first and most enduring monopoly in the film industry, the hijack of the Paris Convention was only a preliminary skirmish. In Germany, where the chemicals industry was particularly advanced, a non-inflammable film stock was in the process of development; Eastman was much concerned. Then Pathé reneged on Eastman's overtures and began an association on Eastman's own home territory with Kodak's major competitor, the chemicals trust of Du Pont. Other competitors appeared in Italy, Belgium, and even Britain – the Austin-Edwards company; though after Eastman built their own plant at Harrow, this latter company was never a serious challenger.

The convention was due to open in Paris in November 1908, but it was postponed until December and then postponed again. Meanwhile the Motion Picture Patents Company (MPPC) was formally created, at a meeting in New York on 18 December 1908, and immediately began its battle to exclude the films of the independents from the screens of the nickelodeons. Shortly after the Paris Convention finally opened in February, a group of European companies operating in New York, which the MPPC was equally devoted to eliminating, met together to set up the International Projecting and Producing Company. The British members were Clarendon, Williamson, Wrench, Cricks and Martin, Walturdaw, Warwick, Paul, and Hepworth. A separate grouping was formed by Pathé and the four next largest European houses in New York (Gaumont, Urban's Paris studio Urban-Eclipse, Cines, and Nordisk), who opened their own negotiations with the MPPC. The two European groupings both proved ephemeral. The Patents War redefined the shape of the US film business, which was soon united in the exclusion of European films from the North American market. European films became unnecessary to it (while they poached the artistes and technicians who made them). The United States became the one country in the world able to provide enough films to satisfy its own market. But the carrot of access to the North American market, which Eastman had dangled in front of Pathé so effectively, remained a powerful dupe that has repeatedly reared its ugly head in later years – especially in Britain, where it represents the generally elusive aim of producers down the generations.

*

It was originally the dealer who was faced with the biggest risks. He was the person who had to recoup the money from the market, from exhibitors who fell behind in their payments or were forced out of business, or who moved around all the time so that it was difficult to keep track of them. In addition, to prevent competition between several copies or suppliers of the same film in the same area, it was in the dealers' interests to develop a system of rental, preferably exclusive. The benefits would also accrue to the producer. It would decrease the dealer's risk; it would reduce the number of copies that were needed; it would allow an increase in price, albeit at the discretion of the dealer. The rationalization of the business was thus placed on the agenda – the complete abolition of sale and its replacement by universal rental.

With this as its principal aim, the third major trade organization, the Incorporated Association of Film Renters, was called into being in 1910 – but in secret. Again it was given weight by the presence of such important renters as William Jury, and spent its first, secretive months aiming for an agreement with the KMA, whose purpose was also to limit the circulation of films, fix prices and thus control the market. It took a year to reach an agreement, which was implemented in December 1911. Designed to check illegal duping and sale of films before official release dates, implementation took the usual form of boycott and rapidly provoked a howl of accusations about interference and monopoly, as both exhibitors and small and second-hand renters found themselves threatened. A year later the agreement was dead. The majority of small renters decided that it was not to their advantage to work with the manufacturers, and declared that all attempts to substitute hire for sale should be resisted. For their part, the opposition of the exhibitors led to the formation of the Cinematograph Exhibitors' Association (CEA).

At this point Pathé intervened, with the declaration that the company would no longer sell its films to renters but rent directly to exhibitors itself. The industry responded in knee-jerk fashion by uniting in condemnation of the French company. But as soon as the exhibitors perceived how the renters were flung back into the arms of the manufacturers as a result, this united front was broken. The renters were induced to sign an agreement with the manufacturers and, as Rachael Low puts it, the CEA 'promptly stood on its head and saw Pathé as the Showman's Friend' (Low, vol. 2, p. 83). A fight to the death was announced, and CEA membership increased. The process was repeated. Negotiations issued in a new agreement which was unfavourable to the exhibitors and fell through almost before it was implemented. The conflict was not to be resolved by means of trade agreements. The changing character of the films themselves – their growing length and expense as a result of developments over which the exhibitors were powerless – forced them to buckle under. The consequences – a fatally weakened exhibition sector, open to domination by the distributors – would be felt in the chronic vulnerability of future British film industry to the hegemony of Hollywood.

In this first stage of the process, from the time the first fixed cinemas appeared to the moment rental finally ousted sale, not only did the renters come to the fore and transmogrify into distributors, but many of the pioneer producers lost the battle for survival. Paul himself gave up production at the end of 1909 and returned to the manufacture of precision instruments; the company was amalgamated in 1920 with Cambridge Scientific Instruments. Haggar gave up production and settled down as a cinema owner. Indeed, most of the provincial film makers stopped production. In 1909/10 British production accounted for only about 15 per cent of programmes, with 40 per cent going to the French, 30 per cent to the North Americans, and 10 per cent to the Italians. During the course of the next few years the Italian proportion rose to about 17 per cent – this was the period in which they led the world in large-scale production, precisely the kind of films which aided the renters in the transition to universal rental

But the North American share of the British market increased even more rapidly, reaching 60 per cent by 1914. In the London area it was even hitting 75 per cent, and *The Times* estimated pessimistically that British production had fallen to only 2 per cent of its own home market. This was probably an exaggeration – the figures were in any case difficult to calculate – but a highly indicative one. Take the case of James Williamson, established as a film maker in Brighton since the very first days, who announced in 1909, after the Patents Company was set up, that he was curtailing the production of dramatic and comic films in favour of educational and industrial films. Three years later the British company declared that the formation of the Edison Trust had led to the death of English production through the closure of the North American market. Williamson, like Paul, was to survive into the wartime period as a manufacturer of equipment; Walturdaw was yet another. However, it was not the closure of the US market by itself that caused the collapse, but the beginning of the American invasion of the British market which accompanied the growing power of the distributors.

Sadoul called this period in British production one of stagnation, which is broadly true. But although several British producers gave up, others rose to the challenge. Attempts were made to develop the aesthetic form of most early film genres, and experiments were undertaken in the use of sound and especially colour. Another of the Brighton pioneers, G. A. Smith, gave up making films to develop a colour process, called Kinemacolor, which he patented jointly with Urban in 1906. Urban launched the process with great panache and maintained strict controls over its use, by means of a licensing system giving exclusive rights to individual showmen in each locality. Imitations soon abounded, and an eager reception by audiences encouraged patent infringements, which involved Urban in considerable legal expenses. Friese-Greene briefly re-enters the story here. He had produced a colour process which went under the name of Biocolour, and was backed by a financier called S. F. Edge. The Urban and Friese-Greene companies were involved in a series of declarations and counter-declarations, proceedings and counter-proceedings, over alleged infringements of each other's patents. Urban managed to hold on to his monopoly for five years and probably made a great deal of money through selling it abroad, but in the end the Court of Appeal decided that the wording of the original patent was inadequate. The episode is a clear example of effects resulting from the changes in the Patents Law enacted in 1907.

More important, however, for the developing shape of the industry were the films of Will Barker, Urban's managing director until 1909 when he set up on his own. Barker established a new pattern with his first important film in 1910, a production of *Henry VIII* (curiously the same subject with which Alexander Korda was to change the pattern of British production twenty-three years later). Barker announced that this film was so expensive to produce that no single dealer or exhibitor could afford to buy it outright, and he therefore proposed to grant one distributor exclusive rights to rent, but not sell, the film, at high prices which he deliberately drove up by declaring that he would withdraw the film totally after a short period. He made much steam out of the fact that he had paid the film's leading actor, Sir Herbert Beerbohm Tree, £1,000 for five hours' work to appear in the film. No doubt this fee helped to account for the film's high cost, and no doubt it was necessary, to persuade such a distinguished actor to appear in a film at all. But the film was a successful gamble, and Barker was able to follow it up with other 'spectaculars'. With *Sixty Years a Queen* he made a profit of £35,000 – an amazing figure for the time. The same intensive exploitation of another film, *Princess Clementine*, required only twenty copies. Thus it is clear that there was reason in his madness, though he did not repeat on later films the drastic measure applied to *Henry VIII* of withdrawing the film and burning it.

Barker thus played a major role in establishing what came to be known as the 'exclusive' or 'quality' picture – the terms were interchangeable. The characteristics of the exclusive film, according to a writer in *The Bioscope* in 1913, were 'special quality of the film (plot, staging, etc.), special hiring terms for territorial areas, and special prices of rental charges'. In other words, the concept of the 'quality' film, which has held sway in one way or another ever since, is as much commercial as aesthetic. The two aspects were inseparable and the commercial film industry has always believed, with little exception, that the more money you spend on a film the better it is. While this is obviously, in aesthetic terms, untrue, nevertheless, in the early period the production of such films was a vital step in the aesthetic as well as the commercial development of cinema. It is true that even then objections were made: once again, some people were afraid that if uniform prices were not maintained the result would be overproduction and a loss of quality. Although in the long run these fears have, ironically, proved to be wholly justified, nevertheless the aesthetic development of film in the early stages depended clearly enough on the development of more sophisticated production techniques, which is just what the increased spending on production stimulated by the notion of 'quality' films guaranteed. But then it was hardly possible in the beginning to distinguish between technical and aesthetic improvements.

*

It took about ten or fifteen years for the special character of film as a commodity to emerge. This is also the time it took for film to take on the first hues of a new narrative art form. There was nothing mysterious involved in this process. What happened, to put it crudely, was that film makers began to develop greater sensitivity towards the expressive possibilities of the new medium; audiences began to demonstrate preferences; and dealers began to realize the consequences: that film was no ordinary commodity, and more effective means could be developed for its exploitation.

In taking on the hues of art, film production also began to develop the intense division of labour with which it is now associated. In the beginning, this division of labour hardly existed. Since the earliest films were scarcely more than moving photographs, short scenes ranging from public events to comic sketches, they were made with little sophistication and at ridiculously little cost – hardly more than the price of the film stock. Camera equipment and other overheads were not counted into the costs of production, and even with the first 'made-up' films some of the labour went unpaid. Someone like Haggar had no need to pay his actors when he made *The Maid of Cefn Ydfa*, since they were members of his own theatre company. By this time, Cecil Hepworth had settled at Walton-on-Thames, and was producing short films in his back garden or by the river. He says in his autobiography that the 'actors' in these films were generally members of his company, family or friends, who appeared in front of the camera. The camera was operated by someone who wasn't 'acting'. Other jobs – printing, processing and so forth – were also shared. The first time Hepworth paid actors a fee was in 1905, for *Rescued by Rover* (a film which also had its own 'director', Lewis Fitzhamon). The principals, who came down from London to augment a cast which included Hepworth, his wife, his baby and his dog, were paid half a guinea each – to include travelling expenses. Even so, the total cost of production was only £7 13s. 9d. The film ran 425 feet, about seven minutes, and prints sold for £10 12s. 6d. (6d. per foot). A total of 395 prints were sold, and this required two remakes of the film because the negative wore out in the printing. Even considering the remake costs and the cost of the raw stock for each copy, it is clear that the profits must have been proportionately enormous.

Gradually, of course, people began to show aptitudes for particular jobs. Clearly one of the first specialized jobs to emerge, as the techniques of filming developed their first elements of judgement and choice, was that of the cameraman, who also fulfilled the functions later ascribed to the director, such as deciding where to place the camera and how to divide the film up into its constituent shots. But even when the cameraman began to evolve a distinctive role, in an outfit like Hepworth's everyone still contributed to a general pool of labour. Indeed, without such an arrangement, the task of manufacturing the hundreds of copies needed of the more successful films, using the crude equipment then available, would have been too formidable, even though Hepworth himself had partly mechanized the process.

It was with films like *Rescued by Rover* that the novelty of film as a phenomenon gave way to the novelty of individual films. As the profits flowed in, production facilities were improved and budgets increased. Hepworth, for example, built a large indoor studio to avoid the vagaries of the weather, although it was glass-covered because films were still being made with natural light. But soon electric lighting was introduced (this is connected with the development of new film stocks by the film manufacturers) and thus a new grade of specialist worker moved into the studios – the electrician. As sets became more elaborate, the carpenter became another recognized special grade. Some of these workers came to film from the theatres, and brought with them their trade union cards as members of the National Association of Theatrical Employees. But if theatres had become entertainment factories, film studios were like backroom workshops, totally resistant to the importation of workers' rights, and it would take until the 1930s before trade unionism took root among film technicians (see Chanan, 1976b).

At the same time there emerged the distinctive role of the producer, who was much more than an owner-manager: he was a figure who combined entrepreneurial thinking with the showmanship of music hall and circus. It soon became apparent that this required different talents from those required in the actual shooting of the film. With the growing complexity of the operation, the role of director would take shape as the necessary complement to that of the cameraman. From this tripartite split would come an uneasy balance, which has never disappeared since, between the aesthetic insight born of technical knowledge and practice, and the 'insight' which the producer claims to derive from knowledge of the audience. The separation of the roles of producer and director began in Europe and America at about the same time, but underwent much more forceful development in the United States. Hepworth later recalled that the term 'director' was still rather new and unfamiliar in Britain in 1912, when an American friend of his advised him to concentrate on directing rather than producing.

Film production stumbled towards its formal division of labour from two directions – the same two directions which Marx identified in *Capital* as the twofold origin of manufacture. On the one hand, it evolved its own specialized jobs in the areas of its own specific technology – the camera, editing, the laboratory and, later, sound. On the other, it brought in workers from different and independent or semi-independent crafts – electricians, carpenters, scene painters, hairdressers, costumiers, etc. The hierarchy among these jobs was in part derived from the internal organization of the crew and partly the hierarchy which already existed among the different types of imported workers. The effects were felt as the job functions began to split up under pressure of the growing complexity of the production process. For example, with the separation of set-design and set-construction, the designer would acquire higher status than the carpenter. The process echoed the split between mental and manual labour which had already occurred in the theatre, but it happened in the technical jobs too. Electricians who set up the lights were subordinate to the cameraman, until the job of lighting the shot and operating the camera were divided. The latter became subordinate to the former, who would come to be known as the director of photography, with the electricians working under him. In this way the division of labour in film production came to partake in the generalized division between mental and manual labour which in precisely the same period was emerging under the guise of 'scientific management' in regular industrial production outside the film studio. Conventional wisdom, in viewing the resulting hierarchy as the natural order, overlooks the convenience of the arrangement from the point of view of capital and the disadvantage to art. The result, in the fully fledged studio system, is to place both director and producer in the position of agents of capital in the control of the labour process. Their essential function is time management. The celebration of the director as the true and original 'author' of the film thus becomes problematic. This is a question which indeed needs a much more extended analysis.

The division of labour was necessary as much for aesthetic reasons as economic ones. As the early film makers learnt the effects of moving the camera, of multiplying the number of set-ups from which scenes were shot, the effects of lighting, the advantages of retaking shots which didn't quite work the first time, and so on, so the film crew inevitably grew in size to cope, and the variety of special talents emerged. The process was a halting one. George Pearson, a schoolmaster who began in films in 1912 writing scripts for Pathé and then directing them as well, speaks in his autobiography, *Flashback*, of the conditions in the Pathé studio in London in that first year of his. His crew numbered only five: a cameraman, an electrician, a carpenter, a scene painter and a handyman. But Pathé's production methods were below scratch for the day, and they were already losing ground to other producers. Pearson soon left them, he tells us, because he found their production methods inflexible. They hadn't yet got round to using a mobile camera. Their camera was still fixed to the floor, with a chalk mark drawn in front of it to indicate the forward point which the actors were forbidden to cross, because if they did so their feet and legs would be cut off by the bottom of the frame.

If this inflexibility was one of the reasons for Pathé's decline as a production company, the example confirms the link between the commercial and the aesthetic in the early period. By this time equipment was beginning to appear which made the camera a much more versatile instrument: tripods with heads to mount the camera on which tilted and swivelled, and soon tripods with wheels on them too. Distinctions were beginning to be made between different types of cameras, according to their intended use. The original basic instrument with no frills was coming to be known as a 'topical' camera, though it was already starting to serve only for amateur and beginners' work. The addition of a few frills, such as a film footage counter, a variable shutter and a lens with adjustable focus, came to merit the term 'improved topical' camera. Before long, this was distinguished from the 'Professional' or 'Field' camera, which came to be regarded as the standard general-purpose instrument of the industry. The professional camera took longer lengths of film, 300 or 400 feet, and incorporated such further improvements as a film speed indicator, to help the operator turn the handle steadily, a single frame forward and reverse facility, and a reflex focusing attachment. (Reflex viewfinders which operated during filming had not yet been developed, however.) Finally, a 'Studio' camera was developed, whose main difference from the field camera was that it was adapted to be driven by an electric motor. In Britain, the manufacture of these more sophisticated cameras and other specialist equipment became the business of companies such as Williamson and Walturdaw, whose qualifications lay largely in their practical experience during the first few years, their trial-and-error discovery of the nature of the specialist needs of the art. There is a close relationship between the technical specifications of the standard pieces of equipment produced by these companies and the stylistics of production, but this relationship is very much two-way. The manufacturers cannot determine these standards alone. There is a continuing need for equipment makers to respond to the stylistic needs of those who use their gear, for they will otherwise go out of business.

If the relation between technology and style is a delicate and difficult one, technophobia is liable to produce explanations of stylistic development which privilege the aesthetic instead. But consider a key element in the evolution of early film style, the question of the mobility of the camera, which took several years to discover. Why not sooner, if, as everyone agrees, it is such a basic and 'natural' property of the medium? The answer is not simply the inertia of inherited modes of vision. Cinematograph cameras were originally mounted in the same way as still cameras – where locking the camera into position was a paramount consideration. It took time for various practices such as tilting and panning to become general primarily because the equipment was not, as a result, originally designed with these operations in mind. But even when they became obviously desirable, the technical solution was dependent on other design factors. Early cameras, like projectors, were hand cranked. This made for difficulties even with the simplest movements. As late as the 1917 publication *The Guide to Kinematography, For Camera Men, Operators, and all who 'want to know'*, the author advises:

> If the camera should need panoraming or tilting, the necessary motion may be imparted by turning the handle of [the] panoram or tilting head with the left hand, while keeping up a steady twice a second with the right. Making delicate contrary motions with each of the two hands at the same time is always a difficult art to accomplish. Experience alone gives proficiency. If possible, get an assistant to operate the tripod controls *under your orders* instead, and confine most of your attention to steadying and turning the camera. Tilting or panoraming done by an assistant will be more even, and the film will be steadier for your own left hand remaining upon the camera top.
>
> (Bennett, p. 4, italics added)

In other words, with a hand-cranked camera, failure to keep the operating handle turning at an even pace results in a critical unevenness both of exposure and of the passage of physical movement across the screen, which has its effect from frame to frame. The problem is not so much the imposition of some idealized notion of beauty and harmony of composition, but adequate control over technical operation. Clearly, the basics of operating technique exercised a primary constraint on the development of early film style.

\*

The enormous social impact of cinema reached the most remote corners of society long before the upper echelons knew what it was really all about. Previous new inventions, like the telephone and the phonograph, entered the market somewhere near the top and then filtered down. Film, after initial screenings for society audiences, went the other way. Thus *The Times*, after its initial report on Lumière's show in 1896, lapsed into silence on the subject for the next eight years, by which time film had spread throughout the land. The music halls, the town hall shows, the travelling shows and the penny gaffs were soon followed, however, by the more genteel bijou theatres, which drew in the more genteel classes; and in order to cater for this new element in the audience, Hepworth and others began adapting established literary classics, or contemporary plays and novels in a traditionally moulded bourgeois form. Hepworth, says Rachael Low, 'sought perfection in established usages' (Low, vol. 2, p. 107) – in contrast, she says, to W. G. Barker, who 'sought new ways of surprising people'. Both tendencies, however, were a function of the development of narrative technique, the transition from what Hepworth at first called 'made-up' films to what is properly called fiction. But the genteel classes were still clothed in the dead weight of Victorian moral armour, and they were not easily appeased. There were things which they were prepared to read about, as long as they were narrated in a suitably moral tone, and even to see illustrated if the illustration was delicate enough, but which they were unprepared to see flicker animated across a screen in darkened rooms – especially since respectability recedes in darkened rooms into the shady and sometimes unguarded behaviour of people who imagine themselves unseen, even hidden from each other's view. The following letter, which appeared in the *Kinematograph and Lantern Weekly* in 1907, expresses these sentiments to a tee:

> Sir, Where will animated photography stop? A few nights ago I was at a kinematograph entertainment when a film was shown depicting the body of a fisherman being cast up by the tide. Surely this is too revolting to be popular with the crowd, and too morbid to be termed 'entertaining'. If it served any good purpose none would object, but the tragedy of the sea is too well known to need any reminder in this way. A few months ago I saw a kinematograph picture, which, if anything, was even more morbid than the one I have just mentioned – a scene in a lunatic asylum. Yet another – that of a suicide by hanging. A considerable sensation was created a short time ago by a series on 'The Birth of Christ'. To say the least it was indelicate, and from a religious standpoint blasphemous. At the time I expected some protest, but none came. Personally

I feel there is a need for a strong expression of public opinion on the subject.

I am, etc.,

G. S. B.

As it became increasingly evident that film was no fad but was here to stay, the establishment clearly felt the need for new official attitudes, in order to bring the new medium under some form of social control, which led to a good deal more moralizing. Lower down the social scale, the agencies of the state – police, magistrates and local government – began having to deal with the disruptions which cinema caused. There was legitimate concern with safety, since film was inflammable and fires occurred. Sometimes the panic which resulted when a film burst into flames in the projector – a not infrequent happening – had disastrous results. Fire was not the only culprit. In the worst British cinema disaster of the period, which happened in Barnsley in 1908, sixteen children were crushed to death simply through a failure in crowd control. Incidents such as these led to pressures for legislation to cover safety in cinemas, and the first Cinematograph Act was passed in 1909, just as the cinema building boom got under way. This Act, ostensibly concerned with safety, allowed local authorities to attach other conditions as they saw fit. 'Nobody but a town councillor could possibly see any harm in the cinematograph', said an exasperated writer in *The Bioscope* in 1911. The trouble was that it was precisely into the hands of town councillors and Watch Committees that the 1909 Act delivered the matter, and they were supported in their prejudice by a rising tide of moral concern on the part of all the would-be town councillors in the world. As Audrey Field puts it:

> From the moral point of view, the cinema was a fascinating focus of attention. For one thing, people were enjoying themselves in a dark place, and this was very fishy: how could you love darkness rather than light unless your deeds were evil? It is easy to dismiss this as merely morbid and prurient-minded; but if we have had the experience of power cuts we realize that it makes better sense when light is hard to come by and correspondingly cherished, as it was [then].

> (Field, 1974)

For a start the moralists set about banning Sunday shows.

This action prompted the exhibitors to form the Cinematograph Defence League in 1910 (to replace the Cinematograph Trade Protection Society). All those who expressed concern at the fact that people were flocking to the cinema on Sundays and not going to church ignored the equally palpable fact that they had already stopped going to church anyway, so that the one was not a cause of the other. Nevertheless, the Christian lobby was sufficiently strong to close cinemas down on Sundays for a good number of years. A similar confusion of cause and effect, equally convenient for moralistic purposes, applied to the demoralizing influence which film was held to have, especially on children. An increasing number of boys charged with petty theft found it convenient to claim that they got the idea from the pictures. The moralists ignored prior evidence of petty crime among the working classes and found it more convenient to agree. Newspapers began to carry headlines like

the cinematograph and juvenile crime

and

cinematograph blamed for boy's downfall.

For a proper perspective on these charges, there is no better account than that of Robert Roberts in *The Classic Slum*:

Cinema in the early years of the century burst like a vision into the underman's existence and, rapidly displacing both concert and theatre, became both his chief source of enjoyment and one of the greatest factors in his cultural development. For us in the village the world suddenly expanded. Many women who had lived in a kind of purdah since marriage (few respectable wives visited public houses) were to be noted now, escorted by their husbands, en route for the 'pictures', a strange sight indeed and one that led to much comment at the shop. Street corner gossip groups for a time grew thin and publicans complained angrily that the new fad was ruining trade: men were going to the films and merely calling in at the tavern for an hour before closing time. The disloyalty of it! Children begged, laboured and even thieved for the odd copper that would give them two hours of magic, crushed on a bench before the enchanting screen.

Moralists were not long in condemning the cinema as the tap-root of every kind of delinquency. Cinema owners protested virtue: one kept an eight-foot long poster across his

box-office: 'clean and moral pictures. Prices – 2d. and 4d.'
In our district the Primitive Methodist Chapel, recently bankrupt and closed, blossomed almost overnight into the 'Kinema'.
There during the first weeks would-be patrons of its twopenny
seats literally fought each night for entrance and tales of
crushed ribs and at least two broken limbs shocked the neigh-
bourhood. In the beginning cinema managers, following the
social custom of the theatre, made the error of grading seats,
with the most expensive near the screen and the cheapest at
the back of the house. For a short time the rabble lolled in
comfort along the rear rows while their betters, paying three
times as much, suffered cricked necks and eye strain in front.
Caste and culture forbade mixing. A sudden change-over one
evening, without warning, at all the local cinemas caused much
bitterness and class recrimination. By 1913 our borough still
retained its four theatres, but already thirteen premises had
been licensed under the Cinematograph Act.

Yet silent films for all their joys presented the unlettered
with a problem unknown in theatres – the printed word. Often
in the early days of cinema, captions broke into the picture
with explanations long, sententious and stage-ridden. To bypass
this difficulty the short-sighted and illiterate would take
children along to act as readers. In this capacity I saw my own
first film. When picture gave place to print on the screen a
muddled Greek chorus of children's voices rose from the
benches, piping above the piano music. To hear them crash in
unison on a polysyllable became for literate elders an entertainment in itself. At the cinema many an ill-educated adult
received cheap and regular instruction with his pleasure, and
some eventually picked up enough to dispense with their
tutors.

Moralistic demands for censorship did not abate. This turned
out to be the one issue on which manufacturers, renters and
exhibitors proved able to unite, even if only out of desperation.
In any case, none of them was prepared to accept that town
councillors and local Watch Committees had any right to push
them around. As a result, and in response to an enquiry early in
1912 from the Home Office, the trade united to put forward plans
for self-censorship by a joint committee, which was to be called
the British Board of Film Censors; its financial independence

would be guaranteed by the payment of an examination fee by manufacturers to have their films certified. The government decided to give the scheme its support.

In so far as the British Board of Film Censors – which has retained its basic form to this day – is a classic and institutionalized example of the famous 'British genius for compromise', it reveals the ideological function of such an approach rather well. By this means, Parliament was able to avoid the necessity of intervening with legislation on such a touchy issue as freedom of speech, and was thus able to preserve its appearance as impartial defender of democratic freedoms. But at the same time the fact that existing legislation remained unaltered meant that local authorities retained such de facto power as would serve to ensure that the Board of Censors would actually behave with due 'responsibility'.

The Board began life with only two specific rules: nudity and the material figure of Christ were both forbidden. Although neither of these rules is still applied it is certain, nonetheless, that the Board has exercised a far more wide-ranging influence. In its first year of existence (1913), 7,488 films were submitted for examination, and the Board took exception to 166 of them, for a variety of reasons which included 'indelicate sexual situations' and 'scenes suggestive of immorality', 'scenes tending to disparage public characters and institutions' and 'the irreverent treatment of sacred or solemn subjects'. The Board did not at any time issue an explicit and restrictive code such as the infamous Hays code later issued in the United States. But it clearly performed its job efficiently, discouraging commercial cinema from indulging in any effective social criticism either. However, as an unofficial body it did no more than articulate the inherent conservatism of those who controlled the film industry.

\*

Music hall exerted not only aesthetic and economic influences on early cinema but also political: it was in the halls that workers in film were first properly organized into a trade union. At the end of 1906 the Variety Artistes' Federation led the great music hall strike which forced proprietors to recognize unions and accept the principles of collective bargaining. However, the settlement which followed the strike included no special provision for cinematograph operators, largely because most of the operators in the halls were electricians for whom operating was a perk, half an hour in each performance for which they might get paid an extra ten shillings a week. But a number of full-time operators decided to set up their own organization, and approached the National Association of Theatrical Employees (NATE), the union which organized backstage workers, whose history went back to 1890. As a result, the National Association of Cinematograph Operators (NACO) came into being, affiliated to the NATE. Its membership was at first very small, numbering only hundreds, and based in London. But the explosive expansion of cinema exhibition quickly produced a huge labour force. It has been estimated that between 1907 and 1913 the number of people employed rose from only a thousand or two to 120,000 – a phenomenal growth. However, it was an extremely fragmented body of workers. The vast majority of them worked in small establishments run by the men who owned them in a proprietorial manner which harks back to an earlier stage of capitalist forma-tion. The early cinema proprietors were mostly small-time petit bourgeois on a level with successful publicans and shopkeepers, and they naturally cultivated a personal relationship with their employees. Often they were not much better off than their workers. Naturally, therefore, organization was extremely difficult, both because of the isolated conditions in which most operators worked and because of the ease with which proprietors were able to employ unskilled labour. The operators regarded themselves as craftsmen, but the skills originally needed in the travelling shows, where operators were responsible for setting up the equip-ment and adapting to local conditions, lost their importance as more and more permanent installations came about. This is reflected in the conflict between the skilled operators and the others, whom they called mere 'handle-turners', which dogged the union in its early days. Operating still required skill, especially to keep the flicker of the picture to a minimum and in order to minimize the risks of fire in the handling of inflammable film stock, but most proprietors were perfectly satisfied as long as there was a picture on the screen. The public dubbed film with one of its first nicknames, 'the flicks'. For these reasons the orig-inal objectives of the NACO were not only a minimum wage but also legal registration of operators, and it saw itself more as an old-style Friendly Society than a new union. It was successful in neither of these objectives, but it soon proved to be a thorn in the proprietors' flesh nonetheless.

The NACO was founded at the very moment when film exhibition took on a new shape and began its fantastic expansion. The first custom-built cinema in Britain was erected in 1907. In 1908 there were still only three registered exhibition companies, with a total capital of £110,000. The take-off came in 1909; 103 new exhibition companies were registered that year, with a total capital of £1,341,824, and the boom gathered such speed that in 1914 there were 1,833 registered exhibition companies, with a total capital of £11,304,500. These included 109 circuits, representing between 15 and 20 per cent of the total number of cinemas, which was somewhere between 4,000 and 5,000, making Britain the second largest market for films in the world after the United States – which helps to explain why it suffered the interest of the United States film industry more than any other country at the time. The number of cinemas in each circuit ranged for the most part between five and twenty. There was only a handful of larger circuits. The penny gaffs had disappeared and the travelling showmen were squeezed out. (The few itinerants who were left enjoyed a brief respite during the First World War when cinema building was curtailed.) Cinemas began to grow more and more lavish, equipment improved, and they became more costly. At the beginning of the period it was possible to build and equip a modest cinema for little over £2,000. The cost of building a new cinema to the latest standards reached around £20,000 within a few years. The boom naturally had its side effects. In 1913, for example, there was a major and successful strike among furniture workers in factories in High Wycombe engaged in the manufacture of tip-up cinema seats.

The NACO had failed to get a provision for the legal registration of operators written into the 1909 Act, though they conducted a legitimate campaign on the issue of safety. On the problem of Sunday closing they were more successful. They were naturally in favour, not for bourgeois moral reasons, but because operators were working a seven-day week for low pay (less than the agreed minimum for theatre electricians). The exhibitors sought to counter the growing influence of the NACO by surreptitiously supporting the formation of a rival union, which argued that many proprietors were dependent on Sunday profits and therefore Sunday closing would threaten large numbers of jobs,

though they tempered the argument by conceding that proprietors should accept basic agreements for a six-day week. The
opportunistic nature of the union can be seen in its very name:
it was an attempt to take advantage of the skating-rink boom of
the period, and was called the National Association of Kinematograph and Skating Rink Employees (NAKSRE). The NACO
brought evidence before the London Trades Council, which was
dominated at the time by the left-wing Social Democratic Federation (part of the extra-parliamentary left which eventually
formed the core of the Communist Party when it was founded in
1920). The Council happily repudiated the NAKSRE. When
Sunday closing became a fact, cinemas did not collapse as a
result.

*

Despite the rapid growth of the early cinema, and the inventiveness of early British film makers, the City adopted what Sadoul
describes (using the English words) as a 'wait and see' policy
towards it, which delayed the entry of finance capital into British
film production. This policy, which exacerbated the exposure of
British cinema to North American penetration, accorded with the
strong orientation of British finance capital towards the exploitation of imperialist super-profits from abroad. On the other hand,
while the City was disinclined to invest in film production, it was
better prepared to invest in the means of consumption, which in
cinema means exhibition. The process began when the cinema
boom brought the end of the open market for the sale of film,
and the transition to universal rental was confirmed by the formation of the first cinema circuits.

The first premonitions of the capital development of exhibition
can be found in the example of Electric Theatres – almost the
only example from these years to anticipate future patterns of
development in the late 1920s. Electric Theatres was an exhibition
company formed in 1907, with a capital of £50,000. Within a year
the company owned five cinemas and was paying shareholders a
dividend of 40 per cent. The directors proposed increasing the
capital to £400,000 in order to build new theatres and to purchase
the London Cinematograph Company, a production and renting
firm, in order to secure the supply of films. Rachael Low says
that 'This interesting scheme for vertical, as well as horizontal
integration fell through because of the opposition of the alarmed

shareholders, who felt that dividends of 40 per cent were not to be lightly risked in this way.' The company managed to continue its expansion, but by 1912 dividends had fallen to 5 per cent. The problem was the basic condition of its theatres, which were already in need of modernization in order to stand any chance of competing effectively against the more grandiose buildings sprouting up every year. However, the thwarted forethought of the directors of Electric Theatres was successfully pursued by another circuit, Provincial Cinematograph Theatres, a company formed in 1909 by Ralph Jupp with backing from the financier Sir William Bass, the first British finance capitalist to show any serious interest in cinema. The firm quickly grew to be one of the largest circuits of the period. In 1913 it became the first cinema company to have its shares quoted on the Stock Exchange; at the same time it established a production subsidiary, the original London Films Company, with studios at Twickenham in the suburbs of London. Bass and Jupp were quite aware of the pressures of United States competition: they recruited directors, technicians and their star, Edna Flugrath, from across the Atlantic in an effort to ensure the commercial success of their enterprise.

The star system began in moves made in the United States by Carl Laemmle to beat the Patents Trust. Until then, performers had been anonymous, and correspondingly low-paid. Laemmle lured Florence Lawrence away from Biograph, with whom her face was identified, and gave her individual billing. The public response was delight. The stars who now emerged constituted by far the most concrete point of identification for the audience with the screen. The stardom of the screen is a new phenomenon, nothing to do with the charisma of great performing talent, but a special dimension which the screen loans to certain personae. There is a critical difference between the stage actor and the screen actor. Stage actors interpret roles, work themselves into roles, which exist independently of them. Screen roles, on the other hand, are inseparable from the actor, who becomes incarnate in their role. Their roles live and die with them, as Panofsky put it. The stage actor projects; the screen actor is projected. As Cavell (p. 28) expresses this:

> 'Bogart' means 'the figure created in a given set of films'. His presence in those films is who he is, not merely in the sense in which a photograph of an event is that event; but in the

sense that if those films did not exist, Bogart would not exist, the name 'Bogart' would not mean what it does. The figure it names is not only in our presence, we are in his, in the only sense we could ever be. That is all the 'presence' he has.

Naturally the independents who began to entice actors and actresses away from the Patents Trust (and then from each other) had to pay for it. And at the same time directors, writers and others had to evolve their roles to support the star system. The producers arbitrated the work of all putative screen authors The stars quickly came to represent their greatest labour invest-ment. They had to be well protected. Films had to be designed as their vehicle.

There were a great many parameters in this process. For one thing, the budgeting of film production eventually left the realms of rationality and sanity. The general rule, that the more the money spent on a film the better it was likely to be, ceased in time to apply. More and more capital came to be involved merely in promoting and bartering the stars. But at the same time, film was only just beginning to evolve those stable aesthetic forms which came automatically to support the star system. What American cinema discovered in the years leading up to the First World War (and continued to develop during the war while pro-duction in Europe was mostly severely curtailed) wasn't only the star system, but the aesthetics that went with it. There is no denying that the aesthetic development of North American film played an extremely large part in its commercial success. This was the moment when Hollywood was born, not just in the physical sense of the independents escaping the Patents Trust by moving to the West Coast, but conceptually, in the imagination, as the mythical home of the stars.

Confronted with these developments, British film makers tried to imitate the American example. They quickly adopted the star system, bringing over American stars as well as trying their own. But the Hollywood offensive was something the hardly capital-ized British film business was in any position to rebuff. Among the advantages which Hollywood enjoyed was the fact that their home market was roughly four times the size of the market in Britain. This made it easy for them to recover the costs of pro-duction at home, which enabled them to undercut local producers abroad – at the very moment when costs of production were being forced upwards in Britain by the attempt to compete. More-over, as Hollywood burgeoned, North American exhibitors needed foreign films less and less. And then the intervention of the First World War only increased the North Americans' advantages, because it effectively gave them economic protection. Europe's production fell drastically, but not that across the Atlan-tic. The North Americans emerged from the war not only com-paratively unscathed but in a mood of irresistible expansionism.

The effects of the populist aesthetics of North American cinema were already felt in Britain before the war. In 1914 Will Barker was involved in the following exchange during an investi-gation of cinema by a Select Committee of the London County Council:

> Mr Balfour Browne: You have taken a special interest in what I may call the natural side of cinematography?
> Mr W. G. Barker: Yes, events and Nature.
> Mr Balfour Browne: You do not go in for drama and comic things?
> Mr W. G. Barker: I am doing a little now because I find I have been forced into it, but I consider that all that is a prostitution of cinematography.

The exchange illustrates, in classic understated form, both the suspicion of the establishment towards the cinema, and the crisis of confidence into which British film makers were thrown by developments across the Atlantic whose implications were both commercial and aesthetic.

# Chapter 12

# The foundations of the film idiom

The fact that in a moving picture successive film frames are fit flush into the fixed screen frame results in a phenomenological frame that is indefinitely extendible and contractible, limited in the smallness of the object it can grasp only by the state of its technology, and in largeness only by the span of the world. Drawing the camera back, and panning it, are two ways of extending the frame; a close-up is of a part of the body, or of one object or small set of objects, supported by and reverberating the whole frame of nature. The altering frame is the image of perfect attention. Early in its history the cinema discovered the possibility of calling attention to persons and parts of persons and objects; but it is equally a possibility of the medium not to call attention to them but, rather, to let the world happen, to let its parts draw attention to themselves according to their natural weight. This possibility is less explored than its opposite. Dreyer, Flaherty, Vigo, Renoir, and Antonioni are masters of it.

Stanley Cavell

The purpose of technique is to be able to do again deliberately what you first did by accident.

Jean Renoir

The history of the early cinema first came into being as an oral history, a folklore belonging to the industry itself. This is the source of many of the stories in the books which form the first generation of accounts of cinema's history, including Frederick Talbot's *Moving Pictures, How they are Made and Worked*, which first appeared in 1912, and Terry Ramsaye's *A Million and One Nights*, an American book which first appeared in 1926 and earned its author the title of 'the first authentic film historian'. Further volumes, by British writers, which also belong to this category, although they represent the tail-end of the genre and appeared in the 1930s, include Low Warren's *The Film Game* and Leslie Wood's *The Romance of the Movies*. To these must be added, as important sources for early film history, the memoirs of pioneers and early participants, including Cecil Hepworth's *Came the Dawn* and George Pearson's *Flashback*.

Often the same stories reappear in these books in different versions, attributed here to one character and there to another. This does not necessarily mean that these writers stole them from each other, but rather that they come from the folklore; and this is also a good reason why they should be taken seriously, though treated with care, by the modern film historian. This kind of situation is perfectly familiar to the anthropologist. As Lévi-Strauss recounts:

> One ethnographer working in South America expresses surprise at the way in which the myths were conveyed to him: 'The stories are told differently by almost every teller. The amount of variation in important details is enormous.' Yet the natives do not seem to worry about this state of affairs: 'A Caraja, who travelled with me from village to village, heard all sorts of variants of this kind and accepted them all in almost equal confidence. It was not that he did not see the discrepancies, but they did not matter to him. . . .' A naive observer from some other planet might more justifiably (since he would be dealing with history, not myths) be amazed that in the mass of works devoted to the French Revolution the same incidents are not always quoted or disregarded, and that the same incidents are presented in different lights by various authors. And yet these variants refer to the same country, the same period, and the same events, the reality of which is scattered throughout the various levels of a complex structure. The criterion of validity is, therefore, not to be found among the elements of history. Each one, if separately pursued, would prove elusive. But some of them at least acquire a certain solidity through being integrated into a series, whose terms can be accorded some degrees of credibility because of their over-all coherence.
>
> (Lévi-Strauss, 1975, p. 12)

The real problem, therefore, in writing film history – like any kind of history – is the question of the criteria which are used to discover coherence and give the individual elements of the history their 'solidity'. But there is a paradox about film. On the one hand, it is a unique object of study: the only example of an art form whose birth and infancy belong to historical times – and recent historical times at that, with records that are reasonably complete. On the other, however, it is relatively easy to discover coherence in the domain of the technical and the economic when compared to the aesthetic. The foundations not of cinema as an economic form but of the film idiom, the language of cinema, as it is sometimes called, are not so easily located (whether or what kind of language this is, is yet another question). Not because many early films are lost or damaged, but rather, as we shall see, because simple chronology has little meaning here. To identify the first uses of various formal devices – close-ups, pans, tilts, tracking shots, direction matching, continuity cutting, reverse angles, and so forth – is not in itself a reliable guide to the evolution of film form, first because only sometimes is the device in question quickly taken up by others, second because even when it is, this doesn't mean it fulfils the same functions that it develops later, when it becomes part of the grammar of montage.

Nor are the first serious aesthetic speculations on cinema, which date mostly from the 1920s, of much help to us in this regard, for there is a degree of mythology here too. Georg Lukács, for example, did not merely insert cinema into a certain history, but appealed to a certain aesthetic myth when he said in the 1920s that 'In the movie, everything that Romanticism hoped in vain to accomplish in the theatre can come true' (Lukács in *New Hungarian Quarterly*). Later on, Bazin too, who remembered the popular theatre origins of cinema, but in an idealized kind of way, saw film as a means of overcoming the limitations of the theatre:

> As for Charlie Chaplin, apart from his indebtedness to the English school of mime, it is clear that his art consists in perfecting, thanks to cinema, his skill as a music hall comic. Here cinema offers more than the theatre but only by going beyond it, by relieving it of its imperfections.
>
> (Bazin, p. 79)

In terms of aesthetics this is highly debatable. As a piece of philosophical reasoning it commits a simple category mistake: it's like calling an apple an imperfect orange. The main value of these remarks is rather to remind us that the relation to theatre is one of the first problems which arises in the process of constituting the history of cinema. But you could just as well say that it was cinema, not theatre, which was more restricted in the beginning – because it was mute, and because the camera of early film was often little more than a surrogate for the spectator in the theatre. However, this is just as problematic. It would more accurately capture the sense of the time to say simply that film offered a mass of indistinct possibilities, some of which were shared with theatre, which the early film makers set about exploring with considerable energy and in many cases, great inventiveness. But there was no royal route to the discovery of what the art historian Erwin Panofsky called 'the unique and specific possibilities of the new medium', on which Stanley Cavell comments that 'it is not as if film makers saw these possibilities and then looked for something to apply them to. It is truer to say that someone with the wish to make a movie saw that certain . . . forms would give point to certain properties of film' (Cavell, p. 31). This may sound like quibbling, he adds, but what it means is that the aesthetic possibilities of the medium are not given in advance, but have to be created.

The aesthetic simplicity of the first films derives in the first instance from the technical simplicity of early film equipment, and there is a sense in which early film style was little more than a by-product of the basic technical capacities of the prototype gear. The first movie cameras, for example, were mounted like still cameras on tripods with fixed heads. No following the action with the camera was normally possible, until the benefits of doing so were sufficiently developed through trial and error to elicit tripod heads which could pan and tilt. (Later still would come extras like wheels and tracking dollies.)

Similarly, early lenses and film stocks required daylight exposure, which prevented shooting real indoor locations. Early 'studios' were simple stages erected in the open air, until lights allowed studio shooting to move indoors. Even in the case of exteriors, early narrative films seem to show no particular preference for real locations over studio sets. A rooftop chase in Walter Haggar's *Life of Charles Peace* (1905), in which a policeman crashes through a skylight, uses a stage set with the skylight made of paper; a similar chase in Mottershaw's *A Daring Daylight Robbery* (1903) uses a real location (though here no one falls through a skylight). In short, in these films the *mise-en-scène* is indifferent to the surface attractions of naturalistic representation, which it can apparently take or leave.

But the look of early narrative film not only comes from the simple and basic *mise-en-scène*, but also derives from the style of acting, a subject which is much more elusive and thus little commented upon. The standard placement of the camera in early cinema renders the scene in long shot. Accordingly the players' principal means of expression is a language of bodily gesture, since their faces remain at a distance, and subtleties of facial expression remain unseen. It is dangerous, however, to assume either that they therefore exaggerated, or that what we see is simply a rendering of the established acting styles of the day. A comparison can be made with the effects of the phonograph. Before 1877, no musician could ever have heard themselves play; conversely, our knowledge of performance styles before the invention of sound recording is only indirect, based on written description and visual iconography, and no real comparison is possible (see Chanan, 1995). Similarly, before 1894/5, no actor could ever have seen themselves act (what photographs showed were, at best, poses). Consequently no actor (or anyone else) could have known what it meant to act *for a movie camera*. What we see in early screen acting therefore has to do with a distance between the camera and the players which is not just physical but also conceptual.

If early film manifested a strong affinity with the popular stage, the reason is both a matter of commercial logic and the pull of popular acting styles, which preserved such traditions as mime. This preference was reinforced by the fact that straight actors found the transition from stage to screen more difficult, because they were too firmly locked in the literary character of their art. Robbing actors of their words, the camera rendered only the outward appearance of acting. No wonder so few theatre players took to the screen in its early years.

There was also a major difference between straight theatre and music hall in the relationship of the player to the character to be played. Straight acting called for the actor to serve the character, whereas music hall artistes depended primarily on the projection of their own personalities. Music hall artistes did not play characters: they adopted characterizations, which were born in the dialogue with the audience. If film robbed straight actors of words, more important to music hall artistes, it robbed them of the presence of the audience on which they thrived. But early film *needed* the music hall, a world peopled by characters like the toff and the henpecked husband, the gormless country lad or the country lass who is more canny than city folk suppose. These were stereotypes which translated easily on to the screen. The situations of early narrative films, comedy and melodrama, were readily built around them. (The ease with which one can generate an infinite series of situations around known characters finds its expression today in television soap operas and situation comedies.)

Music hall had evolved in part from the traditions of popular itinerant theatre, where the fluid and constant action of the itinerant stage demanded from the actors a facility for characterization and rapid character changes, and the capacity to establish instant rapport with the audience. If the travelling theatre companies thus provided a hard but vital training ground for a good many popular entertainers who subsequently entered the halls, then the comic routines which were the ancestors of early film plots go back a good way. An example is provided by a Billy Purvis sketch known as 'Stealing the bundle'. A countryman enters and carefully leaves his bundle outside the door of a public house. Enter Billy, in his clown's costume. As he begins to make off with the bundle after delivering a monologue, the countryman reappears. Billy explains himself: 'Aw thowt it wor lost, aw wis just teykin care on't, aw lives roond here.' The bundle is replaced and its owner returns indoors. With no further delay or pretence, Billy kicks the bundle round the corner, knocks on the door and warns the man that the bundle has been stolen. He sends the man off after the supposed thief, triumphantly picks up the bundle and walks off in the opposite direction.

Martha Vicinus, who quotes this example in *The Industrial Muse*, remarks that this sketch

> differed from later music hall turns because Billy did not treat the foolish countryman who leaves his bundle outside as a comic butt; he is simply the device that sets the scene for Billy. Moreover, contemporaries commented on how each performance differed, as Billy responded to different audiences. The

music hall was far more mannered, and audiences expected their heroes and heroines to repeat the same turn without variation night after night.

(Vicinus, p. 243)

The mannerisms which thus became established on the music hall stage helped the translation of the style to the screen, but here, too, film could do little more than take the outward form of the stage sketch; inevitably the translation of the material from one medium to the other meant that more changes would take place in the import and slant of the material.

Vicinus remarks how 'the comedy rested on Billy's moral duplicity but it was also an indirect attack on the moral pretentiousness of society'. By the time this type of material had moved from the itinerant stage through music hall to the screen, the element of social critique would be much less explicit. But other elements, which the film medium found it more easy to play up, were soon amplified. In a sketch like 'Stealing the bundle' transposed to early film, Billy's monologue would be dropped, and a chase would be added at the end in which Billy would of course get caught and suitable punishment ensue. There would be nothing left of the social critique of the original except the liability of the villain to cock a snook at authority.

The chase, which is found in many of these early sketches, is a key component of early film. Several writers consider it to lie at the origin of filmic narrative, because it provides a model framework for the principles of linearity and continuity of action. At first it was simply a question of exploiting movement within the fixed frame by having characters rushing around backwards and forwards across the screen as they did on stage; the characters had to be easily recognizable, otherwise audiences would be liable to confusion, hence the efficacy of the stereotypical characters of music hall. But given the standard lenses and film stocks of early cinema, there was sufficient depth of focus to allow characters to move, within the frame, from long shot to medium close-up – Lumière exploited the effect in films like the train arriving at a station – and by the turn of the century chases were being staged in depth in suitable exterior locations. To extend the action meant firstly to allow the characters to disappear off screen and then to pick them up in another more or less contiguous space. But as Burch remarks, the earliest films of the genre, like Williamson's

*Stop Thief!* of 1901, are already made up of at least three shots, because 'a series of only two shots would have given the impression of a chase stopping as soon as it had started' (Burch, 1990, p. 149).

However, movement in these films shows no consistent sense of direction; there is no direction matching at the cuts. The cuts in *Stop Thief!* function merely to join a succession of separate shots. They are perfectly intelligible within the unfolding of the action, which begins in the first (a tramp steals some meat from a butcher's boy), continues in the second (pursuit by the boy and several dogs), and concludes in the third (the tramp hides in a barrel where the dogs find him, he gets dragged out and the boy grabs the stolen meat from him). There are various entries and exits in the three successive shots, but they are not coded to maintain continuity of direction across the screen. Characters move out of one shot and into another haphazardly, from different sides of the frame. The result is a simple succession of short scenes in spatial proximity, leaving an amorphous off-screen space in the gaps, so to speak, between the scenes, which occur at the cuts.

There is also no internal sense of temporal organization. The third shot of *Stop Thief!* goes on after the end of the story, as the characters continue to rush around. In other words, there is no proper sense of narrative closure. Neither are there real actors in films like this, only players. It will take longer, however, for the screen to develop actors adequate to the camera's scrutiny than to discover the codes of movement and direction and the art of the matching cut. And when the film idiom developed its own means of punctuating the player's portrayal and articulating it according to its own devices, this would change the nature of acting. None of this was experienced at the time as any kind of lack or insufficiency, however, except by those whom social or cultural elitism rendered blind to the pleasures of the moving pictures.

\*

The dream factory of the corporate film studio produces a rationalized magic. The early film was more like a magic act in itself, presented by magicians on the stage, whose acts would also be filmed and turned into subjects on the screen. These subjects would be re-enacted using filmic tricks like interrupted action and superimposition, which also gave rise to new magical effects, including films within films – films in which inanimate objects would suddenly become animated. In one remarkable example of the genre, a British film distributed in the USA in 1904 called *An Animated Picture Studio*, the scene shows a young woman dancing for a camera and then sitting on the photographer's knee. The photograph of her dance appears within a picture frame standing on an easel in the centre of the scene, and comes alive. When the dancer protests and throws the picture on the floor, the shattered image continues to dance. (The dancer in the film is thought to be Isadora Duncan, says Ian Christie, adding that this 'makes an already intriguing little allegory even more poignant' (Christie, p. 127).) Visual metaphors for the dangerous magic of the film camera, the mastery of the trick effects on which these films depended was extensively pursued.

The first explicitly magical films are usually attributed to Méliès, theatrical illusionist and owner of the Robert Houdin Theatre in Paris. The story of how he hit upon the idea of the camera tricks which his films employed is well known: one day, according to the legend he fostered himself, he was filming in the Place de l'Opéra in Paris when the film in his camera jammed. He fiddled with the machine to get it going again and continued filming. When he projected the film he discovered that an omnibus was suddenly and magically transformed into a hearse. Thus, by accident, was born a crucial discovery – and this was clearly a discovery, not an invention – namely, that film doesn't just reproduce the profilmic scene, but can also be manipulated to present as apparently equally genuine, the unexpected, the unlikely, and the completely impossible. Substitution by stopping the camera and replacing an element in the scene in front of it is known as stop-frame technique. The visual effect is a magical transformation.

There is no reason why it could not have happened that way, and every reason to suppose that it might well have done so, not only in Méliès's case but also others, for ever since Archimedes we have known about the role of the happy accident in the process of invention and discovery. At the same time, however, such techniques were often derived from the adaptation to film of photographic practices used in magic lantern entertainments. Méliès's English counterparts were the members of the 'Brighton School', who, along with Paul, were the protagonists in the development of trick effects during the early years in Britain.

In 1897, one of them, G. A. Smith, patented a method of double exposure – though the technique was common photographic knowledge – and began to make trick films like *Photographing a Ghost*:

> Photographing a Ghost . . . causes astonishment and roars of laughter. Scene: A Photographer's Studio. Two men enter with a large box labelled 'ghost'. The photographer scarcely relishes the order, but eventually opens the box, when a striking ghost of a 'swell' steps out. The ghost is perfectly transparent so that the furniture, etc., can be seen through his 'body'. After a good deal of amusing business with the ghost, which keeps disappearing and reappearing, the photographer attacks it with a chair. The attack is amusingly fruitless, but the ghost finally collapses through the floor. A clean, sharp, and perfect film.
>
> (Smith's catalogue description)

It was not only the illusionism of magic which provided themes for trick films. So did the panoply of scientific and technological marvels of the times, from automobiles to X-rays. Smith himself made films of both. In this way film seemed to become the medium of the emerging technological age par excellence. Its images encompassed every other invention of the day, not just picturing them in action but in scenarios that on the one hand expressed wonder and fascination, and on the other, exorcised fear and suspicion.

Films about motor cars and their effects were legion. Paul made a film in 1897 entitled *On a Runaway Motor Car Through Piccadilly Circus* which showed the view from a car 'speeding' through the streets, photographed according to the catalogue description in some kind of accelerated motion (the film itself is lost). The effect was probably achieved by steady under-cranking of the camera. No great act of imagination was needed to know the impression under-cranking produces on the screen: that it speeds up the action (just as over-cranking slows it down). This would have been obvious to all operators of hand-cranked cameras.

Another example of a trick-effect motor car film is Williamson's *An Interesting Story*, made in 1905, where the multishot format of the short narrative elaborates a running gag. A man is so engrossed in the book he is reading that he has his breakfast, prepares to go out and leaves the house with his eyes continuously glued to the pages. Oblivious to the world, he gets run over by a motor vehicle, and is flattened to the thinness of a sheet. Two passing cyclists stop and pump him up again with their bicycle pumps. The whole thing is done by stop-frame technique, just like Méliès's magic transformation. The resulting 'jump cuts' can be easily discerned – today.

No such 'rescue' was available to the victim of Hepworth's earlier two-shot *How It Feels to be Run Over*, a film of 1900 which combines a joke on the motor car with another self-conscious play on the illusionism of film. The film shows a car approaching the camera, and apparently running it over. According to the catalogue description:

> The eccentric artist Wiertz has powerfully depicted the supposed feelings of a decapitated head, but it has remained for the cinematographer to show large audiences what it feels like to be run over. In this very sensational picture a pretty country road is seen, and in the distance a dog-cart travelling at a fair speed. The road is narrow, but the cart successfully passes, and as the dust which is raised clears away, a motor car is seen approaching very rapidly indeed. Perhaps it is the dust of the previous vehicle, or perhaps sheer carelessness on the part of the driver, but he does not see the obstruction in the road until it is too late to steer past it. The car comes forward at tremendous speed, and the occupants, realizing the danger, get wildly excited in their efforts to clear the obstruction. The steersman makes one or two frantic swerves, and is seen to apply the brake with all his might, but to no purpose, the car dashes full into the spectator, who sees 'stars' as the picture comes to an end.

These 'stars' comprise the second shot of the film, which does not, however, take the appearance of a cut. What we see as the vehicle supposedly runs us over is the screen going dark and a rapid succession of drawings in white-on-black of stars and exclamation marks, ending with the words 'Oh Mother will be pleased.' The effect is a displacement of identity between camera and viewer. The camera is acknowledged by the characters within the film, and the viewer is thereby inserted into ('inscribed in') the camera's position, becoming part of the scene – and suffering the consequences.

This process is the reverse of the early 'voyeur' films, ranging from Smith's *As Seen Through a Telescope*, in which a young woman is spied through a telescope by a middle-aged man, to 'erotic' views of female nudity, where film makers quickly learnt to present the scene with someone in it watching. The viewer is thereby able to displace the role of voyeur on to a delegate within the picture   while the woman who is the object of the voyeuristic gaze refrains from acknowledging the camera and thereby embarrassing the spectator in the cinema. It is no accident that these films are usually cast in the form of comic sketches, which make much out of catching the voyeur in the act and meting out immediate punishment, which further assists in assuaging the potential shame of the spectator.

Now clearly the condition of voyeur is an inescapable facet of the medium of film, and it is not surprising that, in an age governed by patriarchal values, the male gaze should have been taken as the norm and the female figure viewed in this way. At the same time, in terms of emergent filmographic values, the voyeuristic gaze plays a special function, which is complementary to the self-conscious displacement of identity from viewer to camera in the trick film by Hepworth. These two kinds of displacement are opposite sides of the same coin. Taken together they hint at a double process, which is central to the discovery of 'the unique and specific possibilities of the new medium': the viewer learns to assimilate the point of view of the camera, which at the same time becomes invisible to the characters within the profilmic scene. Becoming invisible, the camera will be able to learn a new type of narration, in which the scene is split up into different views, and these views alternate. The result, when the synthesis of these partial views is first achieved at the end of the early period, is a highly plastic virtual space where there is no threat of disasters like being run over, or if they do occur, the spectator is able to experience the event vicariously without becoming disoriented; and at the same time, moral judgement is strangely suspended.

Smith's telescope film is one of a pair. In *Granma's Reading Glass*, Granma's little grandson looks through the reading glass and the screen shows us what he sees: within a circular mask representing the field of vision of the glass, we see a series of images of the interior of a watch, a canary, Granma's eye. While these are not true close-ups – the modern close-up lenses we are now used to give a far more magnified image – they clearly function as point-of-view shots, in which again the film viewer identifies the picture on the screen with the view of a character within the film. Celebrated by many film historians as the first examples of their kind, Smith told Sadoul in 1946 that the idea was completely instinctive, and derived from magic lantern practice (Sadoul, 1948). And indeed Smith was soon using similar inserts, but without explicit pretext, in films like *The Little Doctors* of 1902 – again doubtless without realizing their significance.

The principal difference between *Granma's Reading Glass* and *The Little Doctors* is that in the former the insert is framed by a circular black mask representing the field of vision of the reading glass; in the latter, this frame-within-the-frame is dropped. Reissued in a shortened form as *The Sick Kitten* (1903), this later film contains a straight edit, of the type which would later be called a 'matching cut', from a general view of two children administering a spoon of medicine to a kitten, to a medium shot of the kitten licking the spoon. A 'matching' or 'continuity' cut is one in which the action across the cut appears uninterrupted. It is one of the most basic syntactical devices of classic narrative cinema, where it is accomplished so deftly that the cut itself recedes from conscious attention and remains unobserved. In this case, as in numerous other examples for several years to come, the match is not very precise, though it can be assimilated easily enough. But if Smith took the device from magic lantern practice, he may not have been aware of the notion of continuity – indeed, it seems unlikely. He would only have been thinking in terms of succession. To think in terms of continuity involves a conceptual jump which is still some years away.

The difference is significant. *The Little Doctors* is a precocious film which anticipates the arrival of the conditions for making the conceptual jump to continuity thinking. It should not surprise us that the technique was not developed without some delay, for the other elements with which it comes to be articulated, like direction matching, are in a similar embryonic state. It recurs only sparingly over the next five or six years, and its use during this period is often imperfect. Why it represents such an innovation is that it plays a key role in establishing the camera not just as a recording device, whether magical or scientific, but also or rather as a narrator, which does not merely display a scene but directs the viewer's attention within it. In the process, when the frame-within-a-frame is eliminated, two theoretically distinct levels of classification of the image are collapsed into one. The level which signifies 'This is what the camera sees' and the next level, 'This is what is seen by someone within this film', are elided. Two things happen: the spectator displaces the identification of the view from camera to character, and the camera enters the scene. But it does so surreptitiously, like the voyeur film and in contrast to examples like *How It Feels to be Run Over*, becoming invisible in the process. The result is that the eye inscribed in the camera position also becomes disembodied.

Paul returned to the motor car as a subject in a film listed in his 1905 catalogue, strangely entitled *The ? Motorist* – a true silent film title, designed to be read and not spoken – and a satire on reckless motoring. This multishot fantasy is obviously made in the same spirit as Méliès's 'magic' films, and in particular the fairy story ones, which eschew attempts to depict naturalistic settings and instead continue the use of painted stage scenery combined with special effects.

A motor-car is seen at the gateway of a villa, with [the] motorist carefully handing his lady into the car, and they drive off and soon set up a good speed. A careful policeman thinks they are exceeding the limit, and waves to them to pull up, but they decline, and he stands right in the way of the car, being caught up by the front gear, and carried away for some yards, until he is eventually dropped off, and one of the car wheels goes over him. The policeman collects the pieces of himself, and resumes his attempt to uphold the law. The motor-car then goes on, until a public house is seen to entirely stop the way, and the policeman thinks he has now caught his prey. The car, however, does not stop, but continues its journey right up the front of the house, to the dismay of the fast assembling crowd. The car goes motoring right across the clouds, makes a friendly call on the sun, calmly circling round its circumference, then resumes its cloudy journey, and reaches the planet Saturn. The motorist continues his wild career round the highway of Saturn's rings, but eventually rides off the unusual track into space, and the car is seen falling gracefully through the clouds to earth, until it drops through the roof of a building which turns out to be a Court of Justice. Great confusion is naturally caused, though the car continues its journey unhindered out of the Court, followed by a policeman, magistrate, and other officials, but to their astonishment, while they yet look at the car, and endeavour to arrest the delinquents, a countryman's cart in place of a motor, and a smock-frocked man and his wife appear, and start moving off, until they get out of the reach of justice, when the countryman's cart suddenly again becomes a motor, which now succeeds in making good its escape.

(Catalogue description)

A reference to this film turns up in an essay by the Russian Symbolist Andrei Bely dating from 1907 (which confirms the wide international distribution of early films), who draws from this fantasy of automobile omnipotence the moral that 'walls and peaceful domesticity cannot protect us from the arrival of the unknown' (Christie, p. 22).

Hepworth too made another motor car film, one of the most gruesome of the genre. *Explosion of a Motor Car* is not yet a sustained narrative, and it still uses nothing more sophisticated technically than stop-frame technique, but manifests a peculiarly nightmarish feel. A car is driving along. An almighty explosion takes place and by means of stop-frame an imitation motor car is substituted. As the explosion clears, debris falls from the sky, including clearly discernible dismembered limbs. A policeman passes by and examines the wreckage; he picks up the limbs one by one and tries to assemble them into people.

The film illustrates another motif in early cinema, that of a kind of infantile aggression, which Burch likens to an acting out of the effect of the 'dissecting eye' of the camera on the fragmentation of the body, which some early viewers found shocking. The optical and mechanical trickery, says Burch, which the cinema discovered almost from its inception 'gave this theme an extraordinary, a delirious impetus during those first ten years' (Burch, 1979). Doubtless derived in part from the circus and the popular stage, where women were gleefully sawn in half by conjurors and the villains of Grand Guignol, it also invokes a comparison between the infancy of cinema and infantile aggression fantasies of the kind studied by the psychoanalyst Melanie Klein. According to Klein, the newborn infant relates to its mother only as bits of body such as the breast, or what she calls part-objects; this is what she calls the 'paranoid-schizoid position'. Only when the infant moves into the 'depressive position', which begins around the age of four months, is it able to see the mother as a whole person. The infant's successful passage through these positions produces the integration of human personality, but the process, according to Klein, is forever repeated in fantasy (which is why she calls them positions and not just stages or phases of development) as the individual is constantly required to negotiate the tensions and conflicts of existence. The suggestion, then, is that of a homology between human infancy and the infancy of film, as if film must enact the process by which the human infant learns to integrate its perception and its personality in the process of growing up. In that case, perhaps, the development of the cinematic codes begins with the appearance of the positions of fantasy life in a childish aesthetic form, which film must learn to sublimate in order to constitute itself as a narrative art *sui generis*. When this sublimation is achieved, the problematic identification of the spectator with the camera is transformed. The camera enters profilmic space where it loses physical extension and becomes ubiquitous, constantly displacing its position between the various points of view of the characters in the scene and none of them, while the spectator, submitting to the camera's eye, becomes invisible and bodiless.

\*

If dramatic realism counted at first for little, the power of the camera to present a naturalistic spectacle was another matter altogether. 'Nature on the stage!' was the motto Charles Urban used to advertise the films he presented at the Alhambra Theatre in 1903; or a little later, 'We put the world before you.' The genres to which these mottos referred were actualities, travel and 'scientific' films, whose origins were not music hall but the magic lantern lecture. This tradition produced a strong strain of simple direct observation, which Kracauer described as 'the seizure of physical reality' and identified with the documentary instinct: the act of recording events in the 'real world' 'almost without creative aspirations' (Kracauer, ch. 2). The trend was encouraged by dealers and exhibitors who, eager to establish the respectability of their business, emphasized the moral and educational values of the new medium, thus lending to the process of empirical observation a certain ideological slant.

Actuality is not a precisely defined genre but a range of genres, from the 'typical scene' to events like horseraces and boxing matches. The form of exhibition allowed these films to grow in length by a simple process of accretion. Several typical scenes of a foreign country strung together became a travelogue (a term coined by an itinerant American exhibitor called E. Burton Holmes in 1904; in France the genre was called the *documentaire*). Topicals included state occasions and royal processions, which could be filmed by several cameras along the route. Another variant is well represented in a thirty-minute film made by Cricks and Sharp in 1906, *A Visit to Peak Frean and Co.'s Biscuit Works*. One of the first instances of company sponsorshop, the film consists of a series of long takes of the process of manufacture from raw materials through to finished product, and an amazing shot, which shows that Lumière's original instincts were still active, of hundreds upon hundreds of workers streaming out through the factory gates. Later examples of the genre sometimes take the form of 'a day in the life of . . .', like *A Day in the Life of a Coalminer* (1910) and *At Messrs Pilkington's Glassworks* (1913). Again there is definite ideological intent behind these films, for they are meant to demonstrate how modern and efficient are the companies concerned; as a result they have considerable value for the social historian studying the conditions of labour in the period.

In other early topicals, there is little in the image except ideology. Hepworth is a case in point. Many film historians credit him with the idyllic portrayal of the English countryside, but there was quite another side to his work. In common with other producers he brought to life the cartoon tableaux to be found in magazines like *Punch*. His *Peace with Honour* of 1902 is described in the catalogue thus:

> On a marble dais there is a group of British flags guarded by a 'gentleman in khaki' with a big Union Jack. Britannia enters and drawing aside a central flag, discloses a fine portrait of Lord Kitchener, whereat the soldier cheers lustily, Britannia offers up a laurel leaf to Britain's hero and she then leads in a conquered and dispirited Boer. The Briton shakes him heartily by the hand and the Boer, pleased and pacified, sits down beside him on the dais, and smokes the 'pipe of peace' with his late enemy. The picture closes with Britannia smiling on the two – now the firmest of friends. May so end all Great Britain's wars.

Hepworth went on to make other films which were politically propagandist in even more discomfiting ways. *Aliens' Invasion* of 1905, for example, showed the arrival at London Docks of a steamer crowded with immigrants of a Central European Jewish variety. Again the catalogue provides a description of the film:

> The film follows one 'invader' taken home by a relative to a tenement room. Twenty other aliens are already crowded into the room. Here they live and eat, their breakfast consisting of the strange viands which are purchasable in the neighbourhood of Petticoat Lane. . . . These are the people who oust the honest British toiler from his work and this the manner of their living.

Another, *The International Exchange*, criticizes free trade and puts the case for tariff reform. Films like these clearly reflect the ideology of a petit bourgeois Englishman in period of crisis of Liberal politics.

In due course 'topicals' began to show signs of their own idiosyncratic development, perhaps partly under the influence of the increasing sophistication of 'story' films. In June 1908, for example, a picture called the *Suffragette Film* postrays a sequence of scenes which culminated in a mass meeting in Hyde Park. Suffragettes themselves were involved in its making and were evidently well aware of film as a means of propaganda. An account in the *Kinematograph and Lantern Weekly*, 25 June 1908, reads:

> From certain sources whispers had reached us anent Mr. Harrison Ward's secret conclaves with Mrs. Drummond and Miss Christabel Pankhurst, and as we surmised the plottings of the trio within the suffragettes' fortress have taken definite shape in the form of a picture history of recent performances of the 'great shouters' during their campaign. Mrs. Drummond is seen despatching her corps of lady newspaper sellers upon their rounds, views of Mrs. Drummond and others chalking the pavements, women street-organ players, and scenes at dinner-hour meetings outside Waterlow's, Crosse and Blackwell's, etc. etc., are amongst the features ending in the remarkable sights in Hyde Park on Sunday last. . . .

Whether or not this film was a precocious piece of reportage, the tendency it represents was subsumed by the appearance in 1910 of the first weekly newsreels, introduced by Pathé. Here topicals reverted to what Rachael Low describes as a petrified formal dissociation of events from their context.

Another genre launched by Urban in 1903, under the name of 'Unseen World', was the scientific subject filmed through a microscope, with individual titles such as *Birth of a Crystal*, *Cheese Mites, Circulation of Blood in the Frog's Foot* and *Anatomy of the Water Flea*. (Hepworth immediately produced a parody, *The Unclean World*, in which a scientist inspects his food through a microscope and discovers two large insects; two hands appear in the frame and pick them up, revealing them to be clockwork toys. Here too early cinema reveals one of its most characteristic traits: a penchant for self-satire.) The technique of microscopic filming produces a double magnification, first through the microscope and then the projector, which appears to reveal an entirely new spatial dimension. A similar discovery in the dimension of time takes place through time-lapse photography, originally known as 'speed magnification'. This is simply the logical extension of the stop-frame technique employed by the trick-film makers, where instead of stopping once and starting again, the frames are photographed one by one. Since this is also the basis of animation, it is not surprising that animation films appear around the same time. But animation is not so much a new branch of activity as the resuscitation of a technique which was first discovered far back in the prehistory of cinema, in the drawings made for the Wheel of Life, which Emile Reynaud had perfected in 1892. In this context one should add that the principles of time-lapse photography are already present in Janssen's photographic rifle, and like Reynaud's anticipation of film animation in his Théâtre Optique, could also have been developed before the invention of the cinematograph.

Early examples of time-lapse films include a series shown at the Royal Horticultural Society in 1906 by a Mrs Scott. Another amateur experimenter was Percy Smith, who started out as a junior civil servant at the Board of Education. Encountering Smith's lantern slides of animal and plant life, Urban encouraged him to graduate to film. After trying unsuccessfully to interest the Board in the idea, Smith left his job and teamed up with Urban, constructing his own equipment for time-lapse filming and shooting on the colour film developed by another Urban associate, the Brighton film maker G. A. Smith. Percy Smith's *Birth of a Flower* (1911) was the first of more than fifty natural history subjects distributed by Urban as a series called 'Secrets of Nature' which he made before the First World War. The recalcitrance of the Board of Education should not go unremarked. It is fully symptomatic of the resistance of the social and political establishment in Britain towards the new medium, especially in contrast to its reception across the water, in France in one direction and America in the other.

The scientific genre transformed the dimensions of time and space through cool empirical observation. The spectacle provided by the royal and state occasions which embodied the glory of Empire carried the act of observation into complicity with the function of the event itself, and the political message which is always communicated by such display, which film, again, magnified. Hepworth had been scoring notable successes with films of royal spectacles such as Edward VII's coronation. At the end of the decade Edward graciously provided the film makers with another royal funeral and a coronation to follow, with the Delhi Durbar thrown in for good measure. Urban had the Durbar filmed in Kinemacolor. Here, from the start, film demonstrated the powerful ideological service it was capable of rendering to the state. It projected the reputation of power which, as Thomas Hobbes said, *is* power.

Film portrayed the show of force and status which the state had always employed, carrying it into the furthest corners of the kingdom. If the hegemony of the ruling class ultimately depends on the actual use of force wielded on its behalf by the state, the success with which this force can be wielded when it comes to confrontation is prepared by the regular ritual of its display. As Walter Bagehot, one of the founders of modern political liberalism, put it in *The English Constitution* in 1867, the use of 'theatrical elements' is necessary in order to induce reverence on the part of the 'ruder sorts of men' towards the 'plain, palpable ends of government'. Film extended the projection of the spectacle of the state at the same moment that the working classes were learning how to mobilize their own forces more effectively, through the growth of trade unionism and the beginnings of the parliamentary labour movement. It strengthened state spectacle not merely because it carried it into every corner of the land, but also because it endowed it with a new dimension, in which it was both magnified and multiplied. Probably no state at the time managed its spectacle with so much aplomb as did Britain, at the height of the most powerful and extensive Empire of the epoch. Film enabled Britain to export its spectacle, to the Empire itself and throughout the civilized world. A large number of the orders Hepworth received for his coronation film came from Europe and North America, and it was partly on the strength of this that he became probably the first British film maker to open his own office in New York.

The spectacle of state is structured around central figures of authority or symbolic leadership. Royalty everywhere were quite conscious of the service which the film camera rendered them (though perhaps it also sometimes contributed to their undoing): Hepworth remembered that during Queen Victoria's funeral, Edward VII, hearing the sound of the camera, stopped and provided the cameraman with a particularly good view of his personage. Meanwhile British political leaders took part, as subjects, in early experiments with sound which involved synchronizing film with gramophone records. In the United States, Theodore Roosevelt was particularly aware of the publicity value of film. The cameraman Albert Smith reported that during the march up San Juan Hill in the Spanish–Cuban–American War of 1898, he was well prepared 'to halt . . . and strike a pose' (Smith, 1952). Three years later an American film called *Terrible Teddy, the Grizzly King*, satirized his tough image as a big-game hunter (he is accompanied by a press agent and a photographer), and in 1907 came a successful fake by William Selig of Chicago, *Hunting Big Game in Africa*, which purported to be a film of one of Roosevelt's hunting trips and used a double to impersonate him, although without mentioning his name. The upshot was that in 1908 the English cameraman Cherry Kearton accompanied Roosevelt on a real hunting trip. The resulting film was one of the first of an extended form of travel documentary in which British cameramen, schooled in the tradition of empirical observation and amateur scientific investigation, excelled. Kearton himself went on to film in India, Borneo and South America. As one account puts it, expeditions constituted ideal subjects for extended narratives, enabling audiences to experience vicariously the thrills of the veld and the jungle, the hardship of the desert and the polar explorer (Christie, p. 106).

No expedition was complete without provision for its film record, and a stream of well-funded British explorers travelling to remote corners of the globe took the cameramen on as official photographers. Like the nineteenth-century gentleman photographers who travelled to distant lands with a camera instead of a rifle, or the artists who accompanied the Elizabethan explorers 300 years earlier, the images they brought back added to the catalogue of the exotic. Here again the documentary instinct for 'the seizure of physical reality' turns out to carry ideological implications. Not least because the genre makes celebrities out of the hunters and explorers who embody the idealized man-of-action abroad in the Empire.

The genre reached its climax in 1912, with Herbert Ponting's celebrated film of Scott's Antarctic expedition, *With Captain Scott, R.N. To the South Pole*, which first reached the screens some months before the outcome of the expedition became known, turning Scott into one of the first tragic heroes of the screen. Twice reissued, once in 1924 following the success of Robert Flaherty's *Nanook of the North*, and again in 1933 in a soundtrack version, Sadoul calls this film an ancestor of the fully fledged documentary which emerged with Flaherty, for it is far in advance of the early travelogue (Sadoul, 1972). Here is a film of seven reels – an hour and a quarter – a powerful story told with a strong sense of narrative, with a panoply of highly varied visual images and lots of human detail.

If no other early genre displays more dramatically the distance travelled by the medium in its first fifteen years, the travelogue is also the site of key developments in both cinematography and narrative form which for long escaped the attention of film historians, who like critics generally have always been far more attentive to fiction.* It was in travelogues that the camera first moved, beginning with the view of Venice taken by one of Lumière's cameramen in 1896 from a gondola sailing down the Grand Canal. By 1901 tripods were available fitted with a swivel head, and panoramic shots, in which the camera swung slowly across the landscape, became familar (hence the term 'pan' for a side-to-side movement of the camera). These scenes were often strung together to any desired length, not by the film maker or even the dealer, who listed and sold them individually, but by the

---

* I cannot exclude myself from these remarks. Although a film maker my *métier* is documentary, my treatment of this question in the first edition of this book was skimped. The issue has been addressed by both Bottomore and Musser, in Elsaesser.

exhibitor; and this practice constitutes one of the hidden origins of editing.

These early multi-scene travelogues were unified by the discourse of the lecturer. In Ponting's hands, the expedition film not only provided the audience with figures of identification up on the screen, but also, more invisibly, inserted the point of view of the film maker, again adding a dimension to the basic documentary instinct. The power of Ponting's Antarctic film lies in the variety of imagery photographed at close quarters – the bows of the vessel ploughing through the icy sea, the expedition team erecting their tents and huddling together in the cold, playing football on the ice, or chasing penguins – in which the camera is a palpable participant in the scene, juxtaposed with the terrible beauty of the frozen continent which overflows the frame of the camera's frail human point of view.

But if the travelogue becomes the paradigm of filmic naturalism, the ethos of music hall and popular culture which dominated the reception of early cinema observed no distinction between the real and the fabricated. The popular press carried articles about the ease with which photographs could be faked, but the popular stage was a locus where the issue of authenticity was masked by the practice of magic, and the more effective the illusion the more it was applauded. In these circumstances, where eyes were not yet alert to the perceptual differences, there was a good deal of faking. Films were shown in which the audience are deceived about the veridical content of what they are seeing. Even when no such claim was explicitly made, the ill-defined relationship of spectator to screen allowed the image to be taken for actuality when for one reason or another it was not. The characteristic scenario for this deception was the war subject.

The big early producers like Lumière, Pathé and Urban established networks of cameramen around the world, and prototype 'news footage' continually flowed in. But whenever, for whatever reason, cameramen were unable to film the real thing, they resorted to fakery. James Williamson filmed *Attack on a China Mission Station* in the garden of a rented house in Hove in 1900, and later staged scenes from the Boer War on a local golf course. Albert Smith, returning in 1898 from Cuba to New York during the Spanish–Cuban–American War, boasted that he had taken footage of the Battle of Santiago Bay when he hadn't, so he faked it, using models and cigarette smoke. It was a hit, and the public did not apparently suspect its real nature. (For a full account of the episode see Chanan, 1985.) Not surprisingly, when he then went to South Africa, he felt no compunction about dressing up British soldiers as Boers and passing it off as footage of the Boers in action. Nor was he the only one to claim he had filmed what he hadn't. The film business from the start recognized as enterprise every kind of exploitation of people's imagination within its means.

In many respects, given the intense suggestibility of the medium which we have been tracing here, this is not difficult to understand. But it ought to forewarn us against discussions of the nature of realism and truth in the cinema, or the veracity of the image, which fail to take account of the poor fit between truth as concept and as image. This difficulty, nowadays associated with ideas of postmodernism, is not unique to the visual culture of the late twentieth century. The problem of the simulacrum and the simulation of the image was born with photography and enormously extended by film, whose appearance rode roughshod over all existing aesthetic categories. There is only a thin line (perhaps one should call it a fuzzy one) between the discovery and exploitation of 'special effects' in scientific films (like time-lapse and magnification); the use of similar techniques (especially stop-frame and reverse motion) in trick films, which belong to the realms of humour, magic and fantasy; and the deception of the fake actuality.

Williamson's *Attack on a China Mission Station* has attracted attention from several commentators on account of its novel editing. This simple film, which shows a mission under attack and its rescue by marines during the Boxer rebellion, is singled out as one of the first staged films with a reverse angle in it, a shot which shows the scene unfolding in the opposite direction to the first shot, as if the camera had been turned around 180°. It is not unique, but is more clearly articulated than most other early instances, for this is not a single reverse cut: the alternation of the shots is repeated as the action unfolds. By thus placing the spectator in the crossfire of the battle, an impossible position for a real observer, *Attack on a China Mission Station* demonstrates a new kind of dramatic space, which like other devices examined in these pages, does not become general currency until several years later.

However, the film is something of a conundrum. For one thing, it exists in two versions. The first, dating from 1900, has only one shot – the mission under attack. The reverse set-up is found only in the second version, which dates from 1903, and careful comparison reveals that in both versions the first shot is the same: it is not refilmed. It therefore looks as if Williamson added the second shot later, probably, says Noel Burch, on the model of films in that year by Mottershaw (*A Daring Daylight Robbery*), Hepworth (*Firemen to the Rescue*) and Haggar (*A Desperate Poaching Affray*), all three of which show precocious editing (Burch, 1990, p. 107). If this is true, it is strong evidence that the period between the two versions (1900 to 1903) saw a qualitative shift in the perceived properties of the screen, with the first manifestation of a new sense of spatial articulation among a broad group of film makers in Britain.

The film is also a conundrum as a piece of staged actuality. Several films were issued of incidents from the rebellion, which broke out on the eve of the new year and had collapsed by the end of August 1900. They included four by the Mitchell & Kenyon company of Blackburn, released in July, while the rebellion was still headline news. Williamson's film did not come out till November. Does this mean it was not intended as actuality? Could an audience which had no concept of 'enactment' or 'dramatic reconstruction' have perceived it in any other way? At a conference of film archivists some years ago devoted to the early fiction film, no one doubted the classification of this film as a piece of fiction – but then no one thought of offering a definition of fiction either.

As in many other cases, the action of Williamson's film, even in the second version, is rather less clear than the catalogue description makes it sound, and the film historian Martin Sopocy comments that 'the man who made it could still rely on the circumstance that any ambiguities ... would be cleared up for its audience in the commentary of the master of ceremonies'. In a word, the printed description was of great advantage for the speaker who, in the style of the magic lantern lecturer, talked the early audience through the film, directing their eyes to significant details which their untrained perception might otherwise miss. But it also has another significance, especially when the film is made by someone who belongs to the tradition himself, like Williamson. In that case the description can be read almost as an embryonic script. Not that a film like this required a script to be

written before it could be shot, but because it represents the form
in which the film maker conceives the narrative. The need for a
script – or scenario, as it was first called – developed with the
growing length and complexity of the fiction film. It is in use in
America by around 1910 (when the standard length for a fiction
film had reached two reels or around twenty minutes), though it
is by no means universal; and it represents a critical step towards
the visual articulation of filmic narrative developed by directors
like D. W. Griffith. By contrast, the script-like quality of the early
catalogue description corresponds to a stage when the narrative
thrust of the film images was still subservient to the logic of
verbal description. As Sopocy puts it, 'the stories were meant to
be listened to, the pictures merely forming the illustrations for
this spoken narrative'. We are back with the paradigm of the
illustration. The film was enacted in order to provide pictures to
accompany the telling of the story, even though the story is not
fiction, not 'made-up', but based on incidents which had been
widely reported. Indeed, this is precisely why the audience would
have been able to identify what was going on.

A film like this is an intrinsically slippery object. On the one
hand, the lecturer's speech anchored the ambiguous images on
the screen. The narration would be amplified by the speaker's
informal knowledge of the events portrayed; it would become the
prototype of the commentary, a mode of address which would be
incorporated into the fully fledged documentary with the coming
of sound. On the other hand, as Sopocy puts it, 'the music hall
patrons who watched its first showings did not need a commentator to tell them the fate that awaited the missionary's family,
and we can imagine how they must have cheered at the timely
arrival of the rescuers'. But if this is a consequence of the absence
of any clear distinction between the genres of fiction and non-
fiction, it is also a portent, for it is not as if the distinction between
the two genres will ever become absolute. Quite the contrary, the
cinema will always feel a strong pull towards what one might call
the *film-à-clef*, on the model of the *roman-à-clef*, which introduces
real characters under fictitious names, except the other way
round: by creating fictitious characters who have real names.

*

The 'cheating' which went on in the early topicals, the comic
exploration of trick devices, and the special effects of the scientific

film are inevitable concomitants of the same process. The motivation varies – the enactment of human drama, the pursuit of
magic, illusion and fantasy, the seizure and penetration of physical
reality – but all were equally pertinent to the development of an
awareness of the capabilities of the medium, its capacity to reshape space and time.

Some theorists have suggested that fascination with 'trick'
devices in the early days of cinema may be equivalent to a
fascination with *trompe l'œil* effects, or with anamorphic distortion, both of which occurred in painting in the period following
the invention of artificial perspective.* Photographers, however,
who engaged in comparable practices, were liable to arouse sus-
picions, as if guilty of some kind of transgression. Just before the
turn of the century, a new monthly pictorial called the *Harmsworth Magazine* carried an article entitled 'PHOTOGRAPHIC LIES.
With Remarkable Photos, proving the uselessness of the Camera
as a Witness'. A photograph, the article warned, 'is absolutely
inadmissible as evidence of anything, unless it is proved conclus-
ively that it was in nowise faked after being taken. The faking
can be carried on almost to any extent. In fact, nothing is impossible to the clever knight of the camera.' After illustrating and
explaining photographs of ghosts, of the same man in two positions, and such-like, the author reassures the reader: 'we doubt if
photographers, amateur or otherwise, were ever guilty of using
their knowledge of fakes for any purpose other than that of
amusement, and that indeed was our idea in shedding light on this
comparatively unknown subject'. The *Harmsworth* was a typical
miscellany. It carried short stories and poems with titles like
'Gascoyne's Terrible Revenge, A Story of the Indian Mutiny', 'A
Telegraph Mystery', and 'In Praise of Baby'. There was a
'Monthly Gallery of Beautiful and Interesting Paintings', and
items like 'Nature's Danger Signals, A Study of the Faces of
Murderers' and 'Famous Railway Smashes', by the same Frederick A. Talbot who later wrote *Moving Pictures, How they are
Made and Worked*. One issue includes a demonstration of the
principles of the cinematograph, in the form of a set of 140 tiny

---

* Anamorphic distortion is the painting of an object in such a way that it only
  appears correct – that is, undistorted – from a specific position other than the
  normal frontal position for viewing a painting. An example can be found in
  Holbein's *The Ambassadors* in the National Gallery, London, where a skull
  is painted anamorphically and only appears undistorted when the painting is
  approached obliquely from below while mounting a staircase.

photographs taken from a Lumière film of children playing, printed on the top right corner of every right-hand page, so that the fingers could flip through them and 'see them move'.

But with moving pictures the scope for entertaining deception is hugely augmented, and film makers begin to exercise new forms of mendacity. Film, like photography, was not just a technology of reproduction but a system of representation, which is by no means the same thing. It is not a language in anything like the full sense, but a diverse set of fragmentary codes. And as the elements of these codes first appeared, in necessarily piecemeal fashion, the intensified sense of photographic authenticity also brought with it the seeds of greater and more intense fabrication.

A strong case can be made, independently of any theoretical definition of the properties of illusion, for the role of trickery in upsetting the assumptions of normal vision and established habits of perception. For while reality was given by the camera, illusion was produced by the screen. The screen itself, and not merely the images on it, was felt to be alive, animated in a metaphorical as well as a literal sense.

Consider another film by Williamson, *The Big Swallow* (1901). According to the catalogue description:

> 'I won't! I won't! I'll eat the camera first.' Gentleman reading, finds a camera fiend with his head under a cloth, focussing upon him. He orders him off, approaching nearer and nearer, gesticulating and ordering the photographer off, until his head fills the picture, and finally his mouth only occupies the screen. He opens it, and first the camera, then the operator disappears inside. He retires munching him up and expressing his great satisfaction.

It is curiously difficult to describe this short film accurately. In one account, by Barry Salt,

> a photographer about to take a picture of a reluctant pedestrian is succeeded by a photographer's point-of-view shot of the man approaching till his head fills the screen, at which point he opens his mouth to almost full-screen size. There is a cut to a shot of the photographer and his camera falling around in a black void, and then a final long shot of the pedestrian walking away munching.
>
> (In Elsaesser, p. 41)

But without the catalogue description you cannot tell from the opening shot what is happening (unless the first shot has been lost). The background of the scene is blank, and what you see is the figure of a dandy gesticulating: there is no photographer, and, as Noel Burch observes, the dandy's look is not directed at the camera but about thirty degrees off screen, so that 'the modern spectator even finds it quite difficult to grasp that this look is directed at the "camera fiend" ' (Burch, 1990, p. 220). Then the figure approaches the camera (the camera that is filming) till the frame closes in on his head to a big close-up, his mouth opens, and there is a (nowadays) clearly discernible cut to an inserted over-the-shoulder shot of a hooded photographer and his camera. They proceed to tumble forwards away from us into a black void, then the film cuts back to the open mouth and the figure backs away munching; and only now, as Burch points out, is he looking straight at the camera lens (the one that is shooting the scene).

Salt mentions, in addition, that as the figure approaches the camera the focus is adjusted to keep the image sharp, and such focus pulling is extremely rare before the First World War. But this is another precocious film. What we have in this 'experimental gag film' (as Burch calls it) is an attempt at continuous action with not just one but two continuity cuts, and a frame which moves between medium long shot and extreme close-up. The execution is faltering: the opening framing is unanchored; the follow focus is shaky; in the insert one can clearly see a low edge which camera and photographer dive over; the action on the cuts only approximately matches. Yet these three shots successfully constitute a visual paradox, a passage from external reality into a fantasy space and back again. Moreover, the space of the third shot is a reality which has been transformed by the displacement of identity between camera and viewer which renders both invisible and disembodied.

If this confirms the key role which is played in early cinema by displacement between camera and viewer, it returns us to the question of the way early audiences perceived what was passing on the screen. We are bound to ask on seeing this film today: didn't anybody mind that it was so shaky? Did they even see it as unsteady? One is tempted to say they could not have been as discerning of the execution of such techniques as we are now, and this would not be surprising: we have a great deal of practice behind us; above all, we grew up with it. But what does this mean? Simply that early cinema was crude and primitive? That the early viewer was naive? Is this the same as describing early cinema as childish? Or infantile in a psychoanalytic sense?

There is a pertinent distinction in the work of the psychologist Piaget on the development of the child, which suggests an analogy with all these positions. Piaget observes an opposition between two different mentalities, the syncretism of the child's perception up to the age of seven or eight, and the analytic perception which then develops, and is expressed in the child's burgeoning grasp of abstract reasoning in the form of arithmetic and geometry. Syncretism is a term that goes back to Plutarch, which refers to attempted union or reconciliation between divergent religious systems; hence its modern use by anthropologists to describe phenomena like the fusion of African religions and Catholicism found in the Caribbean and Latin America. Piaget, however, used the term to indicate the distinctive quality of children's vision and children's art in which diverse or opposite tenets are combined without any sense of contradiction; hence the opposite of the analytic. As the psychoanalyst Anton Ehrenzweig explains, the child is unconcerned with the matching of detail to detail. 'A scribble can represent a great number of objects that would look very different to the analytic spectator. However "abstract" the infant's drawing may appear to the adult, to him himself it is a correct rendering of a concrete individual object' (Ehrenzweig, p. 6). Wittgenstein has described the same thing:

> Here is a game played by children: they say that a chest, for example, is a house; and thereupon it is interpreted as a house in every detail. A piece of fancy is worked into it. And does the child now see the chest as a house? 'He quite forgets that it is a chest; for him it actually is a house.' (There are definite tokens of this.) Then would it not also be correct to say he sees it as a house?
>
> (Wittgenstein, p. 206)

In a comparable way, perhaps, the early film viewer, living in the infancy of cinema, would overlook or discount the kind of technical mismatch which we now see so clearly, and accept the intended unity of the film uncritically. Does this mean, in the language of semiology, that the early viewer had not yet learnt to 'read' the images as we have? Not at all. A film like *The Big Swallow* was not unintelligible. Perhaps we should say, historically speaking, that the perception of early film was, so to speak, unreconstructed.

Syncretism is opposed to analytic perception because it is non-rational; this doesn't mean it is not purposeful, as it evidently is in games. But there is more. Wittgenstein adds that if you know how to play the game, and you begin by exclaiming 'with special expression "Now it's a house!" you would be giving expression to the dawning of an aspect'. In order to demonstrate the non-rationality of such a procedure we can add, in the spirit of Wittgenstein, that if you then said half way through the game 'this isn't a house, there are no windows', you would be introducing rational criteria which did not apply, and to do this would be to spoil the game. Why? Because as Ehrenzweig points out, analytic perception has an ineluctable tendency to suppress syncretism, because syncretism is inarticulate, undifferentiated, and therefore subversive in respect to the analytic. (On the other hand, it would be possible for the child to reply, 'Yes it is a house, it's an igloo, igloos don't have windows.')

The tension between the two modes is inevitable, because aesthetic expression is itself grounded in syncretism, through a series of operations – ambiguity, metaphor, condensation and displacement of imagery, etc. – which defy the rational structure and orderly perceptual grid of the analytic. In Freud, these are the qualities associated with the 'primary process' which is manifested in dream language and normally remains inaccessible to the conscious waking mind. By some strange and ironic historical coincidence, Freud arrived at his theory and the cinema was born at the same time; *The Big Swallow* and *The Interpretation of Dreams* appeared within a few months of each other. The affinity between dream and screen becomes a cultural fact. The result will be a major shift in the perception of human psychology, as each – psychoanalysis and film – becomes a laboratory for the findings of the other.

There is a double displacement in Williamson's film: the devouring look of the camera is displaced on to the subject, who devours camera and photographer; and the photographic camera is displaced by the film camera, which thus becomes all-seeing. What the screen offers its audience here is an analogue of its very own animation: its capacity not just to see but to look and to swallow up the object of its look. Even if the film was still set up for the audience by a lecturer, busily commenting on the cinematograph's remarkable ability to perform tricks, it made a hugely filmographic symbol out of the magic power of the screen itself.

*

A film like *How It Feels to be Run Over* raises another significant question: that of endings. It is unusual for its time in the decisive nature of its closure, which transforms it from a moving photograph into a narrative. As long as films consisted only of the single short lengths originally available, they mostly didn't so much end as come to a stop; nor did they begin, they just started. With a few exceptions, they had no internal shape, and are thus correctly described as moving photographs. Many early 'story' films were hardly any different from 'views' in this respect, in spite of the action they contained, since the action was often spun out until the piece of film in the camera came to an end. The practice of joining scenes together to make longer films at first did nothing to alter the timing of individual scenes. It was a matter of simple succession, without any kind of elision. But this was quite enough for the first extended narratives to appear. These, as Burch points out, included boxing matches and passion plays; examples of both occur as early as 1897. In both cases the viewer is already in possession of the code needed to interpret the succession of scenes, especially when prompted by the commentary of the lecturer. And the ending is known in advance.

The techniques of succession extended the range of early cinematic story telling on condition that the story could be rendered in suitable form. This was easily accomplished by mounting a series of tableaux. Another dimension entirely was added in genres like the chase and the rescue. In the former, screen time was articulated in terms of successive narrative steps, with no internal rhythm. Duration is arbitrary. The latter, however, demand the adjustment of duration to the action, and the modulation of succession by internal narrative considerations. By about 1904, these two strategies were being pursued in the same film. The outstanding example of this hybrid genre in Britain in that year is Haggar's *Life of Charles Peace*, a story of the railway age, which celebrates the villainy of a notorious criminal who had been executed some fifty years earlier.

In fact two films were made on his life, one by Haggar and one by Frank Mottershaw of the Sheffield Picture Company.

Haggar's film runs a little under ten minutes and consists of eleven scenes, each identified by a title card. Three of these scenes, however, contain more than one shot. (The National Film Archive holds a copy in which each scene is tinted a particular colour, according to what was deemed thematically or emotionally appropriate to it.) The use of title cards is telling. They are not yet inter titles, that is, captions inserted into a scene which carry the words spoken by a character within it. What they do is replace the lecturer (though in some instances they may have required the participation of members of the audience able to read in calling them out for the benefit of those who couldn't).

The first title announces 'Peace's First Burglary'. The scene is a stage set of an interior, with a wall lined with furniture facing the camera, and containing a large curtained window. Peace is seen poking his head through the curtains, while a woman inside goes about her business. He wears a mask of white make-up in the style of popular stage melodrama. The action is not terribly clear, and passes rapidly. It seems that the woman notices him and exits, but without him realizing that he's been spotted. He climbs in, followed by his accomplice. As they rifle through a chest, the woman returns, followed by other members of the household. A scuffle ensues and Peace manages to escape, but his accomplice is shot as he tries to follow. The camera is completely static, framing the playing area rather than the action, as in all subsequent interiors.

The second scene is entitled 'Peace at Dyson's House', and it runs a few seconds longer than the first at a little more than half a minute. Again an interior stage set, with the wall facing the camera. Peace is discovered playing the violin in a domestic scene with Dyson and his wife. A piece of mime follows in which Dyson offers Peace a drink and exits to get it. Peace and Mrs Dyson move their chairs close together and Peace takes Mrs Dyson in his arms and kisses her. Dyson returns and finds them, and he and Peace fight. Peace and Dyson are contrasted by means of a very simple visual iconography: their faces are made-up differently, and Peace wears a dark suit while Dyson wears a light one.

The third scene is entitled 'The Murder of Mr Dyson', and runs about the same length as the second. Here for the first time the shot is a real exterior location, presumably in some kind of garden. Peace leaves a note in a bush and retires into the foliage. Mrs Dyson enters and finds the note, which she glances at and reacts to melodramatically before hiding it in her bosom. But Dyson enters and snatches it from her. His entry is completely unexpected; there is no attempt to show any anticipation of it. Dyson then discovers Peace emerging from the bushes and again they fight. This time Peace pulls a revolver and shoots Dyson. Mrs Dyson swoons over the body.

Fourth comes 'Chas Peace at Home'. This scene consists of two shots, connected by a straight cut. The first of them lasts about the same length as the previous shots. Peace is once again playing the fiddle in a domestic scene with his family. One of them starts gesturing to warn of the arrival of the police and to indicate that Peace should get into bed and pretend to be asleep. He dons a woman's night-cap and shawl and lies down, covering himself well. The police enter and search around, without realizing that the figure in the bed is Peace. As they leave, Peace begins to get up from the bed, but too quickly and they spot him. A brawl begins, but Peace manages to escape up a ladder standing to one side against the wall opposite the camera, and the picture cuts to the rooftop on to which Peace has climbed. It is not a matching cut. Again this scene is a stage set, but the shot which follows is almost twice as long as any which has yet been seen. It consists of Peace repelling the police, who have followed him, as they struggle on the roof. He shoots two of them in the course of the struggle. One of them falls through a skylight in the roof (which was evidently made of paper). Like all the stage sets used in the film, the sets in these two shots use stage-type iconography. In the very first shot of the film, the moon is visible through the window as Peace climbs in. In the first shot of this scene, the painted view through the window shows an industrial landscape.

The fifth scene is entitled 'Burglary at Blackheath' and consists of three shots. The first runs about three-quarters of a minute. Here, for the second time in the film, a real exterior location is used, the frontage of a respectable-looking house, although the camera is nonetheless placed almost directly opposite just as if it were a stage set. Peace enters with an accomplice and forces entry through the window (back to camera). The accomplice waits outside. Three policemen enter from behind the accomplice's back (all these entrances are like stage entrances) and nab him. One of them takes his place and receives the loot which Peace, unsuspecting, hands out to him through the window. Then the police nab Peace too as he climbs out after it. He manages to fight them off and escapes, running out of frame on the left towards the camera.

We cut to the second shot, another exterior location, which lasts less than half a minute. Here, for the first time, the camera position seems to have been chosen to benefit from depth of field, since it allows, with considerable economy, for three distinct 'areas' of action. First, Peace climbs over the section of the wall facing the camera. Then a fight with the policemen takes place in front of the wall, but again Peace manages to escape, fleeing up the side lane away from the camera.

As he disappears in the distance we cut to the third shot of the sequence – we speak of 'sequence' here for the first time – the continuation of the chase across a mound of rubble, another real exterior location. The cut reverses the direction, for in this shot Peace is running towards camera. The shot lasts only a few seconds, and suggests that here the film maker is beginning to sense the need to pace the action through cutting. Is it an accident that this occurs at a point which does not advance the narrative, but rather, by delaying the passage to the next scene, provides a moment of emotive affect which increases its tension? And is it a coincidence that in these shots real use is made of picture depth, with movement away from and towards the camera instead of simply from side to side? Only the first shot of the sequence really conforms to a stage-bound *mise-en-scène*, although the whole sequence could have been played on stage with characters chasing each other across the proscenium and back again. But it wouldn't have had as much tension and fluidity that way.

The sixth scene is entitled 'Peace, the Parson and the Police'. Again a real exterior location, a country lane. The shot lasts about three-quarters of a minute. Peace enters from the rear and proceeds to disguise himself as a parson. Trick photography – stop-frame or 'interrupted camera' action – is used to allow him to complete his transformation as if by magic. Then three policemen enter, one by one, searching for their man, and Peace sends them off in different directions. The scene provides an opportunity for a kind of comic play which firmly roots the appeal of the film within working-class culture, since it takes two forms of authority, police and parson, as the butts of its humour. As Peace the Parson directs the policemen in their pursuit, he offers them a pamphlet. The first two policemen accept politely, but the third knocks the pamphlets out of Peace's hand impatiently. Peace cocks a snook at him, then promptly turns tail and runs.

The seventh scene is entitled 'Peace captured by P.C. Robinson' and runs just over a minute, the longest shot in the film, as if, although we know the outcome in advance, the film maker is trying to spin out the suspense as long as possible. Again an exterior location, on a heath. Peace is captured only after a fight in which he twice shoots at his pursuers. One of the policemen, repulsed by Peace, rushes away from the action, which takes place in the middle distance, towards the camera, exiting very close to it on the left of frame. Again, in other words, the use of picture depth for effect at a moment which doesn't directly advance the narrative. It must have been a very startling moment. (It still is.)

The eighth scene is entitled 'Peace being taken to Sheffield for Trial'. It lasts about a quarter of a minute and continues the use of real locations, taking place on a railway station platform. Peace is wearing gaolbird dress and cowers before his captors, but he still has enough insolence left to make a couple of half-hearted attempts to escape them.

We are now approaching the film's central tour de force, a portrayal of the episode which made Peace particularly famous – his attempt to escape the police by jumping through the window of a moving train. We can well imagine the audience being on tenterhooks as they wondered how the film was going to manage to portray the incident. It was one of the cinema's first real stunts, a moment when the screen reached beyond all known limitations of art and entertainment by conquering the need for the suspension of disbelief, so that each member of the audience could come out afterwards and say, 'I saw it with my own eyes.' The sequence in which the event occurs is entitled 'Struggle in the Railway Carriage' and consists of three shots. All use real locations. The first is taken with the camera outside the railway carriage facing it and shows Peace sticking his body out of the window trying to escape. Faint wisps of steam crossing the bottom of the frame give a slight impression that the train is in motion, though we cannot see any scenery, and the shot was obviously (to our more analytic eyes) taken with the train stationary. We then cut to another angle of the same action – for the first time a shot in strict continuity with the preceding one, an intended matching cut. This shot looks as if it was taken by holding the camera outside the window of the train as it rounded a bend, which emphasizes the movement in the shot. Peace is seen struggling with his body half out of the window. He gets pulled back in, and then you see his figure shooting through the window and completely out of shot to the right of frame. Close examination of the film reveals that the figure which shoots through the window is a dummy, but the action is too fast for it to be clearly spotted. We immediately cut to a chase along the railway line towards the camera. Peace stumbles (perhaps he's sprained his ankle) and the police catch up, and finally exit with him towards camera right.

The penultimate scene, 'Chas Peace in Prison', shows an identity parade in a real exterior location, with Mrs Dyson making the identification. Finally comes one of the most controversial scenes, 'The Execution'. A procession of Peace, a parson and the warders mount a platform, the rope and hood are placed over Peace's head, and he disappears through the floor. Mottershaw's version does not include the execution; the catalogue description states, 'It has been decided not to reproduce the Execution scene, as we believe it is too ghastly and repulsive.'

If Haggar's film stands as a paradigm of early cinema at the end of its first decade, it is not because its aesthetics are out of the ordinary but rather because they are entirely symptomatic. What is remarkable about it is the indicative, almost didactic way in which it combines so many facets of the filmographic object of the time. First, the subject of the narrative speaks of the audience's foreknowledge, without which a film like this would hardly have been conceivable. This is related to the question of endings. The ending is known: the only question is whether to show it. The idea of dramatic closure motivated from within by the filmic narrative itself has not yet arisen. Second, the opening scene raises the issue of the difficulty of following the action, because the framing is wide and the camera has not yet learnt how to draw attention to significant elements. Third, we find the use of stage iconography and theatrical sets, but also the interpolation of real locations; this refers us to questions of naturalism. Fourth, we find the use of trick photography in the form of stop-frame technique. Fifth, we see the emergence of a sense of continuity. It is no accident that the stunt scene works because it is bound together by continuity cuts; it is unimaginable otherwise. Lastly, there is the discovery of picture depth, clearly linked with the entry of the camera into profilmic space, even though here it still remains mostly at the edge. Nevertheless what is happening here is the discovery of the plasticity of screen space, and we observed that it occurs at points where it does not advance the narrative but elaborates upon it in a new dimension. (This is one of our most curious and paradoxical findings.)

Other film makers go rather further than Haggar in the direction of naturalism, in terms of both acting and *mise-en-scène*. Williamson, in films like *The Soldier's Return*, made a marked attempt to cultivate naturalistic acting. This film, which survives incomplete, tells of a soldier returning from the war to find that his ageing mother has been removed from her cottage to a workhouse, from which he then 'retrieves' her; Williamson boasted about the naturalistic acting in his publicity for the film. Certain films of Hepworth, such as *John Gilpin's Ride* and *Falsely Accused*, strive for naturalism in both acting and setting. His most popular film of the period, *Rescued by Rover*, displays an admirable consistency in its use of interiors with naturalistic lighting and exteriors with perspective and depth, which are filmed with direction matching. But because the camera in these films is still positioned at the edge of the profilmic space, and the characters are mostly still seen, especially in interiors, from a full frontal view, such naturalism as the acting possesses is still enveloped in a sense of theatre with its transparent fourth wall – which leaves the dog to steal the show.

Mottershaw's version of the Peace story is lost, but a film of his from the previous year (1903), *A Daring Daylight Robbery*, which also includes a shot of a convict escaping over a rooftop, uses real outdoor locations entirely and is devoid of theatrical iconography. This film occupies a notable position in the early history of film genres. The story it tells – of a criminal who escapes pursuit by jumping on a train, only to be captured by the aid of a telegraph message sent to the next station – was a modern folk tale going back to 1845, when a suspected murderer, seen boarding a London-bound train at Slough, was arrested when he got out at Paddington; the incident received huge publicity and speeded the railway companies' adoption of the telegraph. Mottershaw's film was bought by Urban, who sold it to America, where it was distributed by Edison under the title *Daylight Robbery*. Here it was remade by Edison's leading cameraman-director, Edwin S. Porter, under the title *The Great Train*

*Robbery*, which combines a mighty locomotive, the telegraph, a 'Western' setting (though it was actually shot in New Jersey), a gallant heroine and a swaggering band of desperadoes – a key film in the evolution of what would later become the most classic of all Hollywood genres.

The passage from Sheffield to New Jersey parallels what Stephen Heath calls 'the passage from views to the process of vision' (Heath, 1981, p. 26): the transition from the tableau narrative to the creation of the specific narrative space of cinema. The screen becomes a fluid space where the narrative is enfolded in a camera which is discovering a sense of direction and learning to alternate its point of view. The process is essentially that of the coding of relations of mobility and continuity, in such a manner that space becomes pregnant with the anticipation of action. The dimensions of this dramatic space are constructed by means of what the French call *découpage* – cutting the scene up into more than one shot. If the necessary counterpart of *découpage* is *montage*, putting it back together again, then the process requires and produces a refinement in the audience's perception comparable to the conceptual shift by which the film maker learns to think in terms of continuity.

This process involves the suppression of disruptive detail. There are some tracking shots in Hepworth's *John Gilpin's Ride*, frequently remarked on because they are among the earliest instances of tracking shots with a clear dramatic function. To achieve these shots the camera was evidently mounted on some kind of moving vehicle, whose direction of movement was apparently controlled by a driving wheel at the front, just below the camera's field of vision, for it becomes visible once or twice at the bottom of the frame: you can see it turning as the direction of the shot changes. In one shot, the camera begins to tilt upwards a little, as if the operator was aware that the edge of the wheel might have been in view and ought not to be. He could not have been certain, since reflex viewfinders had not yet been developed and framing therefore had to be judged subjectively. Something similar occurs in Haggar's *Life of Charles Peace*. In one shot, while a fight takes place in the middle foreground, a figure appears momentarily in the background and disappears again. If examples like these are rarely discussed, this is either because early film scholars have not noticed them themselves, or else because they're dismissed as unimportant accidents. But this is exactly their significance: precisely because they are accidents, they raise questions about the powers of vision and perception. Are they there because the cameraman didn't notice them, or because he thought the audience wouldn't notice?

The latter is surely the more likely, but either way, their presence supports the suggestion that the audience had yet to develop analytic perception; otherwise the accidents in these shots would have mattered and they would not have been acceptable. That they were acceptable is revealed by comparing them with the 'carelessness' with which the earliest examples of matching continuity cuts were made. What this in turn suggests is that the developing powers of analytic attention produce tensions between the primary centre of focus and the periphery.

Another pertinent example is a film called *Drink and Repentance*, subtitled *A Convict Story*. In the final scene, entitled 'Just in time. A dying forgiveness', a drunkard who had gone to prison for beating his wife arrives at his home, having escaped from prison, to find his wife lying in bed, dying. He enters through the door, screen right, and makes for the bed, screen left. While he embraces his wife, the nurse remains at the door trying to delay the entry of the pursuing prison officers. The two actions continue simultaneously, and it is not possible to watch both at the same time. You naturally watch one or the other. Because of the dramatic exigencies of the situation, one is drawn to watching what is going on at the door (a response confirmed by others seeing the film with me when I viewed it). In short, there is parallel action within a scene filmed by a static camera in long shot, which divides attention and detracts from narrative efficacy. It is not an isolated example but a moment of a kind that crops up in many of the dramatic situations portrayed in early films. It is partly scenes like this which gives rise to *découpage*, when the division of attention impinges on analytic consciousness, and the response is to film each action separately in succession.

The film maker develops greater analytic powers in articulating the system of representation; the viewer develops greater analytic powers in viewing. The fusion of the two produces the sublimation of syncretistic perception on to a new level, which preserves the aesthetic illusion that would otherwise be shattered by increased analytic powers. The key to this process of sublimation is the realization that syncretistic perception is not passive but active. Nor is it opposed to analytic perception by simple lack of structure, in which case the analytic would always succeed in imposing itself, but on the contrary, by its power of synthesis.

Analytic reason, which defines, distinguishes, classifies and opposes, is the expression of Freud's Secondary Process, governed by the Reality Principle. The syncretistic qualities of ambiguity, metaphor, condensation and displacement are the highly struc tured aesthetic equivalent of the mode which Freud called the Primary Process, which accounts for the nature of dream language, and is governed by the Pleasure Principle. If effective aesthetic communication depends on a reciprocal relationship between the two – it is this, after all, which distinguishes the work of art from the child's scribbles – then film re-enacts the confrontation between the two principles in a form and at a moment in history that places them in an intense new relationship. An intimate symbiosis develops between the sophistication of analytic perception on the one hand, and that attained within the mode of syncretism on the other. While syncretism plays with formal principles and elaborates expressive devices on their basis, disrupting the fixed categories of ideology, analyticity responds by calling up the further reification of both formal principles and symbolic meanings. But the more sophisticated the analytic rules which apply to the formal structure, the greater the scope for syncretic playfulness in the interstices of this structure.

The opposition between the two modes can be seen in theoretical terms in an opposition between two types of psychological approach to aesthetics. On the one hand, there is the Gestalt psychologist Rudolf Arnheim, who is interested in the process of formation of stable perceptual forms. The artist, he says,

> directly grasps the full meaning of nature's creations, and, by organising sensory facts according to the laws of 'Prägnanz', unity, segregation and balance, he reveals harmony and order, or stigmatizes discord and disorder.
>
> ('Prägnanz' means 'pregnant with meaning'. In Hogg, p. 258)

On the other hand, the psychoanalyst Anton Ehrenzweig says:

> There seem to exist in the structure of a work of art complex relationships that refuse to be caught in the stable and neat grid of common-sense visualization. Incompatible outlines and

surfaces permeate and try to crowd themselves into the same
point in time and space.

(ibid., p. 114)

It is the function of montage to bring the two together into a
holistic unity. The techniques of editing were born in the extension of simple succession into expanded narrative structures, in
which the analytic rules of the new system of representation
were elaborated. It becomes the synthesis through which analytic
perception tames the peripheral and subliminal levels of perception. In the process, it articulates a new set of dimensions in
which new expressive forces come into play.

*

Silent cinema was not usually viewed in silence but, from the
very start, with music playing. A piano improvising on popular
tunes accompanied Lumière's first presentation of the Cinématographe in Paris (at the London debut it was a harmonium). Music
was used for various purposes. Mackerness is obviously correct
when he says that to attribute the use of music in the showing
of films to a desire to drown the noise of the projector is quite
inadequate. 'In normal life', he says, 'practically all movement is
associated with some kind of sound: to witness it in complete
silence produces a false or comic effect.' Music was therefore
used to cover an absent dimension, a dimension for which a
verbal commentary is no substitute. It also became an important
economic element in the growing competition among exhibitors.
Obviously the accompaniment was most lavish in the music halls,
since there were bands and even whole orchestras ready to hand.
Fairground showmen, equipped with elaborate mechanical organs,
were able to add all sorts of sound effects, in the form of bells
and whistles, gun-shots, wind machines, and so forth. The same
instinct is echoed by various attempts throughout the early period
to find a way of adding a synchronous sound track by means of
the phonograph. But these were marginal for the same reason
that the use of the phonograph to provide the musical accompaniment was negligible: the acoustic gramophone of the time was
lacking any system of amplification and the sound was too weak
for a sizeable audience.

Mackerness also points out that the use of music to accompany
action without dialogue was already practised in the stage

melodrama; undoubtedly this gave rise to a number of principles that were simply taken over into cinema usage with the appearance of the first story films. However, as many contemporary accounts and reminiscences bear witness, there was often in the beginning very little attempt to match the music with what could be seen on the screen. In his book *Film Music*, dating from 1936 and practically the first serious treatment of the subject, Kurt London says of the early accompanist: 'His repertory remained a matter of complete indifference; he played anything he liked, and there was little or no connection between the music and the film it accompanied.' Such indifference could only pass muster as long as music had to answer to no more than the absence of sound, but the pictures soon began to make their own demands. The response which music provided to these demands closely parallels the evolution of early narrative. It also tells us interesting things about the functions of music and the nature of its expressivity.

In the first place, music becomes another way of setting the scene. It thereby helps to resolve both the distance between the scene and the camera, and the voyeuristic tensions which may arise in the encounter. But as the story film evolved and became more sustained, new demands were placed on music to help make the dramatic shape of these films more intelligible, and thus promote their acceptance by the growing audience. As Rachael Low has recounted,

> Triumphant know-alls wagged warning fingers when the long film appeared. This time, it was felt, the manufacturers were overreaching themselves. The public would never stand it. It was patently absurd to think an audience would endure one film for more than an hour at the utmost, and besides, what would happen if people came in after it had started?

Music provided answers to these questions. Not only did it help to carry the audience's attention along, it also helped to tell them where they were in the flow of the drama.

Music is capable of several different modes of relationship to the screen, which will evolve in stages. The first to develop was dominantly associative, the echo of a mood or link of an impressionistic kind. Later will come more expressionistic uses, in which music projects the emotions supposedly ascribable to the characters in the story. It is as if music takes over not the external role of the magic lantern lecturer, but that of the narrator in the nineteenth-century novel who is somehow inside the events that are told.

The first name in musical impressionism is Debussy. Ian Christie remarks that Debussy's two books of *Preludes* for piano, written in the years 1909–13, consist of 'vividly contrasted short pieces with unusual titles, suggesting a mixed early film programme' (Christie, p. 143). These titles also suggest several different types of relation between music and image. Pieces like 'Steps in the Snow', 'The Wind on the Plain' and 'Mists' evoke a correspondence between the rhythms in the music and the sense of movement (or stillness) to be perceived in natural phenomena, which is also one of the first points of correspondence in matching music to the movement which appears on the screen. Other titles – 'General Lavine – Eccentric', 'Homage to S. Pickwick, Esq.' – indicate certain powers of human characterization which music and moving pictures share, somewhat of the order of caricature, though without being 'sketchy' or lacking precision (they are concrete and syncretistic). But here the paradigms are found in ballet music, with its own visual qualities, in which we hear the way the characters move in the notes – not to mention the tone of their voices, their laughter, their cries. Music was used sporadi cally for these qualities in the cinema from very early on, not least because it constituted an effective means of parody and answered to the music hall aesthetic which already included such practices.

In all these instances, the primary effect of music is to provide an analogue of what is seen on the screen. Expressionistic uses are much slower to develop partly because they are less concerned with the visual qualities of observable behaviour. Again a piece of music inspired by film – this time by the first name in musical expressionism – is exemplary: Schoenberg's short *Accompaniment to a Film Scene* for orchestra, Op. 34, completed in 1930. The film scene in question is imagined. The only scenario is the one provided by the music, which is in three episodes: 'imminent danger, fear and catastrophe'. Remarkably it has no identifiable internal musical structure apart from this – it follows no principles of music form for musicologists to analyse. It constitutes a musical scenario, a model of the function of music in the cinema as the narrator of dramatic action, and had a secret but huge influence on the work of film composers over several decades thereafter.

The demands made on music in the cinema grew precisely in relation to the development of the film idiom itself. We might speculate for a moment on the way this might have stimulated the art of musical improvisation – a part of practical music making which had been very much alive as little as a hundred years earlier in the age of the great Romantic virtuosos, and which was reborn in the same period as early cinema in the quite separate context, in the United States, of the emergence of jazz. But in a world where the commercialization of music hall has already produced the standardization of popular music according to the dictates of the publishers, such a possibility is hardly expectable. It was in the same decade as the birth of cinema that a newspaper columnist dubbed the street in New York to which the music publishers gravitated Tin Pan Alley. A significant part of their business during the early years of cinema came from the purchase of sheet music for picture house pianists. When two-reeler films, with a duration of around twenty minutes, placed new demands on the skills of the accompanist, it was clearly no longer enough to play a selection of popular tunes of the day. A system of music cue sheets began to develop. A downbeat account of this system has been given by Bert Ennis, and although it belongs more strictly to the annals of North American cinema, it is nonetheless worth quoting at length:

> Music cues, we called them. They originated at the old Vitagraph Studios in Flatbush, Brooklyn, New York, in the early part of 1910, when I was assistant publicity worker for the late Sam Spedon, dean of all picture press agents.
>
> Spedon was the editor of the Vitagraph Bulletin, the first moving picture studio house organ. Knowing that I had come from a career of crime in vaudeville and Tin Pan Alley . . . Sam conceived the idea of having me furnish appropriate musical suggestions for the various Vitagraph releases. Fearing nothing, I undertook the assignment with much enthusiasm and a loyal heart for the numbers of the publishers for whom I had worked. . . . I didn't bother to view the various films. I simply scanned one of Sam Spedon's synopses of the current flicker, sat down at the typewriter, and with the aid of a good memory, plus the catalogues of Remick, Feist, Von Tilzer, Ted Snyder, Witmark, etc., proceeded to cue the film for the benefit of the piano player and three piece orchestras which were paid by

exhibitors in 1910 under the belief that they were assisting the picture with harmony and melody. The piano players who received the Ennis system of Vitagraph Music Cues probably felt after a while that there were only a limited number of musical compositions in the world and that Remick and his fellow publishers had the exclusive rights to these compositions.

For an Irish story, for example, Ennis suggested 'Has Anybody Here Seen Kelly?', 'Mother Machree', 'The River Shannon', and similar titles. Tear jerkers meant sentimental ballads. Songs like 'My Gal Sal', 'A Bird in a Gilded Cage', 'The Mansion of Aching Hearts'

> were scored time and again for the Vitagraphs which carried the heart throbs and pathos, as enacted by Florence Turner, Earl Williams and Harry Morey. When a war picture came along the music cues wrote themselves. 'The Blue and the Grey', 'Mama's Boy', 'Good Bye, Dolly Gray', 'Break the News to Mother', 'Good Bye, Little Girl, Good Bye', and numerous other soldier songs did yeoman duty, whether the film was that of Civil or Spanish war period. . . . We showed our class by injecting at times the classical and standard numbers – a few of them, anyhow. 'Hearts and Flowers', 'Melody in F', 'Traumerei', 'Souvenir', 'Pilgrim's Chorus' – they all helped to give helpless audiences a barrage of highbrow music before the present day experts in the writing of music scores for films discovered Debussy, Beethoven, Schubert, Mozart, Wagner and other big leaguers of the classical field.

The cue sheet system, which spread very quickly, institutionalized what had already become an established informal practice, in which a repertoire of well-known music was coded by a loose, impressionistic iconic association. The method thereby perpetrated upon this repertoire an authorized classification according to the crudest possible categories, a reduction and schematization of musical meanings. A manual for the movie pianist published by one of the leading music publishers, Schirmer, in 1924, carries the following index:

*Aeroplane*
*Band*
*Battle*

*Birds*
*Calls*
*Chase*
*Chatter*
*Children*
*Chimes*
*Dances*
   *Gavottes*
   *Marches*
   *Mazurkas*
   *Minuets*
   *Polkas*
   *Tangos*
   *Valses*
   *Valses lentes*
*Doll*
*Festival*
*Fire-Fighting*
*Funeral*
*Grotesque*
*Gruesome*
*Happiness*
*Horror*
*Humorous*
*Hunting*
*Impatience*
*Joyfulness*
*Love-themes*
*Lullabies*
*Misterioso*
*Monotony*
*Music-box*
*National*
*Neutral*
*Orgies*
*Oriental*
*Parties*
*Passion*
*Pastorale*
*Purity*
*Quietude*

*Race*
*Railroad*
*Religioso*
*Sadness*
*Sea-Storm*
*Sinister*
*Wedding*
*Western*

Under 'Sinister' we find one piece: the *Coriolan* Overture by Beethoven. Under 'Religioso' we find Handel's 'Largo', 'the Old Hundredth' by Bourgeois, 'Onward Christian Soldiers' by Sullivan, and the unaccredited hymn 'Lead, Kindly Light'. Under 'Sadness', as many as fourteen pieces, by composers such as Beethoven, Chopin, Grieg, Anton Rubinstein, Tchaikovsky and Massenet (to mention only the best known). And so on. The effects of this kind of classification of music for the screen would reach beyond the cinema. It has created a way of hearing which insists on associating music forever with pictures; and a way of hearing which annihilates listening. Perhaps the most indicative thing about the mentality which produced this system is a link mentioned by Ennis: it was originated by a press agent. Music, in other words, is here regarded not as an aesthetically integral part of the film but as a sales device. In line with the school of thought which believes that all good sales devices must have a subliminal dimension, the belief soon grew up that film music had to be surreptitious (like editing). 'The chief difficulty in score writing', according to Hugo Riesenfeld, an American film music composer, in the 1920s, 'is keeping the music subordinate to the action on the screen. It must never obtrude itself. The audience must never be conscious of hearing a familiar tune.' And yet it consisted of nothing but familiar tunes, and familiar harmonies and familiar rhythms. It is precisely because they are familiar that nobody listens to them, and they thereby provide a ready-made emotive vocabulary. Music is thus used to trigger off established response patterns, to reinforce the conventionality of the plot and the genre. It will need a different conception of the screen, a modernist and perhaps even surrealistic sense, for a different relationship to music to arise.

# Chapter 13

# Epilogue: The dream that kicks

Is film a language? If so, what kind? If the pressure of this question has led to the application of semiotics to the cinema, the answers that have been offered leave several problems, especially when they treat the cinema according to models derived from structural linguistics. For this generally leads to the neglect of the dimension which film shares with music – the ordering of time.

Music, like film, is a kind of language, which possesses a form of grammar, but without words, those units of signification with stable, well-defined meanings of the type that can be listed in a dictionary. It is expressive because, as Lévi-Strauss has put it, it operates across two grids, one physiological and natural, the other cultural: for on the one hand music exploits the natural rhythms of the body, on the other hand it does so in terms of scales and harmonies which vary through history and between cultures (Lévi-Strauss, 1975). The result is that musical time is not a dimension to be measured by the clock. Duration in music is measurable only in terms of sensibilities, tensions and emotions.

Film is remarkably similar: it quickly acquires a syntax, which governs the form and relationships of successive shots, but these are hardly to be compared with words. It is true that film images are denotational (which is not the case with music), but not in the same way as words; they are pre-articulate, belonging to a realm of symbolic connotation which is subject to the attraction of the subconscious. If these images create an illusion of real space in two dimensions which belongs to the realm of the imaginary, on the other hand their duration is not at all imaginary but perfectly palpable; and again it is not chronometric, but like music, plastic and affective.

The marriage of film and music, however, had a paradoxical effect: music, which itself is vague, was pressed into service in order to pin down the emotive content of the image. Nevertheless, within this restrictive classification of allowable emotive responses, the film remains (like music) pre-articulate and non-conceptual, but still immediately intelligible. If the grammar of film is constituted by a series of codes, these are codes which do not need to be decoded in order to be understood (except in special circumstances). The film is perceived and experienced directly, like the dream. Interpretation is secondary.

The language of the film screen is thus more like the language of dream than anything else, or as Christian Metz puts it, the 'filmic flux' resembles the 'dream flux' more than other products of the waking state. A dream is a vision which seems to pass before us without our having to do anything, in which the unconscious embodies itself in images while bodily action is suspended; and 'in the dream as in the film there are not only images; there is, clearly or confusedly woven by the images themselves, a succession, whether organized or chaotic, of places, actions, moments, characters' (Metz, 1982, pp. 124–5).

The analogy is reinforced by the experience of watching the moving pictures within a darkened space where the audience can forget the world outside and lose itself. In an essay of 1911, the French writer Jules Romains likens the process of going to the cinema to the experience of a collective dream, as if the audience are asleep, no longer conscious of their bodies, all attentive to the same passing images (Christie, p. 132). Many early films were the visualization of dreams, where we see a character's dream images. Among the most curious is an English film of 1900 called *Let Me Dream Again*, remade by Zecca in France a year later under the title *Rêve et Réalité* ('Dream and Reality'). Both versions consist of two shots. In the first a man is wining and dining an attractive woman. As they finally begin to embrace, the picture dissolves into a shot of the same man in bed with a different woman, presumably his wife. In the French version, she is embracing him and he, in the act of waking up and discovering her, pushes her away; the action in the original English version is less clear, more ambiguous. The oddity in this film is that the first shot, unannounced by anything except the film's title, is the dream shot. Nothing heralds the dream image, as it usually does in this kind of film. The result is a puzzle: what tells us this is a dream image, and not the characters' waking state? And then how do we know whose dream it is we have been watching? The only reason we have for identifying it as the man's dream is the fact that it is the man who is present, occupying the same position, screen left, in both shots. This is not enough, logically speaking. After all, displacement can operate in the dream not only on those we dream about, but also on the ego of the dreamer, which may be thus dissolved, suspended. Why should one not imagine it as the woman's dream, only a dream in which the dreamer herself is displaced in the first part? The only possible answer is that we read significance into successive film images not only forwards but also backwards, withholding judgement until we have seen what comes next. Or, to put it another way, time on the screen is not linear and unidirectional but moves forwards, backwards and sideways, in a continual flux which is also the property of time in the dream.

There are differences, of course, between films and dreams. As Metz remarks, while dreamers do not generally know they are dreaming, film spectators know they are at the cinema. Conversely, there are states of dreaming when the thought arises within the dream that 'this is only a dream': 'regimes of consciousness in which the subject is sufficiently asleep for his dream to continue but sufficiently awake to know that it is only a dream', thus approaching a very common feeling in the cinema (Metz, 1982, p. 105). Compared to other waking states, then – except for the reverie induced by music, which is very similar – the film 'encourages narcissistic withdrawal and the indulgence of phantasy', the 'inhibition of action' and 'temporary suspension of concern for the exterior world'.

However, the sleep into which the dreamer is induced to fall inside the cinema is a collective and not a private one. Metz observes that the film image belongs to that class of 'real images' (paintings, drawings, engravings, etc.) which psychologists oppose to mental images; a behaviourist would say that what characterizes filmic perception is that it involves an external stimulus, whereas the dream state does not. The obverse of this condition is that the symbolic discourse of these dreams is not private and individual but social and ideological. In these conditions, the very first film makers translated into dreams not just the fantasies of the unconscious but also their social and political prejudices. There is the case, for example, of a film called *Milling the Militants*

– *A Comic Absurdity*, issued by the Clarendon Film Company in 1913, the same year that a film camera captured Emily Davidson's protest suicide at the Derby, when she threw herself under the King's horse. The story is cast in one of the established forms of the time, a sequence of events dreamed by one of the characters. The film opens in a posh-looking parlour with a disgruntled husband holding two babies confronting his wife, who wears an apron inscribed 'Women's Suffrage – Be Militant'. She goes off to join a demonstration in the street outside. The man calls the maid to take the babies off his hands and grimaces with despair. After a shot of women smashing windows, we cut to a title which reads, 'Brown sleeps and dreams that he is the Prime Minister. He legislates for the suppression of the Suffragettes.' The rest of the film shows Brown's new laws being put into effect on the principle of 'make the punishment fit the crime'. This seems to mean making a huge joke out of setting women to work at men's jobs and wearing men's clothes. The most striking thing about this extraordinary film is its duplicity: on the one hand a sexist male wish-fulfilment fantasy, with a henpecked husband – a familiar music hall stereotype – as the main vehicle of the comedy, on the other a satire on bourgeois behaviour. In short, a film which in extracting its laughs at equal expense from the middle classes, politicians in general, and women in particular demonstrates an indifference to ideology which is itself deeply ideological in character – a kind of denial of reality typical of the daydream.

The visual continuum of the cinema screen stretches from the real and veridical to the magical and fantastical. For writers such as Walter Benjamin and George Orwell, who, as we saw at the outset of this investigation, prized the power of film to penetrate the surface of reality, the latter was suspicious. Orwell speculated that

> A millionaire with a private cinematograph, all the necessary props and a troupe of intelligent actors could, if he wished, make practically all of his inner life known. . . . Of course, it is not desirable that any one man . . . should make a show of his inner life. What is wanted is to discover the now nameless feelings that men have *in common*. All the powerful motives which will not go into words and which are a cause of constant lying and misunderstanding, could be tracked down, given visible form, agreed upon, and named. I am sure that the film,

with its almost limitless powers of representation, could accomplish this in the hands of the right investigators, though putting thoughts into visible shape would not always be easy – in fact, at first it might be as difficult as any other art.

He almost seems to be paraphrasing Benjamin's argument that the effect of film is like the impact of Freud's *Psychopathology of Everyday Life*, which 'isolated and made analysable things which had heretofore floated along unnoticed in the broad stream of perception':

> It is only an obverse of this fact that behaviour items shown in a movie can be analysed much more precisely and from more points of view than those presented on paintings or on the stage. As compared with painting, filmed behaviour lends itself more readily to analysis because of its incomparably more precise statements.

But this deepening of apperception was negated, said Benjamin, by the 'ultrareactionary significance' which Werfel gave to cinema in a review of Max Reinhardt's film of *A Midsummer Night's Dream*, when he celebrated its fantasy at the expense of what he called the slavish copying of external reality. Before Reinhardt, said Werfel, film had 'not yet realised its true meaning, its real possibilities . . . [which] consist in its unique faculty to express by natural means and with incomparable persuasiveness all that is fairylike, marvelous, supernatural'. It is of course precisely this principle on which the commercial film industry was based, and the reason why it devoted so many of its resources to turning the cinema building itself into a dream palace.

The dream quality of film relies on the way the mechanical process of projection turns the screen into a public dream-screen, similar to the dream-screen of which psychoanalysts have spoken, an indistinct and intangible mental space on which the manifest content of the dream is projected. The space which the dream-screen seems to hold, according to the psychoanalysts, is undifferentiated: it expands and contracts according to its own dictates. Sometimes it disappears into infinity, sometimes advances towards the dreamer and envelops them. The cinema screen does the same.

Moreover, in the peculiar semi-waking, semi-sleep of the cinema spectator, the film possesses the paradoxical power of momentarily reconciling three very different mental regimes: the normal waking sense of reality, the perceptual illusion of the dream, and the evocation of the daydream – conditions which cease to be contradictory and mutually exclusive, as they are ordinarily, in order to enter into new relations where they overlap, coincide and intersect with each other. The screen is thus, according to Metz, a potentially confused territory, a place 'consisting of actions, objects, persons, a time and a space (a place similar in this respect to the real), but which presents itself of its own accord as a vast simulation, a non-real real' (Metz, 1982, p. 141).

All of this and more is involved when film in the camera is exposed to the photogenic aspects of the phenomenal world, then developed and recombined to become a means of projecting a world of the imagination. Since this projection is psychological as well as mechanical, and since the profilmic events are cut up and reassembled in a pattern in which film discovers its own laws, the result is in some sense obviously fantastic and unreal. This fantasy may shock, or it may lull – like dreams themselves. The effect is reinforced by the disappearance in the act of viewing of all the props of artifice which may be employed in this process. The camera disappears, the crew, the lights, everything Benjamin referred to as the spectacle of the shooting of a film, 'unimaginable anywhere at any time before'. Finally, when the projector lights up, the screen itself disappears. The spectacle of shooting a film, says Benjamin,

> presents a process in which it is impossible to assign to a spectator a viewpoint which would exclude from the actual scene such extraneous accessories as camera equipment, lighting machinery, staff assistants, etc. – unless his eye were on a line parallel with the lens. This circumstance, more than any other, renders superficial and insignificant any possible similarity between a scene in the studio and one on the stage. In the theatre one is well aware of the place from which the play cannot immediately be detected as illusionary. There is no such place for the movie scene that is being shot. Its illusionary nature is that of the second degree, the result of cutting. . . . The equipment-free aspect of reality here has become the height of artifice; the sight of immediate reality has become an orchid in the land of technology.

The artifice of film remains, whatever the developments in

technology and technique. A century after the birth of film it is present equally in the films of documentarists who claim that their work is free from artifice, because of modern, agile equipment, and the latest Hollywood blockbusters, although their respective relation to reality is utterly different. Nevertheless, the facts of projection render the artifice invisible, because the viewer is situated only by what passes on the screen from moment to moment. Stanley Cavell has described the force-field which film turns on here:

> The world of a moving picture is screened. The screen is not a support, not like a canvas; there is nothing to support, that way. It holds a projection, as light a light. A screen is a barrier. What does the silver screen screen? It screens me from the world it holds – that is, screens its existence from me. That the projected world does not exist (now) is its only difference from reality.

This difference is highly persuasive. The illusion of the film screen, says Metz, is less absolute than the total perceptual illusion of the real dream, but it is perhaps more formidable, because it is the delusion of someone who is awake. Although what the screen holds is part of the world, the picture we see becomes a world apart. To play on this facet of film effectively is generally to neutralize its subversiveness. But to fight this neutralization is not necessarily to deny the dreamlike qualities of cinema; it is rather to turn the film into a dream that kicks

> the buried from their sack
And lets their trash be honoured as the quick.
This is the world. Have faith.

# Bibliography

Aaron, Will, 'Walter Haggar', *Barn*, October 1975.

Adorno, T. W., *Minima Moralia*, New Left Books, 1974.

Allister, Ray, *Friese-Greene, Close-up of an Inventor*, Marsland, 1951.

Arnold, Matthew, *Culture and Anarchy*, Cambridge University Press, 1963.

Bachlin, Peter, *Histoire Économique du Cinéma*, La Nouvelle Edition, Paris, 1947.

Bakhtin, M. M., *The Dialogic Imagination*, University of Texas Press, 1981.

Barker, W. G., Paul, R. W. and Hepworth, Cecil, 'Before 1910: Kinematograph Experiences', *Proceedings of the British Kinematograph Society*, no. 38, 3 February 1936.

Barnes, John, *The Beginnings of the Cinema in England*, David & Charles, 1976.

Barnouw, Erik, *Documentary, A History of the Non-fiction Film*, Oxford University Press, New York, 1974.

Barthes, Roland, *Image-Music-Text*, Fontana, 1977.

Bazin, André, *What is Cinema?* vol. 1, University of California Press, 1967.

Benjamin, Walter, *Charles Baudelaire: A Lyric Poet in the Era of High Capitalism*, New Left Books, 1973.

Benjamin, Walter, *Illuminations*, Schocken Books, 1969.

Benjamin, Walter, 'A Small History of Photography', in *One-Way Street*, New Left Books, 1979. For another translation as 'A Short History of Photography', see *Screen*, vol. 13, no. 1.

Bennett, Colin N., *The Guide to Kinematography*, E. T. Heron, 1917.

Bernal, J. D., *Science and Industry in the Nineteenth Century*, Indiana University Press, 1970.

Booth, Charles, *Life and Labour of the People in London*, vol. 8, Macmillan, 1896.

Booth, Michael R., 'The Metropolis on Stage', see Dyos and Wolff, eds.

Bratton, J. S., *The Victorian Popular Ballad*, Macmillan, 1975.

Brockmann, Friedrich, *Celluloid, Its Raw Materials, Manufacture, Properties and Uses*, Scott & Co., 1921.

Bromhead, A. C., 'Reminiscences of the British Film Trade', *Proceedings of the British Kinematograph Society*, no. 21, 11 December 1933.

Brown, J. F., 'The Thresholds for Visual Movement', in M. D. Vernon, ed., *Experiments in Visual Perception*, Penguin, 1966.

Burch, Noel, Notes to accompany 'Correction Please, or how we got into Pictures', Arts Council, 1979.

Burch, Noel, *Life to those Shadows*, BFI, 1990.

Canetti, Elias, *Crowds and Power*, Gollancz, 1962.

Cavell, Stanley, *The World Viewed, Reflections on the Ontology of Cinema*, Viking Press, 1979.

Ceram, C. W., *Archeology of the Cinema*, Thames & Hudson, 1965.

Chanan, Michael, 'Art as Experiment', *British Journal of Aesthetics*, vol. 12, no. 2, Spring 1972.

Chanan, Michael, ed., *Chilean Cinema*, BFI, 1976a.

Chanan, Michael, *The Cuban Image, Cinema and Cultural Politics in Cuba*, BFI/Indiana University Press, 1985.

Chanan, Michael, *Labour Power in the British Film Industry*, BFI, 1976b.

Chanan, Michael, *Musica Practica, The Social Practice of Western Music from Gregorian Chant to Postmodernism*, Verso, 1995.

Cheshire, D. F., *Music Hall in Britain*, David & Charles, 1974.

Christie, Ian, *The Last Machine: Early Cinema and the Birth of the Modern World*, BFI, 1994.

Clerke, Agnes M., *A History of Astronomy During the Nineteenth Century*, Adam & Charles Black, 1887.

Coe, Brian, 'W. Donisthorpe', *Cinema Studies*, vol.1, no. 3, August 1961.

Coe, Brian, *George Eastman and the Early Photographers*, Priory Press, 1973.

Coe, Brian, 'William Friese-Greene and the Origins of Kinematography', *Photographic Journal*, March–April 1962.

Cole, G. D. H., and Postgate, Raymond, *The British Common People*, Methuen, 1961.

Commolli, J.-L., 'Technique and Ideology', BFI, Education Dept, duplicated translation.

Couzens, E. G., and Yarsley, V. E., *Plastics*, Penguin, 1941, or *Plastics in the Service of Man*, Penguin, 1956.

Crowther, J. G., *British Scientists of the Nineteenth Century*, vol. 1, Penguin, 1940.

Crowther, J. G., *Famous American Men of Science*, vol. 2, Penguin, 1944.

Daney, Serge, 'Sur Salador', in 'Travail, lecture, jouissance', *Cahiers du Cinéma*, no. 222.

Derry, T. K., and Williams, Trevor I., *A Short History of Technology*, Oxford University Press, 1970.

Deslandes, Jacques, *Histoire Comparée du Cinéma*, 2 vols (vol. 2 with Jacques Richard), Casterman, 1966–8.

Dobb, Maurice, *Studies in the Development of Capitalism*, Routledge & Kegan Paul, 1963.

Dyos, H. J., and Wolff, Michael, eds, *The Victorian City, Images and Realities*, Routledge & Kegan Paul, 1977.

Ehrenzweig, Anton, *The Hidden Order of Art*, Weidenfeld & Nicolson, 1967.

Ehrlich, Cyril, *The Music Profession in Britain since the Eighteenth Century*, Clarendon Press, 1985.

Elsaesser, Thomas, with Adam Barker, eds, *Early Cinema: Space, Frame, Narrative*, BFI, 1990.

Engels, Friedrich, *The Condition of the Working Class in England in 1844*, Allen & Unwin, 1952.

Falconer, D., *et al.*, *Terrell on the Law of Patents*, 12th edn, Sweet & Maxwell, 1971.

Farson, Daniel, *Marie Lloyd and Music Hall*, Tom Stacey, 1972.

Field, Audrey, *Picture Palace, A Social History of the Cinema*, Gentry Books, 1974.

Fielding, Raymond, ed., *A Technological History of Motion Pictures and Television*, University of California Press, 1967.

Foucault, Michel, *The Order of Things*, Vintage Books, 1973.

Francastel, Pierre, 'Espace et Illusion', *Revue Internationale de Filmologie* (Deuxième Année, no. 5), tome II, 1951

Frank, André Gunder, *Capitalism and Underdevelopment in Latin America*, Penguin, 1971.

Friese-Greene, William, 'Affidavit', *Moving Picture News*, no. 49, 3 December 1910.

Frisby, David, *Fragments of Modernity*, Polity, 1985,

Gaunt, William, *The Aesthetic Adventure*, Penguin, 1957.

Gernsheim, Helmut and Gernsheim, Alison, *The History of Photography*, Thames & Hudson, 1969.

Gombrich, E. H., *Norm and Form*, Phaidon, 1966.

Gorki, M., 'You Don't Believe Your Eyes', *World Film News*, March 1938

Greenfield, Susan, Royal Institute Christmas Lectures 1994, BBC1 Television.

Gregory, R. L., *Eye and Brain*, Weidenfeld & Nicolson, 1966.

Grierson, J., *Grierson on Documentary*, ed. F. Hardy, Collins, 1946.

Gubern, Roman, *Historia del Cine*, Ediciones Danae, Madrid (undated).

Haber, Ralph Norman, ed., *Information-processing Approaches to Visual Perception*, Holt, Rinehart & Winston, 1969.

Haber, Ralph Norman, and Hershenson, Maurice, *The Psychology of Visual Perception*, Holt, Rinehart & Winston, 1973.

Halévy, Elie, *History of the English People in the Nineteenth Century*, several vols, Ernest Benn, 1961.

Harvie, Christopher, *et al.*, eds, *Industrialization and Culture, 1830–1914*, Macmillan for the Open University Press, 1970.

Heath, Stephen, 'Narrative Space', *Screen*, vol. 17, no. 3, Autumn 1976.

Heath, Stephen, *Questions of Cinema*, Macmillan, 1981.

Heath, Mrs Syd, *The First Thirty Years, A Record of the N.A.T.T.K.E. 1890–1920* Civic Press, 1973.

Hendricks, Gordon, *The Edison Motion Picture Myth*, University of California Press, 1961.

Hepworth, Cecil, *Came the Dawn, Memories of a Film Pioneer*, Phoenix House, 1951.

Hepworth, Cecil, 'Those Were the Days', in *Penguin Film Review* no. 6. Reprinted in Harry M. Geduld, ed., *Film Makers on Film Making*, Penguin, 1967.

Hepworth, T. C., *The Book of the Lantern, being A Practical Guide to the Working of the Optical (or Magic) Lantern*, Hazell, Watson & Vinoy, 1894.

Hobsbawm, Eric, *The Age of Revolution*, Sphere Books, 1973.

Hoffman, Banesh, *Einstein*, Paladin Books, 1975.

Hofman, Charles, *Sounds for Silents*, Drama Book Specialists, 1970.

Hogg, James, *Psychology and the Visual Arts*, Penguin, 1969.

Hunnings, Neville March, *Film Censors and the Law*, Allen & Unwin, 1967.

Jacobs, Lewis, *The Rise of the American Film*, Teachers College Press, Columbia University, 1969.

Jones, Gareth Stedman, *Outcast London*, Penguin, 1976.

Jones, Robert, and Marriott, Oliver, *Anatomy of a Merger*, Jonathan Cape, 1970.

Josephson, Matthew, *Edison*, Eyre & Spottiswoode, 1961.

Josephson, Matthew, *The Robber Barons*, Eyre & Spottiswoode, 1962.

Kracauer, Siegfried, *Theory of Film, The Redemption of Physical Reality*, Oxford University Press, 1960.

Kuhn, T. S., *The Structure of Scientific Revolutions*, University of Chicago Press, 1962.

Leeson, R. A., *Strike*, Allen & Unwin, 1973.

Lenin, V. I., *Imperialism, The Highest Stage of Capitalism*, Foreign Languages Press, 1975.

Leslie, C. R., *Memoirs of John Constable*, Phaidon, 1951.

Lévi-Strauss, Claude, *The Raw and the Cooked*, Harper & Row (Colophon), 1975.

Lévi-Strauss, Claude, *The Savage Mind*, Weidenfeld & Nicolson, 1972.

Lilley, Samuel, 'Technological Progress and Industrial Revolution, 1700–1914', in Carlo M. Cipolla, ed., *Fontana Economic History of Europe*, Fontana, 1973.

Lloyd, A. L., *Folk Song in England*, Paladin Books, 1975.

Low, Rachael, *The History of the British Film*, vol. 1 (with Roger Manvell), and vols 2 and 3, Allen & Unwin, 1948.

Lukács, G., 'The Poetry of Film', *New Hungarian Quarterly*, no. 54.

Luria, A. R., *The Working Brain*, Penguin, 1973.

Macinnes, Colin, *Sweet Saturday Night, Pop Song 1840–1920*, MacGibbon & Kee, 1967.

McKechnie, Samuel, *Popular Entertainments through the Ages*, Sampson Low (undated, 1932).

Mackerness, E. D., *A Social History of English Music*, Routledge & Kegan Paul, 1964.

Mandel, Ernest, *Late Capitalism*, New Left Books, 1975.

Mander, Raymond, and Mitchenson, Joe, *British Music Hall*, Gentry Books, 1974.

Manvell, R. and Huntley, J., *The Technique of Film Music*, 1975.
Martin, G. H., and Francis, David, 'The Camera's Eye', see Dyos and Wolff, eds.
Marx, Karl, *Capital*, Lawrence & Wishart, 1970.
Marx, Karl, *Early Writings*, ed. T. Bottomore, Watts, 1963.
Marx, Karl, *Grundrisse*, Penguin, 1973.
Marx, Karl, *Marx–Engels Selected Correspondence*, Progress Publishers, 1975.
Marx, Karl, *Writings of the Young Marx on Philosophy and Society*, ed. Easton and Guddat, Doubleday (Anchor), 1967.
Mayhew, Henry, *Mayhew's London*, ed. P. Quennell, Spring Books, 1969.
Mellor, G. J., *Picture Pioneers, The Story of Northern Cinema 1896–1971*, Frank Graham, 1971.
Mepham, John, 'The Theory of Ideology in Capital', *Radical Philosophy* 2, reprinted in *Working Papers in Cultural Studies 6* and in J. Mepham and D.-H. Ruben, eds, *Issues in Marxist Philosophy*, vol. 3, Harvester Press, 1979.
Metz, Christian, 'The Imaginary Signifier', *Screen*, vol. 16, no. 2, Summer, 1975.
Metz, Christian, *Psychoanalysis and Cinema*, Macmillan, 1982.
Mitry, Jean, *Histoire du Cinéma*, vol. 1, Editions Universitaires, 1967.
Moles, Abraham, *Information Theory and Esthetic Perception*, University of Illinois Press, 1968.
Montmorency, Miles F. de, *A Short History of Painting in England*, Dent, 1933.
Neuburg, Victor E., 'The Literature of the Streets', see Dyos and Wolff, eds.
Nowell-Smith, Geoffrey, 'On the Writing of the History of the Cinema: Some Problems', in *Edinburgh '77 Magazine, History/Production/Memory*, Edinburgh Film Festival.
Orwell, George, 'New Words', in *Collected Essays, Journalism and Letters*, vol. 3, Penguin, 1970.
Palmer, Roy, ed., *A Touch on the Times, Songs of Social Change 1770–1914*, Penguin Education, 1974.
Pearsall, Ronald, *Edwardian Popular Music*, David & Charles, 1975.
Pearsall, Ronald, *The Worm in the Bud*, Penguin, 1971.
Pearson, George, *Flashback, The Autobiography of a British Film-maker*, Allen & Unwin, 1957.
Perkin, Harold, *The Origins of Modern British Society, 1780–1880*, Routledge & Kegan Paul, 1972.
Pleynet, M. and Thibaudeau, J., 'Economique, idéologie, formel', discussion, *Cinéthique*, no. 3.
Ramsaye, Terry, *A Million and One Nights*, Frank Cass, 1964.
Rawlence, Christopher, *The Missing Reel*, Fontana, 1991.
Rendle, T. MacDonald, *Swings and Roundabouts*, Chapman & Hall, 1919.
Roberts, Robert, *The Classic Slum*, Penguin, 1973.
Robertson, J. H., *The Story of the Telephone*, Scientific Book Club, 1948.
Sadoul, Georges, *British Creators of Film Technique*, BFI, 1948–.

Sadoul, Georges, *Dictionary of Films* and *Dictionary of Film Makers*, University of California Press, 1972.

Sadoul, Georges, *Histoire Générale du Cinéma*, vols 1–3, Editions Denoel

Salt, Barry, 'Film Form, 1900–06', *Sight & Sound*, vol. 47, no. 3, Summer 1978.

Scharf, Aaron, *Art and Photography*, Penguin, 1974.

Scholes, Percy, *The Mirror of Music 1844–1944*, 2 vols, Novello and Oxford University Press, 1947.

Slonimsky, Nicolas, *Lexicon of Musical Invective*, University of Washington Press, 1969.

Smith, Albert E., *Two Reels and a Crank*, Doubleday, 1952.

Sopocy, Martin, 'James A. Williamson: American View', *Cinema Journal*, Fall 1978.

Storey, Graham, *Reuter's Century*, Max Parrish, 1951.

Talbot, Frederick, *Moving Pictures, How they are Made and Worked*, Heinemann, 1923 ('Entirely Rewritten' – first published 1912).

Taylor, Richard and Christie, Ian, eds, *The Film Factory: Russian and Soviet Cinema in Documents, 1896–1939*, 1988.

Tharp, Grahame, 'An Appreciation of Percy Smith', *Documentary Newsletter*, January 1941.

Thiesen, Earl, 'The History of Nitrocellulose as a Film Base', in Fielding, ed.

Thompson, E. P., *The Making of the English Working Class*, Penguin, 1968.

Tummel, H., 'Birt Acres', *Cinema Studies*, vol. 1, nos 3, 6.

Vaughan, Dai, 'The Broken Trust of the Image', *Vertigo*, no. 4, 1995.

Vicinus, Martha, *The Industrial Muse*, Croom Helm, 1974.

Warren, Low, *The Film Game*, T. Werner Laurie, 1937.

Weber, Max, *The Rational and Social Foundations of Music*, Arcturus Books, 1969.

Weber, William, *Music and the Middle Classes*, Croom Helm, 1975.

Wenden, D. J., *The Birth of the Movies*, Macdonald, 1975.

White, John, *The Birth and Rebirth of Pictorial Space*, Faber, 1967.

Williams, Raymond, *The Long Tradition*, Penguin, 1965.

Williams, Raymond, *Culture and Society*, Penguin, 1968.

Williams, Raymond, 'A Lecture on Realism', *Screen*, vol. 16, no. 1, Spring 1977.

Williams, T. I., *The Chemical Industry*, EP Publishing, 1972.

Wittgenstein, Ludwig, *Philosophical Investigations*, Blackwell, 1963.

Wood, Leslie, *The Romance of the Movies*, Heinemann, 1937.

Wolff, Michael, ed., see Dyos and Wolff, eds.

Woolf, Virginia, *The Captain's Death Bed and Other Essays*, Hogarth Press, 1950.

# Index

Note: Titles of films are given in **bold** type

Magic silver screen
                    where
spooled in desire
                    our winding lives
cast on a shaft
                    strike our hearts
where dream is clear
                    and far is near
with shadows standing on their heads
inverted by the light –

Is there no other way
to meet our second selves
no way to search our eyes
without a film of tears?

When will be the day
you'll caress the ligaments of the light
and not just obey
the dictates of the night?

                              M.C.